jogger's catalog

jogger's catalog

the source book for runners

by robert e. burger

Foreword by Dr. Joan Ullyot

M. Evans and Company, Inc.   New York, N.Y. 10017

Library of Congress Cataloging in Publication Data

Burger, Robert E.

  Jogger's catalog.

  Includes index.

  1. Jogging—Miscellanea. I. Title.

GV494.B87   796.4'26   78-4271

  ISBN 0-87131-259-X paperback
  ISBN 0-87131-275-1 hardcover

Manufactured in the United States of America

9 8 7 6 5 4 3

acknowledgments

While every effort has been made to insure the accuracy of information included herein, neither the author nor the publisher can be held responsible for changes that occurred after the book went to press.

Thanks are due to the following publishers, magazines, newpapers, newsletters, and individuals for permission to reprint material included in the JOGGER'S CATALOG:

The American Express Cardmember Newsletter for "A New Par for the Course for Businessmen," from their July 1977 issue.

Dr. Tom Bassler for "How to Find a Doctor Who Understands Runners."

The Chico Running Club Newsletter for Walt Schafer's "1977 Ride and Tie."

Clive Davies for material from *The Oregon Distance Runner.*

Mary P. Fitzpatrick for "Special Olympics" (originally titled "Age Has No Priority in the Development of New Interest") from the August 1977 issue of the *Aorta Newsletter.*

Funk and Wagnalls, Inc./Harper and Row for "Stretch It Out" from *Biotonics* by Rex Wiederanders, M.D. with Edmond G. Addeo, copyright © 1977 by Rex Wiederanders, M.D.

Bob Glover for "The Long Blue Line" from the *New York Road Runners Club Newsletter.*

J. B. Lippincott Company for "Running and Time" and "Running Therapy" from *The Joy of Running* by Thaddeus Kostrubala, M.D. Copyright © 1976 by Thaddeus Kostrubala, M.D. Reprinted by permission of J. B. Lippincott Company.

M. Evans and Company for "Twelve Minute Walking/Running Test" and "Point Chart, Running," from *The Aerobics Way* by Kenneth H. Cooper, M.D., Copyright © 1977 Kenneth H. Cooper, M.D. Reprinted by permission of M. Evans and Company.

New Republic Magazine for "Thoughts from a Marathon Man" by Erich Segal.

Gary K. Olsen for material from *The Jogger.*

The Physician and Sportsmedicine for excerpts from Dr. George Sheehan's column for that magazine.

Random House, Inc. for "Sharing an Ancient Kinship" from *The Complete Book of Running* by James F. Fixx. Copyright © 1977 by James F. Fixx. Reprinted by permission of Random House, Inc.

Running for "Heat Tolerance: The Key to the Puzzle" by E. C. Frederick and Jack Welch.

Running Times for "The Hash House Harriers" by Steve Clapp (originally titled "The Night the Hare Was a Bunny") and "Time for Running" by the editors of *Running Times* (originally titled "Finding Time to Run"). Copyright © 1977 by *Running Times.* Reprinted by permission.

The San Diego Union for "Baby Enjoys Mother's Exercise" (originally titled "Jogging Has a Youthful Touch"), which appeared in *The San Diego Union* July 19, 1977 and was reprinted in the *San Diego Track Club News.* Reprinted with permission from *The San Diego Union.*

Michael Stubblefield for "Have a Nice Saturday" from *Body Talk.*

The Village Voice for "Why One Man Runs" by David Bradley (originally titled "The Happiness of the Long-Distance Runner") which appeared in *The Village Voice* August 23, 1976. Reprinted by permission of *The Village Voice.* Copyright © The Village Voice, Inc., 1976.

Ron Wayne for "The Boston" from *Nike News,* Summer 1977.

World Publications for excerpts from *Runner's World* and for excerpts from Age of the Runner by George Sheehan, M.D. (World Publications, 1974); *The Complete Runner* (World Publications, 1974); *The Foot Book* by Harry F. Hlavac, M.D. (World Publications, 1977); *Jog, Run Race* by Jo Henderson (World Publications, 1977); *Women's Running* by Joan Ullyot, M.D. (World Publications, 1977); and *Van Aaken Method* by Ernst van Aaken (World Publications, 1976).

Young Men's Christian Association of Syracuse and Onondaga County, New York, for "On the Trail of Pheidippides" by Laurel Saiz from *Running On.*

picture credits

Adidas: pages 62, 66, 70; Susan Bernard: pages 91 (right), 166; Ed Burger: pages 165 (bottom), 170; Judy Burger: page 77; Shirley Burger: page 167; Theresa Burger: pages 18, 20, 102, 103; Dr. Kenneth H. Cooper: pages 32, 163; Clive Davies: pages 46, 56, 145; Etonic: page 54; Dr. Steve Fredman: pages 126, 174, 178, 179; Rhoda Galyn: pages 2, 11, 15, 24, 26, 28, 34, 48, 63, 73, 75, 81, 96, 100, 108, 111, 112, 115, 118 (top), 121, 128, 133, 140, 150, 154, 157, 161, 165 (top), 173, 177, 184, 190; Peter Gowland: page 183; Grohe: page 94; Dr. Harry Hlavac from *The Foot Book*: pages 49, 50, 53; Janeart/Arthur Klonsky: page 156; Jog-a-Lite: page 98 (left); Kees Tuinzing: page 104; Don Melandry: pages 12, 36, 38, 43, 76, 86, 113, 129, 139, 146, 151, 160, 168, 169; Moving Comfort: pages 90, 91 (left); New Balance: page 55; Nike/Blue Ribbon: pages 61, 65, 68; Oleg Cassini/Osaga: page 92; Rick Reedy: pages 102, 103; Reflexite: page 98 (right); *Runner's World*: page 13; Sealcut: page 118 (bottom); Len Tokar/Courtesy of Total Environmental Sports: page 93; United Feature Syndicate, Inc.: page 175 (top).

contents

foreword

Seven years ago, I took my first hesitant jogging step—shod in canvas tennis shoes with minimal cushioning and support. Like most beginning joggers, I was totally ignorant of the sport. I did everything wrong and knew nothing about proper footwear, clothes, races, clubs, running doctors, or even books that might have helped me. Perhaps as a consequence, I suffered through injuries, layoffs, poor training, and disastrous races. I had nowhere to turn. Books were nonexistent and my few running friends were as naive as I.

Somehow, because the physical and mental benefits of running outweighed my suffering, I persisted in my newfound hobby. I learned through experience and became, with time and assistance, a decent marathoner. Along the way, I discovered by myself the people, the literature, the whole new world that running opens up.

My own progress was slow and decidedly erratic. But must all joggers take years, as I did, to find the sources and information that can help them? Surely there must be a better way. The estimated 25 million Americans who jog as of 1978 should not all be left to stumble around in the dark, courting injury, boredom, or frustration.

With *Jogger's Catalog*, Bob Burger presents a better way to find the answers. Here he compiles,

for the first time under one cover, huge chunks of valuable information bound together in readable fashion by anecdotes, book reviews, profiles of runners and races. As a member of the family-oriented San Francisco DSE (Dolphin South End) Runners, Bob has run with—and interviewed—hundreds of fellow runners of all abilities. And in his catalog, he focuses on matters of greatest concern to them.

Where can one find a local running club? The AAU address? What *is* the AAU, or the NJA, or the RRCA? Where does one look for shoes? A sports-oriented podiatrist or physician? Books and articles written for women runners, or masters (over forty), or midwesterners?

Joggers who refer to this detailed and amusing catalog will find most of the answers they need, or learn where else to go for pertinent information. They can avoid much of the confusion that used to be inevitable for the beginning runner. And, by keeping this book handy for reference through the years, they can more quickly and easily be at home in the wide and exciting new world of the distance runner. I wish them all as much pleasure in reading as in running.

Joan Ullyot, M.D.
San Francisco

introduction

This book brings together, in one place *in the format of a source book,* whatever is worth knowing about running. Such a format allows me to quote freely from what I consider to be the best opinions, to make available to you the whole gamut of products and services, and to offer liberal samples of the best writing in the field. The idea is to give you *access* to the whole world of running. You might well call this book the Runner's Whole Earth Catalog.

As jogging has rapidly become a way of life for some 25 million Americans (according to the most recent Gallup poll), numerous books on the sport have attempted to capture its essence and to instruct its followers. New industries have sprung up to serve its special needs. Because of it, new questions have been raised about exercise, leisure time, work, the environment, and even philosophy and psychiatry. No one book can do justice to it all, but this one book, I hope, can give you entree to it all.

The beginner may use it immediately for instruction and motivation. Through these pages the regular runner will deepen his appreciation for his avocation. Both, I am sure, will be able to take advantage of the many money-saving and time-saving ideas that only a source book such as this can offer. I hope that even the general reader will discover a fascinating world here that he perhaps thought of once as only a passing fad. I can't imagine that anyone will ever need *all* the information between these covers, but, by George, it's *here.*

This is a grassroots book. As much as from well-known sources, my information has come from unstapled, Xeroxed newsletters, from bull sessions after fun-runs, from tips and hints over the phone. Before long, the opinions of the people work their way into the slick magazines and well-publicized books. I have tried to listen to these opinions unedited, and to hasten their journey to print.

I have kept a sharp eye out for addresses, for places to go and things to do, and for ways to buy wisely. Yet all these data do not add up to much without a sense of what's going on in other people's lives. So I have excerpted from my sources the things that move me about jogging: stories, jokes, pains, deeply felt emotions. I have felt it a duty to interject my own opinions, asking them to be challenged. (The camaraderie of runners is so intense that nobody likes to knock the other guy's club or race or book. But in order to be objective, I have had to do a bit of knocking here.)

I have tried to *label* the material in this book so you can easily place its context without long introductions. "Nominations" are my suggestions for the best of this and the best of that: I welcome your opinions for subsequent editions of this book. "Selections" are samplings of the gamut of writing in this burgeoning literary field. To everyone credited in this book I must acknowledge a debt, but I must also take the blame for every unquoted opinion. "Reviews" are my own. And "Ideas" have come from many sources, not the least of whom are Denis Burger, Ph.D.; Walt Stack; Joan Ullyot, M.D.; and Pamela Veley.

one

the basics

Running is the sport of the people. If it's not the largest participant sport already in terms of numbers, it no doubt is in terms of time devoted to it. It requires little in the way of skills or money, and no particular body type or age or location. It doesn't discriminate; it cuts across all classes. Even at competitive levels it thrives on friendship. Where has it been all this time?

It's not in the sports pages yet—except for the handful of marathons and civically sponsored races held each year. It has few heroes, because it has too many.

You can go out and jog right now, barefoot if necessary. (Do you know how many marathon champions never wore shoes? A cynic has said that the major challenge of shoe manufacturers is to limit the bad things their shoes do to the feet.) When Bill Bowerman, then track coach at the University of Oregon, launched the jogging revolution in the 1960's, he wrote, "Probably the shoes you wear for gardening, working in the shop, or around the house will do just fine."

We've come a long way since that time. We've become more sophisticated. We have theories of glycogen storage and electrolyte replacement and orthotics. Bowerman himself led the shoe revolution by pressing a sole in his wife's waffle iron (thus, the Nike Waffle). But before we essay all of the theories and the developments in equipment that have come along in the last decade, let's consider the simple realities that lie behind it all. Why should you start running, and how?

What is jogging, anyway? It's good to recall that Bowerman defined jogging as part running, part walking. Only a few others, such as Bud Getchell of Ball State University in Muncie, Indiana, have come back to this point. Most joggers who become discouraged think of walking as a sign of failure. Or as a regression to the old Boy Scouts' pace. In reality, run-walk-run sessions allow you to (1) enjoy where you're going, (2) go to more interesting places than you could by running alone, and (3) do simple stretching exercises while walking, which one is inclined to forget. If you are privileged to live near hills, use them with this in mind: walk up the hills until you're ready to run them, and walk down them to save your

Runner's World offers a fun-run kit, complete with certificates for participants, to encourage weekly participation in running activities in your area. Inquire of *Runner's World* for further details. If you decide to have a fun-run, *Runner's World* will list details in the Fun Run section of the magazine.

knees. Or if you're starting out with a slower partner, take advantage of the opportunity to walk when he or she *has* to.

Others define jogging, as opposed to continuous running, by numbers. Ken Cooper, whose breakthrough book *Aerobics* provided the physiological basis for Bowerman's physical insights, first proposed a 12-minute test to measure conditioning. By this standard, a middle-aged man could be considered in good condition if he could cover 1½ miles in that time. So others began to think of the 8-minute-per-mile pace as the dividing line between running and jogging. But, of course, it's all relative: for a postcardiac patient, a ten-minute pace might be running; for marathon runners like Bill Rodgers or Frank Shorter, a seven-minute pace might be jogging.

I like to define running in psychological terms. You've become a runner, whatever your pace, when you achieve that first marvelous feeling that there's a new direction in your physical development. You no longer "die" at the thought of that little hill down the street. You run to the track instead of driving there. You notice a change in your eating habits. You no longer care what the neighbors think as you lean into the lamp post doing your stretching exercises. Bowerman predicts this will happen, at least the fitness part of it, at about 12 weeks. You may even get a "charge," as he puts it, at six weeks.

Then the measurable benefits appear. Frank Shorter says the runner can feel he's getting something important done every day he runs. "You have the tangible sense of doing something significant." Dr. Terence Kavanaugh, Medical Director of the Toronto Rehabilitation Centre, points to the improved self-image of the runner, as well as his improved waistline: "The first time you complete five or six miles, no matter what the speed, you know you have set yourself apart from the majority of your fellow men." For women, a smaller dress size may be the first obvious signal of accomplishment. Men report weight loss. But the scales mean little for the first three months or so of running, since calories burned off are often countered by the higher density of newly acquired muscle. The key to making jogging a regular habit is the realization that, after all the failures of diets

and calisthenics programs and generally good resolutions, *running is changing the course of your life.*

Why run? The most provocative writer in the field, a cardiologist-turned-sports-doctor named George Sheehan, answers this question almost without reference to physical benefits. What happens to the body only confirms what the spirit wants to know, and emboldens the spirit to command the body, "Stick with it." So before you wonder about the importance of your cardiovascular system, listen to Sheehan's *apologia pro vita sua:*

At the age of reason, I was placed on a train, the shades drawn, my life's course and destination already determined. At the age of 45, I pulled the emergency cord and ran out into the world. It was a decision that meant no less than a new life, a new course, a new destination. . . .

The authorities agree that we come upon this stage of our life unprepared for the reality of advancing years and receding rewards. . . .

Most experts suggest we make a new start in a new career, develop new interests. I say begin at the beginning. Begin with the body. The body mirrors the soul and the mind, and is much more accessible than either. Become proficient at listening to your body and you will eventually hear from your totality—the complex, unique person you are.

I did it that way. I stepped off that train and began to run. And in that hour a day of perfecting my body, I began to find out who I was. . . . In the creative act of running, I became convinced of my own importance, certain that my life had significance.

This is only a brief sample of Dr. Sheehan's outlook, in one of his popular columns. His new book, *On Running and Being* (Simon and Schuster, 1978) confirms him in the role of guru to the running world. If you're not persuaded by philosophy, listen to his summation of the physical side of running:

It is a physiologically perfect exercise. Running uses the large thigh and leg muscles in rhythmic fashion at a personally controlled rate. . . . Running has been proven to (a) increase cardiopulmonary fitness, (b) reduce weight, (c) lower blood pressure, (d) decrease the cholesterol and triglycerides associated with coronary disease, and (e) help psychological stability.

Add it all up, and it means not only a longer life in years but fuller years. Occasionally a dissenter will surface—an essayist in *The New Yorker* looking at the sport through a pince-nez, a doctor writing for shock effect in *Playboy,* and Dr. Meyer Friedman, the "Type A, Type B" man (see page 113), who should know better. But the evidence for the physical benefits of running is overwhelming. In fact, many otherwise excellent books on running are ruined by endless repetition of all the studies relating to health and longevity. And I don't think one runner in a thousand wants to see another chart or questionnaire showing precisely how much one has improved or should improve by precisely so much running.

If further evidence were needed for the medical rewards of jogging, it came recently in a report to the American Heart Association and in a new booklet distributed by the AHA, *Beyond Diet . . . Exercise Your Way to Fitness and Heart Health* (see review, page 33). Heart disease, as we all know, now accounts for more than half of all deaths in the United States. The rising incidence of heart attacks may be partially explained by the successful treatment of other diseases. But at least the Heart Association is now backing away from its former insistence on dietary causes.

The study reported to the AHA followed the exercise habits of 17,000 Harvard alumni over periods of more than 15 years. In broad terms, the conclusion was that strenuous leisure-time exercise has a definite protective effect against heart attacks. More interesting, for our purposes here, was the specific determination that the intense physical activities ("like jogging") had no measurable effect unless engaged in for at least three hours a week. This guidepost correlates well with the advice of experienced runners. Bowerman estimates a beginner should spend 30 minutes a day, three days a week. Rory Donaldson of the National Jogging Association (see page 138) would up that to four days a week. Most coaches recommend five days a week. But all would agree that once a level of fitness is achieved (after about three months of regular running) three hours a week is probably less than you'll *want* to spend jogging. So now we come to some specific guidelines:

BASIC NUMBER ONE: Measure your jogging in elapsed time, not total miles. If you run to the edge of your ability, not loafing but not straining, your mileage will necessarily increase. When you start *running* **you may want to count the miles.** *But your first aim is endurance.*

I know runners who count laps on a track by changing to a different lane each time around. One friend even throws in an extra lap at the end to be sure he hasn't missed one! But most joggers (in a broad sense, beginners) are quite content to make a rough approximation of distances—if they want to measure their progress. When you're starting out, ten minutes may be all you can handle at one time. That's not unusual. Be patient.

What's the best way to divide up your total weekly time? Here the experts differ—but more and more it's becoming clear that there's a great variation among the needs of people. Dr. Joan Ullyot, who specializes in exercise physiology (see page 85), writes that "virtually daily running is necessary or the body lapses back to its former state and all that work of adaptation has been in vain." Dr. Sheehan has recently said that as few as two longer runs a week may be quite enough. (He finds himself fit for marathons on a schedule of about 30 miles a week—far below what runners half his age find necessary.) Sheehan cites studies of the importance of rest for the body to replenish its glycogen stores (see page 116). The truth is probably that both points of view apply, but to different situations. The beginner needs greater consistency, but once a plateau of fitness is reached he can settle into a maintenance program. It all comes back to a basic principle dubbed by Bowerman "Hard-Easy":

BASIC NUMBER TWO: Vary your daily schedule from long to short, from fast to slow. This technique not only allows your body to recuperate, but contributes to improvement in a positive way. Muscles respond better to *variety* in stresses and in intervals of use.

The more you run, the more you will want another form of variety: in locales. My wife and I have found about four or five interesting routes, of from three to six miles, from our doorstep. On weekends we try to drive to parks or lakes. The presence of water has some mystic attraction to runners (coolness? fresher air?). As far as I can tell, lap-running is tolerated only by people who have to run on surfaces softer than paved roads.

In a sense, jogging *teaches* us the benefits of variety. A change of shoes is better than wearing your best pair every time. We encounter changes in the weather—and find that it's stimulating! We learn that it's OK to skip a day or two when we simply don't feel like running. We even learn not to pass out iron-clad advice!

At least in my experience, however, the variety rule answers a lot of other questions beginners often ask. Is the morning better for jogging than the evening? Perhaps, as Dr. Cooper says, morning runners tend to stick with it more than nighttime joggers. I say run when you can find the time, especially to replace unwanted eating or drinking. And *vary* it. How does your available time compare with what others have?

Joe Henderson, the editor of that lifeline of information for the beginner as well as competitor, *Runner's World* (see page 25), assures me that he used to run during his lunch hours without benefit of showering. (Now, as head of the maga-

A beginning runner

zine's book department, he has the luxury of working at home.) Dr. Sheehan writes that he runs to and from work frequently, and simply towels off. Let's face it: some people perspire less than others. But the moral is that there is no best time to run physiologically, only psychologically. If a strict schedule every day helps your resolve to run, good! I think it's part of listening to your body to vary your schedule as you feel up to it—and not to feel guilty when you decide not to run.

BASIC NUMBER THREE: Run first and think about it later. Get some firsthand experience before delving into theory, and the theory will mean something.

This principle might apply to a lot of activities, but in a sport (if you can call it that) as simple as jogging, it's especially helpful. Don't worry about holding your arms at a precise angle—they'll fall naturally to your waist. Later, you can read how some runners lower them running up hills, or shake them to prevent tightening up. Here are some other common tips, which you can read about more fully in the succeeding chapters after you've had a few easy outings:

1. *"Consult your doctor."* Follow Joe Henderson's advice (page 42) and do just the opposite—plunge right in. Sure you're going to start slowly, even with a brisk walk if your body tells you that's all you can handle. A stress test? Certainly, even for experienced runners—because the purpose of such tests (on treadmills, with monitoring of the heart as the workload is gradually increased) is to uncover any hidden heart defect (see page 112). But anything less than this, according to Dr. Sheehan and other cardiologists, is worthless as a safeguard against some unforeseen danger of vigorous exercise. If you have a doctor who runs, that's different.

2. *Technique can be improved.* Breathing, for example. Bowerman relates how many beginners ask, "Should I breathe with my mouth open?" Breathe through your ears, if it gets more oxygen into your system! And practice deep-breathing: expand your stomach, not your chest, as you inhale. As Dr. Laurence Morehouse of UCLA says, the military posture of breathing turns the whole system upside down (Dr. Morehouse set up exercise programs for the astronauts.) (See page 82.) And your stride, foot plant, and posture may not be as natural as you think. Bowerman advises to resist the tendency to look at the ground; ask your running partner to tell you when you drop your head from an erect position. Many beginners start on their toes, try to extend their stride by lifting their knees, and kick their heels up—all because this is how they remember sprinting in school. You can diagnose yourself by watching the way your shoes wear and studying your gait in the windows of stores (see page 76).

3. *Make friends with the weather.* Don't mind getting soaked occasionally. But dress for comfort, and you'll get a lot more out of your running time. Forget the "frozen lung" myth, but be cautious of heat (page 31). How important is fresh air? Some say it's better not to run at all than breathe in automobile fumes all the way. But everyone agrees that a fresh-air course adds immeasurably to the enjoyment of a run.

4. *Don't ignore the dangers.* There are minor irritations from dogs and hecklers. Women are the target of wisecracks from the macho element, who don't know any better—but this minor annoyance is fast disappearing as joggers are becoming a visible part of the landscape of most cities. More serious dangers are cars and—yourself. As we will see in the next chapter, running can put you into a trance-like state. You don't realize how close cars are going by at corners. Two well-known runners, Ernst van Aaken (see page 18) and Sig Podlozny (see page 127), were seriously injured by automobiles, the latter fatally. Run on sidewalks (in spite of the slightly better "give" on asphalt) and wear reflective clothing at night (page 97). Avoid surfaces that may have hidden snares for your feet; Dr. Sheehan points out that the pleasure of running in heavy grass or on a plowed field is not worth one sprained ankle. (Running down the middle of a street at night, I once almost broke a leg on one of Berkeley's infamous barriers.) As Dr. Ullyot (*Women's Running*) and Kathryn Lance (*Running for Health and Beauty: A Woman's Guide*) have

pointed out, a running woman discourages a potential rapist more than a walking woman; but at night and in unfamiliar surroundings the best safety is in numbers.

5. *Don't be discouraged by pain.* Common aches and pains in the feet and calves are signals of your body adapting to stress. *San Francisco Chronicle* columnist Charles McCabe writes, "Think of the restorative power of memory. It edits pain into sadness, and sadness into poignancy." There is some sort of a physical memory in our bodies which similarly edits stress into strength and strength into stamina. A good test of whether you should attempt to "run through pain" is to try a brisk walk and then a slow jog and see if the soreness disappears. Unfortunately, most doctors are unqualified in sports medicine, and their routine advice will be to rest. A cold or respiratory problem is another matter: *don't* try to run through illness.

6. *Foot, ankle, and knee problems are something else.* The way your foot strikes the ground is, according to sports podiatrists like Dr. Harry Hlavac (page 53), the key to almost all bone and joint problems, even in the hip. As we will see in detail in the chapter on feet, good shoes and perhaps inserts in your shoes can solve shin splints, "bad knees," and Achilles tendinitis, the most common complaints. But running can also help take the strain off a joint by strenthening muscles around it. I couldn't run for any length of time on an ankle I dislocated some 25 years ago—until I was motivated enough to run through the pain. Since then I've never felt it.

7. *Running is not a complete conditioner.* Write it in your heart: you've got to do antirunning exer-

---

SELECTION:
TIME FOR RUNNING

U.S. Senator William Proxmire, Newark (N.J.), Mayor Kenneth Gibson, *Washington Post* columnist Colman McCarthy, and lots of other people whose lives are unusually "full" share several important secrets about the management of time:

1. They have found that running not only *takes* time, but *gives* it—in the sense that a person who exercises an hour a day can accomplish far more in the other 23 than a sedentary person can accomplish in 24.

2. They have worked out their schedules so that running is substituted for other time-consuming activities, rather than just added on to them. Two of the most popular substitutes are *running to work* and *running for lunch.*

People who get to work by foot instead of by car spend very little extra time. A typical urban commuting trip of five miles might take 20 minutes by car, including the time spent crawling through traffic jams, waiting for lights, and looking for parking. The same trip taken by foot might require 50 minutes, including a quick shower. But the shower can substitute for the shower that would otherwise be taken before leaving for work. So the *net* time required for running to work is only 20 minutes. And the employee who arrives at work by foot will be so invigorated that he/she will quickly make up the "lost" 20 minutes with heightened alertness and energy.

Some people like to do their running during the lunch hour, substituting exercise for the excessive eating they would otherwise do. The secret here is that a large proportion of the food consumed in a typical American lunch is eaten for reasons of habit or taste, rather than of nutritional need. A lunch hour normally spent slumped over a Formica table can just as easily be spent reviving the body and spirit—and reducing excess body fat instead of piling more fat on—with a four- or five-mile run followed by a quick shower and perhaps a piece of fruit to restore some of the blood sugar and electrolytes used in the run.

—*Running Times*, July 1977

The hurdler's stretch, to balance an overtight hamstring

SELECTION:
STRESS AND "THE FREEDOM
OF INDEPENDENT RUNNING"

Stress for a human being is almost anything he may encounter in his environment which is subjectively associated with certain unpleasant feelings. For example: You have to go to the dentist; the boss calls you into his office to bawl you out; you're facing a difficult school examination; you're an engineer responsible for the success of a difficult construction design; you're an athlete facing your toughest competition after years of preparation. There are thousands of situations in life which can unsettle a person.

Stress and its manifold burdens do not inevitably cause damage. . . . People who constantly try to avoid the first stage of alarm reaction become addicted to flight from stress and from responsibility. In a certain sense, they become incompetent for living. They often end up overindulging in alcohol, tobacco, or drugs.

Children should be taught early to confront appropriate stresses and to handle them on their own, without assistance. As soon as the child lets go of its mother's hand and explores and conquers the freedom of independent running, it should be allowed to develop on its own.

This, in fact, should be the rule throughout life.

—Ernst van Aaken
Van Aaken Method
(World Publications, Mountain View, Calif., 1976)

cises or you'll eventually wind up with a problem. There are two kinds of muscles in your body, by position: anterior and posterior, or simply front and back. Running uses only your back muscles: calves, hamstring, buttocks, back. You've got to build up the front muscles which "oppose" those, as the exercise physiologists say. And you've got to stretch the overtrained posterior muscles. Every book on running or exercise gives its own set of exercises to accomplish this anterior strengthening and posterior stretching. The best way to choose a set is to understand the purpose of it all. Then you can make up your own exercises if your prefer. (For suggestions, see page 101.)

Proper exercise technique is, strangely, the only part of running theory which remains muddled. Perhaps it's because there are so many possibilities. As you will see, I recommend Dr. Sheehan's Basic Six, with variations, because I know he suffered once from the most long lasting problem of poor exercise habits—sciatica (see page 101). Here are some of the "reasons why" of exercise, as offered by Ellen Collins, Chief Exercise Physiologist of Vital (see page 114):

• A muscle is strengthened only when it's overloaded, and that takes full flexing for eight to 10 seconds. So don't imagine you're accomplishing much by bouncing up and back.

THE FIVE STAGES OF THE RUNNER

ONE: Impressed by the svelte appearance of friends, who attribute it to running, the potential runner is given shoes and warmup suit, or makes his own way to the local sporting goods store to select a pair himself. Now he's got to get out and use them.

TWO: Runner picks up a book or subscribes to *Runner's World,* further bolstering his resolve to continue.

THREE: Runner attempts his first race, something like a charity three-miler sponsored by the local heart association, and receives his first tee shirt or ribbon for finishing.

FOUR: Runner signs up at a fun-run club, attends the first potluck, starts hailing fellow members on the street. If he has a family, the kids drop out at this point, but continue occasional runs.

FIVE: Runner experiences first breakthrough, starts entering races to improve his time, then suffers first major injury and begins stretching exercises. He now has fifteen tee shirts, four pairs of runnings shoes in various states of repair, and a burning desire to run a marathon some day. He's hooked for life.

• A muscle resists stretching up to a certain reflex point, just to protect itself. In most cases this means you must stretch it for 20 to 40 seconds—

The bent-leg curl up: leave the small of the back on the floor and you still perform 75% of the work.

The sit-back variation of the sit-up, holding just above the ground to strengthen the abdominals.

in the fully stretched position to get substantial benefits from that type of exercise.

• Virtually all of the "work" of many familiar exercises occurs in only a portion of the apparent cycle. For example, in doing a sit-up (on your back, hands behind head, knees bent) almost all the load is put on your abdominal muscles *before* your lower back leaves the floor. So why not do just a "curl-up"—lifting your upper back as far as you can with your lower back flat on the floor? (See illustration.) If you go through any exercise slowly, you can sense when the load is greatest if you "listen to" your muscles.

• Holding a muscle in an overload or tensed position may not necessarily tell you that the muscle is being fully exercised. For example, in the "sit-back" recommended by Dr. Laurence Morehouse (see page 103), you reverse the above procedure and fall back, from a sitting position, until your hands are just above the floor with no part of your back on the floor. Holding this position for ten seconds will put a great load on your stomach muscles, but it won't give those muscles the full *range* of a workout that the curl-up provides.

The moral of these examples is: Don't take anything for granted no matter how basic it may seem. Do you remember how sit-ups were once done—with knees straight? Do you remember doing deep knee-bends in school? Go to any field where people are exercising, and you'll see them springing up and down trying to touch their toes. I have yet to see a book which sets the record straight on this rather important subject.

8. Companionship and camaraderie are natural in running. This is a corollary of the noncompetitiveness of the sport. But subtle forms of competitiveness can creep in, even between you and your stopwatch. It's easy to strain when you're trying to keep pace with a well-meaning but

better-conditioned friend who takes off at his or her own speed. Paradoxically, joining a club tends to foster noncompetitiveness. You'll find more runners of your own level than in your household, perhaps, or your immediate neighborhood. It can even help your resolve if you join the National Jogging Association. (For information on joining of all kinds, see Chapter Six).

BASIC NUMBER FOUR: Don't start running unless you intend not to stop. There are few short-term benefits of jogging. If you start with an eye on the clock or on a cosmetic change, you'll be bored so fast you'll stop faster than you expected.

Included in this precept is the warning "Don't try to buy your way into fitness." Some people must have all the gear and all the books currently in fashion—and then they think they have "done something." Bill Bowerman said a lot of things when he wrote, "The dude buys a stopwatch."

George Sheehan once estimated, in his melancholy Irish fashion, that only 10 to 15% of the population will ever have the body type, the opportunity, or the will to make running part of their lives. He might modify that today. Eighty-eight-year-old Eula Weaver won gold medals in the Senior Olympics in the half-mile and mile in 1977—in her age bracket! That was five years after she came to the Longevity Research Insti-

---

SELECTION:
THE SUBTLE INFLUENCE
OF COMPETITION

Fortunately, most husbands try to help. Many are themselves runners and are delighted when you join them and can *really* understand, finally, their own passion for the sport. I've noticed that almost all male road runners share this delightful attitude toward women who run. They are pleased to be joined by us and are full of helpful advice and encouragement.

But back to the man who shares your home—and, I hope, your enthusiasm. He may wish to run with you and guide your initial steps. Say no. Pleasant as it may be to have company, it is unwise to run with a man until you are reasonably fit and can run under ten minutes per mile.

One of the sad facts of life is that even a paunchy, beer drinking, smoking, middle-aged slob, if he's male, can almost always run a mile faster and more easily without practice than a woman. It's discouraging for you and can lead to understandable feelings of resentment if you set out together. It's unjust, but there it is—your horribly unfit husband is a better miler than you at the start.

If your husband is in good shape, you'll under-stand and tolerate his better performance. But he will have trouble going as slowly as you *must* in your conditioning stage. He will have to jog circles around you, chatter incessantly to use up his excess wind, sprint ahead now and then to stretch his legs. You will feel like a plodder, slow and snail-like, and soon will feel guilty about slowing him down.

Actually, since the pace you'll be going is right for you, you should stick with it and not try to speed up or push too much to keep up with your well-meaning husband. It's much better to go alone or with some women friends. The danger of injury or stress is less and the mental outlook much more upbeat.

Later on, when you can do your two miles comfortably and have progressed to the intermediate stage, by all means accept your husband's offer of company. When you can keep up, chat as you run, and have enough experience not to be lured into a too-fast pace, it's fun to run together.

—Joan Ullyot, M.D., *Women's Running*
(World Publications, Mountain View, Calif., 1977)

tute in Santa Barbara unable to walk a hundred feet. Given the will, *anybody* can make running part of his or her life.

Dr. Ullyot's remarks apply equally well to a father whose daughter is on a college cross-country team, to a mother challenged by a gung-ho teenage son, or to an overweight executive invited to a workout by the newest member of the firm. If you *can* adjust to differences in fitness, running with another person who knows you well has a side-effect beyond companionship. You'll get good advice on how you're doing.

Amby Burfoot, the lanky New England marathoner who won at Boston in 1968, makes this surprising observation: "Most importantly, listen to your mother. Mothers may not know much about running, but they can intuitively tell a lot about your general physical condition. You may think your mother is picking up on insignificant details, but, if you are smart, you will listen. Mothers are the best trainers."

AEROBIC EXERCISE OR MUSCLE EXERCISE?

"After running my daily three or four miles, I cool down with about five minutes of slow walking and then unwind with about 20 repetitions of some basic calisthenics. (As I've said before, I do calisthenics, I just don't count points for them!) The ones I prefer are sit-ups with the knees in a bent position, some toe touches, and some push-ups. . . . Basically, calisthenics are good for maintaining muscle strength and tone. Just use them *in addition to, not in place of*, one of the primary aerobic conditioning programs."

Thus Dr. Ken Cooper, in *Aerobics* (M. Evans and Company, New York, 1968), made the basic distinction in the field of conditioning: exercise requiring oxygen and not requiring it. To measure the effect of oxygen-using exercise on the cadiovascular system, he devised a point system, revised and updated in three succeeding books, which has helped millions by giving them a tangible target: 30 points a week for men, 24 for women. A glance at his tables shows that a regular runner earns enough points a day that he needn't bother to count. Dr. Cooper says, "If you were to

ask me, finally, what exercise can be used most effectively, I'd have no hesitancy about recommending running."

By now it's obvious that the fledgling runner has a few new words to learn, like "aerobic" and

The Point System

WALKING/RUNNING

TIME (min:sec)	POINT VALUE	TIME (min:sec)	POINT VALUE
1.0 Mile		**5.0 Miles**	
over 20:01	0	over 1:40:01	4.0
20:00–15:01	1.0	1:40:00–1:15:01	9.0
15:00–12:01	2.0	1:15:00–1:00:01	14.0
12:00–10:01	3.0	1:00:00– 50:01	19.0
10:00– 8:01	4.0	50:00– 40:01	24.0
8:00– 6:41	5.0	40:00– 33:21	29.0
6:40– 5:44	6.0	33:20– 28:35	34.0
under 5:43	7.0	under 28:34	39.0
2.0 Miles		**6.0 Miles**	
over 40:01	1.0	over 2:00:01	5.0
40:00–30:01	3.0	2:00:00–1:30:01	11.0
30:00–24:01	5.0	1:30:00–1:12:01	17.0
24:00–20:01	7.0	1:12:00–1:00:01	23.0
20:00–16:01	9.0	1:00:00– 48:01	29.0
16:00–13:21	11.0	48:00– 40:01	35.0
13:20–11:27	13.0	40:00– 34:19	41.0
under 11:26	15.0	under 34:17	47.0
3.0 Miles		**7.0 Miles**	
over 1:00:01	2.0	over 2:20:01	6.0
1:00:00– 45:01	5.0	2:20:00–1:45:01	13.0
45:00– 36:01	8.0	1:45:00–1:24:01	20.0
36:00– 30:01	11.0	1:24:00–1:10:01	27.0
30:00– 24:01	14.0	1:10:00– 56:01	34.0
24:00– 20:01	17.0	56:00– 46:41	41.0
20:00– 17:10	20.0	46:40– 40:01	48.0
under 17:08	23.0	under 40:00	55.0
4.0 Miles		**8.0 Miles**	
over 1:20:01	3.0	over 2:40:01	7.0
1:20:00–1:00:01	7.0	2:40:00–2:00:01	15.0
1:00:00– 48:01	11.0	2:00:00–1:36:01	23.0
48:00– 40:01	15.0	1:36:00–1:20:01	31.0
40:00– 32:01	19.0	1:20:00–1:04:01	39.0
32:00– 26:41	23.0	1:04:00– 53:21	47.0
26:40– 22:53	27.0	53:20– 45:44	55.0
under 22:52	31.0	under 45:43	63.0

From *The Aerobics Way* by Kenneth H. Cooper, M.D.

its opposite. Scan the following glossary and come back to it when necessary. Unlike other sports, however, running does not encourage show-offs and runners seldom use "in" words to impress.

THE JOGGER'S GLOSSARY

Many of these terms are explained elsewhere or are evident from the context. They are arranged here for easy reference.

Achilles tendon: The large tendon which connects the calf muscle with the back of the heel. It is often irritated by rubbing against the back of the shoe or by pulling on foot strike.

Aerobic: With air; with sufficient oxygen intake to sustain an activity without depriving any part of the body of oxygen.

Anaerobic: Without air; describing an activity which either (a) does not require oxygen intake, such as isometric exercise, or (b) occurs without a sufficient intake of oxygen from breathing to sustain it over a long period of time, such as sprinting. See "Oxygen debt." Books on running usually refer only to (b).

Athlete's heart: Well-exercised heart, often enlarged (no longer considered to be abnormal in a healthy person).

Body fat: A measurable quantity of fatty tissue expressed as a per cent of total body weight, hence often referred to as "per cent body fat." Measured by total immersion; the normal range is from 6 to 15% with generally higher percentages in women.

Chondromalacia (patella): "Runner's knee," a softening of the kneecap from repeated stress, probably due to improper foot strike.

Cooldown: Tapering-off exercise at end of heavy running, similar in purpose to warmup; also known as warmdown.

Counter: The cup forming the back of the shoe, which supports the heel laterally and protects it vertically.

Fartlek: The Swedish word for unstructured interval training, literally "speed play." Cross-country running with changes in pace according to changes in landscape and mood. See "Intervals."

Flat feet: Flattening of the arch of the foot, sometimes by pronation of the foot, not necessarily pathological.

Heat exhaustion (prostration): State of shock characterized by rapid pulse; sweating; cool, wet skin. Medical attention, water, and salt are required immediately.

Heat stroke (sunstroke): Severe medical problem characterized by diminishing pulse, dry skin, and high fever.

Intervals: Training method involving varying a pace from slow to fast segments, usually on a track and according to a program, as opposed to "fartlek," as described above.

Isometric: Describing a method of exercise in which a muscle is placed under tension without movement, as opposed to isotonic (with movement of the body part controlled by the muscle) and aerobic (with expenditure of oxygen).

Loop: Segment of a race course with start and finish passing through same point, as opposed to point-to-point.

LSD: Long, slow distance, as coined by Joe Henderson.

Magic six: Six miles per day and six exercises, as recommended by Dr. George Sheehan for long-distance runners.

Morton's foot: Foot with excessively long first toe (second metartarsal bone) as compared with big toe, apparently the cause of many foot and leg problems in runners.

Orthotics: Devices or techniques to support the foot in a neutral or corrected position. They are usually plastic inserts made from casts of feet.

Oxygen debt: Oxygen that must be replaced after anaerobic exercise, characterized by out-of-breath feeling.

PR: Personal record; one's best time for a given distance, or best distance.

Pronation: Turning of the outward side of the foot upward, or flattening of the arch.

Runner's knee: Chondromalacia (which see).

Sciatica: Inflammation of the sciatic nerve, from lower back to toe, often caused by "sway back" or weak abdominal muscles.

Shin splints: Pain in lower leg from running on hard surfaces or from lack of training.

Stitch: Sharp pain in the lower torso, of muscular origin, usually temporary.

Stress test: Treadmill test to measure ability of

body to sustain exercise, especially as precaution against heart precondition.

Supination: Turning of the inside of the foot upward, as in normal glide pattern of stride.

Trick knee: Knee prone to buckle or lock due to torn cartilage not properly mended.

Toe-off: Push-off phase of gait that propels the body forward, requiring flexibility of shoe sole and lateral support of toe box.

Warmup: Exercises to stretch or limber muscles before vigorous exercise; opposite of cooldown (which see).

HOW TO START YOUR READING

As mentioned in Basic Number Two, reading should come relatively late in your jogging program. But once you've started, you won't want to stop. A lot of top runners are also excellent writers. And a lot of first-rate talent at the clubnewsletter level awaits your attention. (I don't mean to put blinders on you if you haven't yet started jogging. Actually, it's a see-saw process: run a little, read a little, run some more.)

The problem that faces the newcomer to the field is the great array of books all with promising titles, all with intriguing authors. Perhaps the best known is Hal Higdon, author of 17 books at last count, among which are books on management consulting and the Leopold and Loeb case. His

articles appear in *Sports Illustrated* and *National Geographic* as well as, of course, *Runner's World*. Then there are the training secrets from famous coaches: Arthur Lydiard, New Zealand Olympic coach and now peripatetic spokesman for his E.B. shoes; Bill Bowerman, now vice president at Nike; and Ernst van Aaken, enigmatic West German who was preaching the benefits of long, slow running a quarter of a century ago. Something of a newcomer, but certainly the most inspiring sports author to anyone who has seen one of his columns, is Dr. George Sheehan. More than anyone else he has lifted running theory out of the check-the-charts, look-at-the-statistics stage (see page 79). Quite recently the special concerns of women have been addressed in sensible books by Dr. Joan Ullyot and Kathryn

Young boys starting their own race

Lance. Gary K. Olsen and the tabloid he edits for the National Jogging Association, *The Jogger,* have been equally zealous in the cause of women's running.

On the following pages I will try to pigeonhole the major books on running and exercise as to (1) who should read them and (2) what you can expect to get out of them. But let's start with *the* magazine in the field.

THE BEST, ALL-AROUND MAGAZINE

RUNNER'S WORLD

Three men, each working in his own way and independently, have put jogging on the map: Ken Cooper, with the concept of aerobics; Bill Bowerman, the Oregon track coach who worked out the mechanics of jogging; and Bob Anderson, who put the sport into a magazine. With a sense of dedication possessed by few mortals, Bob has tapped the voracious appetite of the American public for information and news about its favorite *participant* sports. *Runner's World* passed its eleventh anniversary recently and it is just beginning to hit high gear. Its 228,000 subscribers make it by far Anderson's most successful magazine (he also publishes *Soccer World, Bike World,* and several other "Worlds"). Running is also the key to his equally successful book-publishing and sports-equipment spinoffs: World Publications, Inc. and Starting Line Sports, Inc.

You'll hear criticism of *Runner's World*—it's that good. Nobody knocks an also-ran. The editors have their ears to the ground, and they hear well. The magazine serves up a very palatable mixture of homey humor, original research, moments from history, vignettes, and major coverage of worldwide events. But the contributors make the difference: George Sheehan, of course; but also marathoner Brian Maxwell, Bill Rodgers, Joan Ullyot; Ken Young, who heads the National Running Data Center in Tucson, Arizona; Hal Higdon; Dr. Tom Bassler, leading name in the American Medical Joggers Association; and a whole host of unknowns who are paid modestly for their slants on running at the grass-

roots level. And it's a real forum: every viewpoint receives a full hearing, without being tempered with Editor's Notes. Quite a furor erupted over a recent piece on alcohol and athletics, for example (see page 110). But the magazine goes along unselfconsciously, like a patient oracle.

Sooner or later you'll subscribe, as much for the medical advice and instruction as for the titillation of reading about the greats of running.

Runner's World
P.O. Box 366
Mountain View, Calif. 94042

The current subscription rate is $9.50 per year. Don't worry, they'll put you in touch with their book and equipment outlets in short order.

What you can't expect to get in *RW* is good coverage of local events. They compromise by reporting on the bigger marathons, the special runs, such as the 12,000-strong Bay to Breakers in San Francisco, and by listing locations around the country where fun-runs are held on a regular weekly or monthly basis. Fun-runs, in fact, were the invention of Bob Anderson about five years ago. He sees them as the logical extension of Aerobics-a goal-oriented program for those who achieved their 30 points a week and were confused about where to go from there. For more on fun-runs, see Chapter Seven.

With so much to cover I marvel that so little slips by *RW*. And I am also impressed with the degree of person-to-person communication the magazine exudes, even as it has shouldered its way into the big-time of the publishing industry.

Important issues: the annual shoe evaluation issue, October; coverage of the Boston Marathon, June; and (every four years) magnificent accounts before, during, and after the Olympics. (For more on the shoe issue, see page 55.)

Important features: Sheehan's "Medical Advice" column, to which you can bring your own questions (I am told the doctor answers *all* his mail, though of course only the most broadly interesting subjects appear in print. How long can this keep up?); "Runner's Forum" where readers offer viewpoints and sometimes oddball stories and humor; and "Looking at People," a collection profile on runners with a very human touch.

Important articles: coverage of the big races by Hal Higdon (he understands the "older" runner, as he is perhaps the only athlete to win National AAU titles as a junior, senior, and master); evocative accounts of marathoning by Brian Maxwell, assistant track coach at the University of California; perceptive reporting of women's events by a host of women participants. The secret here is that virtually all articles are written from the inside, not by spectators.

There are several magazines which do some things better than *RW* (see pages 123-127), and many that get closer to home, but none with its overall impact and international prestige.

THE BEST BUY FOR BEGINNERS

Bill Bowerman, *Jogging*
(Grosset & Dunlap, New York, 1967)

From all the references in this chapter, you might have guessed this is my favorite. Sure, it's a little out of date, but that's a good part of its charm. All the trappings have been stripped away—or I should say, were never there to begin with. A glance at the photographs tells who this was written for—*you*. There you are, old-timer, in your baggy Bermudas and undershirt. There *you* are, bored housewife, looking as if you're sloshing home from a bridge game in your hooded raincoat. And there's the college crowd in full stride around the track. Where else would you find a writer saying that it's all right for women to run in skirts if they prefer?

The theory is still sound after all these years, and the headlines (there are no chapters, just a running series of headlines) loudly proclaim the main points: "Long Johns in Cold Weather," "Clothes Don't Make the Jogger but They May Help the Spirit," "Jog Anywhere—Open Your Door and You're in Business."

More than half this slim paperback is taken up with a 12-week program: just open up to the right week and you're told what to do each day. And you can choose Plan A, B, or C, depending on your starting condition.

You'll find little here of medical research or advice to the competitive runner—but the title didn't promise that. Just jogging. The focus is right and the price is right: $1.95 (paperback).

Runners stretching their muscles before running

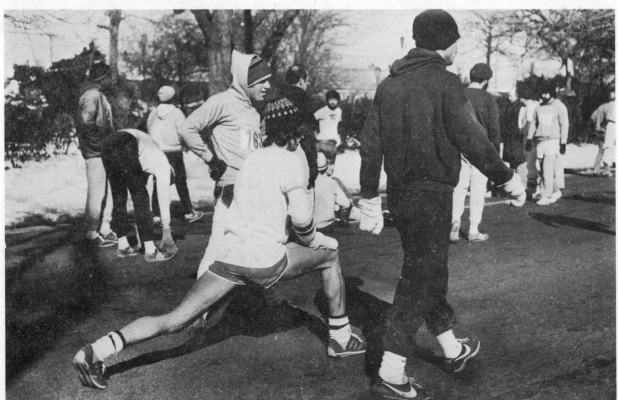

THE METRIC MILER

50 meters = 54 yards 6.5 inches
100 meters = 109 yards 1 foot 1 inch
400 meters = 437 yards 1 foot 4 inches
800 meters = 874 yards 2 feet 8 inches
1500 meters = 1640 yards 1 foot 3 inches
5000 meters = (3.1) miles 188 yards 2.4 inches
10,000 meters = (6.2) miles 376 yards 4.8 inches

One mile = 1609.344 meters
3 miles = 4828.032 meters
6 miles = 9656.064 meters
10 miles = 16,093.44 meters
Marathon = 42,195 meters (26 miles, 385 yards)

Note
one kilometer = 1000 meters (km.)

THE BEST OVERALL ACCOUNT OF RUNNING

James F. Fixx, *The Complete Book of Running* (Random House, New York, 1977)

With the publication of this comprehensive study, the literature of running took a quantum leap. A worthy bestseller, it will open the appeal of jogging to a vast audience which previously might have looked on huffing and puffing as some sort of a fad or cult.

Fixx has etched in his subject painstakingly and patiently, ringing in the appropriate references, talking to fun-runners as well as marathoners, equally balancing 24 topics from "feeling better" to ultralong-distance running, never missing the telling anecdote or the precise detail. The result is at one and the same time an instruction manual, an inspirational tract, and a coffee-table tome.

A better-than-average runner for many years, Fixx also reveals a lot of his personality, which, while competitive, has the human touch runners can identify with readily. He has not skimped, although my personal taste would have thinned out the numerous pages devoted to proving, once again, the case for the medical benefits of running. He has gone and talked to Dave Costill at Ball State University; to Ken Cooper in Dallas; to Joe Henderson in Mountain View. He has run with Bill Rodgers. He has walked down the hospital corridors with George Sheehan. And he has pried loose the dormant fact, the hidden assumption that was there all the time but that we never saw before.

There is a pleasing compression to his reporting that makes this very full book move along swiftly. Unlike many books on sports, it can be read cover-to-cover. For this same reason the illustrations are decorative without being either outstanding art or instructional. And then there's this business of using a full-page chart to make a simple statement appear more scientific. Some important names and institutions are passed over: Arthur Lydiard, Ken Young and his statistical lab, all podiatrists (not even the word is mentioned), and the big runs throughout the country that are the lifeblood of the sport. The generally Eastern orientation of the book makes it sound hollow in parts to readers in other regions of the country.

But he didn't promise us an encyclopedia! His account of the Boston Marathon is at once lyrical and laced with facts. His discussion of young runners, masters, women, and personalities could hardly be improved upon. Tips of the trade abound. But best of all, Fixx makes you feel proud to be a runner, privileged to get up at the crack of dawn, put on your running shoes, and go out for a run. To round it off, the publisher put $10 production quality into this $10 bargain. It's big in every way.

THE BEST SYMPOSIUM OF VIEWPOINTS FOR REGULAR RUNNERS

Editors of *Runner's World* Magazine, *The Complete Runner* (World Publications, Mountain View, Calif., 1974)

Though many of the pieces in this hefty volume are rapidly going out of date, together they constitute just about everything a serious runner is concerned with. Strictly speaking, this book is not "by" the editors of *Runner's World,* as the title page says. It's a collection of some of the best pieces to appear there, up to 1973. In a Foreword, Joe Henderson aptly points out that there is a range of viewpoints here, not just the conventional wisdom. It would have been helpful to preface them a little more thoroughly; as it is, sometimes one can't tell if an article is an original contribution or when and where it first appeared.

Many books entitle themselves "complete" on scanter data. For future editions, I hope more recent articles could be included, such as Sheehan's Basic Six exercises, something on orthotics, and an account of one of the big races, such as the Boston Marathon. It's a milestone in publishing in the field of running. And it may be your only chance to sample some of the best pieces from old issues of the magazine.

The $10.95 price tag is justified by a liberal sprinkling of illustrations and photographs, and good coverage of competitive races, such as sprints, which you're not likely to see in a jogging book. Then why do you want to see them? For just plain good reading, that's why!

THE BEST MOTIVATIONAL BOOK FOR RUNNERS OF ALL TYPES

George Sheehan, M.D.,
Dr. Sheehan on Running
(World Publications,
Mountain View, Calif., 1975)

Sheehan is the most quoted man in running because he generally writes about everything *else*. His iconoclastic attitude toward his own profession invites our credence; his concern for the human condition inspires our confidence (see profile, page 79).

This is the first collection of his columns, mostly from *Runner's World, The Physician and Sportsmedicine,* and a newspaper in his home state, New Jersey. They are arranged in three categories: The Runner, The Doctor, The Thinker; and they are appropriately grouped under conventional chapter headings ("Stress and Rest," "Age and Ability," etc.). But the limits of subject matter cannot restrain this thinker. When he is called upon to discuss "carbohydrate

Dr. Sheehan lecturing on podiatry in Central Park in New York City

loading," for example, he carefully ticks off the facts: an exhausting workout about a week before a race depletes the runner's glycogen stores—three days of low-carb diet exhaust those stores even further—then when the runner loads up with pancakes and spaghetti in the final days before the race his body overcompensates and doubles or triples its glycogen stores, the source of energy. So far, so good. But Sheehan characteristically tops this account off by theorizing that this is what our cavemen ancestors did: when reduced to roots and herbs they were revitalized and went off to a successful (protein) hunt. (Note: Carbohydrates, not protein, are most certainly the body's source of energy, but *loading* in the above manner may be dangerous. Serious runners: check *RW* for the latest theory!)

Sheehan has a new book out, but I prefer seeing him here in transition: doctor turning runner turning writer. He says that he finds writing extremely difficult and apologizes for his efforts. Yet every time he writes, he gives us something of himself, and motivates us to run by showing us that running is a larger thing than technique, or exercise, or good medical practice.

Paperback, $3.95; like most other World Publications, also available in hardcover at $5.95.

THE BEST PHYSIOLOGICAL BACKGROUND FOR RUNNERS

Kenneth H. Cooper, M.D., M.P.H.,
The Aerobics Way
(M. Evans and Company, New York, 1977)

That aerobics man is back again with his eye on

Ken and Millie Cooper

same thing all over the world, for the focus of both is improvement of the cardiovascular system. Jogging is simply the easiest way to amass aerobic points. Unlike most of the apostles of jogging, however, Cooper pays scant attention to the psychological aspects of running. A popular tee shirt reads, "Work has purpose but no meaning—running has meaning but no purpose." Cooper's unstated assumption is that the purpose of jogging is to prevent heart attacks. I lean to the opinion that the physical benefits are just a happy accompaniment of the play, and once one starts aiming for those benefits the play easily becomes work. It's like pursuing happiness.

The Aerobics Way doesn't supersede any of Dr. Cooper's three previous bestsellers. The "chart pack" for various forms of exercise remains basically the same, but the heart of the aerobics message has always been motivation, not simply information. *Aerobics* (M. Evans, 1968), *The New Aerobics* (M. Evans, 1970), and *Aerobics for Women* (M. Evans, 1972) deserve to be read on their own for the uniqueness of their approach to the age-old question, "What, *me* exercise?" I hasten to point out that the latter book is very much Mildred Cooper's, with technical support and an introduction from her husband. Millie writes engagingly for other women faced with the "dress-size crisis"; her message, however, goes much deeper than cosmetics. She's not afraid to tackle the question of how women differ physically from men and what those differences mean in an exercise program. Her case histories ring true: One woman, on being told by her doctor that she must be 29, not 39, sighed, "Ahhhhhrobics!" You get the feeling from reading the aerobics books that the Coopers are the kind of people you'd like to have as friends. In *The New Aerobics*, the doctor takes a closer look at the age crisis, and explains how an aerobics program should be tailored for men and women of all capabilities and interests. As people everywhere become more exercise-conscious, I look for further guidelines from the Coopers after *The Aerobics Way:* the subject is bottomless.

Cooper's ability to hold the attention of a fad-oriented public is all the more noteworthy when you consider the number of excellent physical fit-

the clipboard and his cheerful pen flowing with good news for people who care about their health. Most "son of" books are pale imitations of the original; Cooper seems to improve with age. For one thing, he has more figures (does he!). For another, ten years after his first book he has dozens of imitators springing up around him to act as foils for his sensible approach. He takes them all on—the fad dieters, the "quickee" fitness experts, the miracle-pill people. True, his presentation is awash with statistics and charts. But Cooper has a way of summarizing and finding rules of thumb from years of experience at his clinic; when you're ready for it, you can always go back to the fine print.

Jogging and aerobics are thought of as the

ness books on the market, among them: *Physical Fitness: A Way of Life* by Bud Getchell (see page 81), *Complete Conditioning* by David Shepero and Howard G. Knuttgen (Addison-Wesley, 1975), and *Maximum Performance* by Laurence Morehouse (see page 82). The reason for Cooper's consistent success, I think, is that he avoids a heavy-handed scientific approach on the one hand, and a breezy popularization on the other. Cute drawings and puns won't turn an academic treatise into a book for the average reader—and Cooper doesn't need those tricks. *The Aerobics Way* is the product of a man of strong opinions and with a serious message. If you are taken by the health-promise of jogging, this book will give you its complete rationale, from statistics, to exercise programs, to diet, and even to the "aerobic glow." A $10 book, it will be on your bookshelf a long time after a dozen other current competitors are packed away.

MAKING YOUR WAY THROUGH TRAINING ON ONE-LINERS

This is the short course in jogging instruction. Here are the aphorisms, the quips, and the ripostes that spur runners on in the face of pain and uncertainty. When you can't turn another page or remember who said what, come back here.

The basic plan of training

"Run slowly, run daily, drink moderately, and don't eat like a pig."
    —Ernst van Aaken, *Van Aaken Method*

How much a day?

"More and more as I study positive addiction in its various forms, it seems that about an hour a day does it."
    —William Glasser, M.D., *Positive Addiction*

The only danger in running

"Heat is the only thing that can kill a healthy athlete."
    —George Sheehan, M.D., *The Physician and Sportsmedicine*

On resting

"It takes as much courage to stop training as to go out when not feeling up to it."
    —Roger Bannister, *The Four-Minute Mile*

On breathing

"The basic rule of life is: Never close your glottis."
    —Laurence Morehouse, Ph.D., *Total Fitness*

On drinking beer

"I don't mind getting half-looped the night before a race."
    —Frank Shorter, quoted in *Runner's World*

On mixing sex with athletics

"It isn't sex that wrecks these guys—it's staying up all night looking for it."
    —Casey Stengel

On competing

"Start slowly and taper off."
    —Motto, the Dolphin South End Runners' Club

On the social benefits

"Hills make every man a brother."
    —George Sheehan

Wise and consoling thought

"Train, don't strain."
    —Bill Bowerman

On running and addiction

"For reasons not entirely clear, smokers who become runners always quit smoking."
    —Dr. Peter D. Wood, Stanford Medical Center

On stretching

"There is no special advantage in being able to touch your toes or put your palms flat on the floor. All that indicates is that your joints locked late."
    —Percy Cerutty

BOOKS YOU CAN'T GO WRONG WITH

Beyond the preceding five "best books" there lies a whole range of writing that can't be ignored. The basic information outlined in this chapter is also covered in one form or another in any of the following books and pamphlets:

Jack Batten, *The Complete Jogger,* Harcourt Brace Jovanovich, New York, 1977, $4.95. (Too much promise for a 145-page paperback and out of touch with many forms of running, but still a well-written introduction to the sport.)

Joe Henderson, *Long Slow Distance: The Humane Way to Train,* World Publications, Mountain View, Calif., 1969, $2.50. (The first of a number of inspiring books by the editor of *Runner's World,* about whom see page 44.)

Joe Henderson, *The Long Run Solution,* World Publications, 1976, $3.95. (Meditations on 20 reasons for running.)

Joe Henderson, *Jog, Run, Race,* World Publications, 1977, $3.50. (Step-by-step approach to moving from a loafer to a true competitor.)

Kathryn Lance, *Running for Health and Beauty: A Complete Guide for Women,* Bobbs-Merrill, New York, 1977, $4.95. (Closely parallels Joan Ullyot's book below, with a strong New York City perspective.)

Joan Ullyot, M.D., *Women's Running,* World Publications, 1976, $3.95. (From a woman's point of view but widely applicable; see page 88).

Ernst van Aaken, M.D., *Van Aaken Method,* World Publications, 1976, $3.95. (Somewhat more specialized, emphasizing endurance training, but full of insights and proposing some highly speculative theories, such as running as a preventative of cancer.)

Beginning Running, Runner's World Magazine, 1972, $1.50. (32 jam-packed pages, summarizing the advice of the experts.)

Guidelines for Successful Jogging, Rory Donaldson, editor. Contributions by Dr. George Sheehan, Hal Higdon, Dr. Tom Bassler, Dr. Harry Hlavac, etc. Available from the publisher: National Jogging Association, 1910 K Street, Suite 202, Washington, D.C. 20006, $3.95 plus 40¢ handling and postage. (For more on the NJA, see page 138. *The Jogger*, a monthly tabloid published by the association and edited by Donaldson, offers wise and often whacky advice and psychups for the noncompetitive runner; especially the beginner. *Guidelines* is largely excerpted from *The Jogger.*)

HOW TO BUY BOOKS ON RUNNING WITHOUT RUNNING UP A BIG TAB

1. *Don't buy sight-unseen.* At least get the recommendation of a friend. Even the "best buys" here may not be right for you, for a book is a personal communication of which you are one half. Catalog descriptions cannot convey the spirit of a book.

2. *Look at books in a sports store.* Most bookstores carry only books from major publishers. When you have only a few books to compare, you have no comparison. Running-shoe stores especially carry the most popular paperbacks. If your bookseller has a good line, patronize him. (B. Dalton stores now carry World Publications books.)

3. *Don't be swayed by publication dates.* Some of the original pamphlets published by *Runner's World* in their "Booklet of the Month" program several years ago stand up exceedingly well.

4. *Choose one or two good books.* It's a false economy to buy several inexpensive pamphlets or paperbacks when a solid, bigger book has more to offer between two covers.

5. *Exchange books with your friends.* Put your name on them, and return the books you borrow to get your own back.

6. *Buy through your club.* You or the club may get discounts; your club treasurer will steer you away from lemons.

7. *Trust your fellow runners.* All of the books listed in this chapter are heartily approved by most joggers, and certainly meet the standard of being useful to the noncompetitive runner of any level.

FREE BOOKLETS

Beyond Diet . . . Exercise Your Way to Fitness and Heart Health,
Lenore R. Zohman, M.D.

The American Heart Association has taken several fast jogs forward with the distribution of this well-presented case for aerobic exercise. The illustration on the cover is of youngsters skipping rope, but the message comes through loud and clear in the charts comparing various types of exercise: walking, jogging, running are good, better, best. An excellent feature rarely found in books ten times the size is a thorough discussion of warning signs of physical distress—before or after exercise. Since the publisher is Mazola Corn Oil, the dietary message favoring polyunsaturated vegatable oils receives due prominence—but who are we to argue nutrition when the net effect is excellent?

Call your nearest American Heart Association office for free copies—especially for your school, business firm, or club.

HOW TO START A RUNNING CLUB

This free 16-page booklet published by the Road Runners Club of America gives helpful hints on getting things organized—useful also for the runner who is unsure about the merits of belonging to a club. (See "Joining.") Send a stamped, self-addressed envelope to:

Jeff Darman, President
Road Runners Club of America
2737 Devonshire Place, N.W.
Washington, D.C. 20008

This is an important address, and an important organization. The RRCA also has a "Personal Fitness Program" for the person who wants to get serious about his health. For a flyer describing the program send a stamped, self-addressed envelope to:

Russ Akers
959 Olympia
Walla Walla, Wash. 99362

What they say

You may have read a lot of the good things about running already in the newspapers. Here's what the celebrities are saying: "It's my way of getting centered, of getting a grip on myself" (Farrah Fawcett-Majors); "It's a morning cocktail party" (George Hirsch); "I feel like a man in his 20's or 30's, but I'm 56" (Abe Vigoda); "I sing music in my head—it's a nice way to keep the rhythm and keep grooving" (Lola Falana); "I jog because it helps my love life" (Brenda Vaccaro); "I can lock my brain off and focus on one particular subject—it's hypnotic" (Richard Zanuck).

Corporations are giving employees incentives to jog—they're providing track facilities, and affording employees extra time to use them. Executives use running as a preparation for tough negotiating. Mayors are running for civic unity. Worriers are jogging to avoid heart attacks. Writers are running to unleash their creative minds. But best of all, almost everyone is running *for fun.*

Grab your shoes and let's go.

two

the soul
what running does for your head

That 30 minutes will get us fit and put us in the 95 percentile for cardiopulmonary endurance. At 12 calories per minute, it will eventually bring our weight down to desired levels. It will also slow the pulse and drop the blood pressure. It will make us good animals.

That first 30 minutes is for my body. During that half hour, I take joy in my physical ability, the endurance and power of my running. I find it a time when I feel myself competent and in control of my body, when I can think about my problems and plan my day-to-day world. In many ways, that 30 minutes is all ego, all the self. It has to do with me, the individual.

What lies beyond this fitness of muscle? I can only answer for myself. The next 30 minutes is for my soul. In it, I come upon the third wind, which is psychological (unlike the second wind, which is physiological). And then I see myself not as an individual but as a part of the universe. In it I can happen upon anything I ever read or saw or experienced. Every fact and instinct and emotion is unlocked and made available to me through some mysterious operation in my brain.

Thus Dr. George Sheehan charts the specifics of the psychological benefits of running (*Runner's World,* August, 1977). He also has given us the 19 reasons why runners hurt, his Irish nature coming to the fore. (Don't let the number scare you. See "Compensating," page 101—they're all there.) Most writers are transfixed by the *physiological* benefits of running. Hal Higdon offers 21 questions to measure your life expectancy, many of which involve points for diet and exercise. Likewise Dr. Lester Breslow, as a result of hundreds of case histories, laid down seven good health habits "that add seven to eleven years to your life." But Sheehan waxes poetic and optimistic only when talking about the rewards for the *spirit.*

The jogging "high" is not given to all of us, even after the mandatory 30 minutes on the road. *More convincing to many is the peculiar inversion of cause and effect which running brings about in our daily lives.* Instead of dieting in order to be able to run, running tells our bodies what diet it prefers. Vegetarians and near-vegetarians are numerous among joggers who log at least 20 miles a week. Instead of going to bed early to recuperate from jogging, we get more energy and more waking hours. This unexpected blessing which the avocation confers brightens our lives. Even Sheehan's 19 reasons why runners hurt begin to look like nice ways of diverting deeper pains.

When someone tells you he doesn't experience "runner's high," ask him what else gives him a high. A few martinis? Beethoven's Ninth? Loving without expecting love in return? Trouble is, the word "high" has zen-like, grass-like connotations. I have shed tears, while running, thinking of Sheehan's little story: "I saw this solemn four-year-old just standing with a tiny cup hoping someone would stop. I did and drank two ounces and told her, 'You're my honey.'" But remember, if you like Beethoven's Ninth, don't settle for highlights, don't buy the pop-rock version. Take the full run.

A SENSE OF PEOPLE

Communing with nature and listening to one's *inner* nature are commonly mentioned as the

---

THOUGHTS FROM A MARATHON MAN

"Man in a state of nature is a runner. Look at children: they are always running. Their first halting steps are but a transient stage towards culmination in a sprint. . . . For a child is born free. We grownups must be 'civilized.'

". . . Every time one sole lights upon the earth, the other is aloft. He is at one with nature, and he flies." (Ed. note: In a marathon the runner is completely aloft for at least two and a half miles. See "The Feet," page 48.)

"It is a scientific fact that running is, by chance, salubrious as well. But so is sex. Yet has a man in passion ever cried, 'I only do it for my health'?"
—Erich Segal

spiritual stuff of running. Perhaps writers on the subject haven't fully explored the *social* springs from which runners drink: the teams, clubs outings, relays, parties, camaraderie, and even "dating game" of the fraternity/sorority. One looks in vain to most books and national magazines for a clue to why joggers are joiners, and what sorts of activities they join in.

The "Christmas Relay" is an annual fixture of the running scene in Northern California. It's a 50-mile run in seven legs, roughly 10-5-5-10-5-5-10, from the University of California at Santa Cruz north to Half Moon Bay, along the ocean route of California Highway 1. It typifies the "people" appeal of running, for among the two hundred or more teams which enter are college cross-country teams, A.A.U. clubs, high school students, women's clubs or schools, masters and submasters (30 to 40 years of age) groups, and pickup teams assembled a half hour before starting time. Most of the teams are hardly vying for awards—they start an hour before the "fast race" entrants, identified as intending to run at better than seven-minute miles. Yet there are awards in each of nine divisions, for a total of 245 plaques, with perpetual trophies for the fastest legs and fastest men's and women's teams.

The club I belong to decided to enter two teams and divide the talent among them—with the express purpose of getting everyone involved. With world-class marathoners Ron Wayne and Brian Maxwell in the club, this was a generous deci-

Synanon, which is known throughout the world for its rehabilitation programs, has now taken to running as a form of therapy. Races sponsored by the Synanon headquarters in Marshall, California are open to the public.

SELECTION:
SHARING AN ANCIENT KINSHIP

Mere good health can easily be earned without major dislocation of one's life; twenty or thirty minutes a day four days a week would do it. So why do people run eight, ten, or more miles every day, in summer's swelter and winter's blasts, particularly when they know that they will never become especially distinguished at it?

Many theories have been suggested. Roger Bannister has compared running with music. Both stimulate our nervous systems in ways the human organism finds pleasurable. . . .

Closely related to this theory is one recently offered by Thaddeus Kostrubala, the psychiatrist. Addressing a conference of doctors and researchers, Kostrubala wondered aloud whether a runner might, after forty minutes or so of running, somehow "obliterate" the influence of the right cortex (the logical part of the brain), allowing the left cortex (the intuitive, artistic part) to gain temporary dominance. . . .

Perhaps there is something to all these theories. Still, I have a different one. Most people who have considered the matter have, I believe, posed the wrong question. They have asked why running produces such extraordinary effects. Putting the question that way elicits a certain kind of answer, and I think it is the wrong one. My suspicion is that the effects of running are not extraordinary at all, but quite ordinary. It is the *other* states, all *other* feelings, that are peculiar, for they are an abnegation of the way you and I are intended to feel. As runners, I think we reach back directly along the endless chain of history. We experience what we would have felt had we lived ten thousand years ago, eating fruits, nuts, and vegetables, and keeping our hearts and lungs and muscles fit by constant movement. We are reasserting, as modern man seldom does, our kinship with ancient man, and even with the wild beasts that preceded him. This, I think, is our remarkable secret, one we share every time we go running.

—James F. Fixx,
The Complete Book of Running
(Random House, New York, 1977)

sion, for there were several other sub-seven-minute long-distance runners itching to go after an award. It turned out to be more than generous—a satisfying decision.

Brian led off one team at a blistering sub-five-minute pace, which placed him well in the lead at the first exchange point. There he slapped the hand of our second runner, 11-year-old John Burger, who somewhat hesitatingly took off up the hill in a light rain, all alone in first place, carrying the honor of the club on his gangly legs for the next five miles. After a hundred yards he turned back to look at the crowd lining the highway, smiled the smile of one who has just had the experience of a lifetime, and loped onward. Our "support" car leapfrogged ahead to drop our runner for the next leg, and so on for the rest of the fifty miles. It didn't matter that John's five miles was little faster than Brian's ten. At an impromptu picnic five hours later the fourteen of us—kids, women, marathoners, and graybeards—relished our own little triumphs of the day, challenges overcome, friends met, courses run.

There are many other relays like this throughout the country, though perhaps California has the longest tradition in this one and in the Lake Tahoe relays. Whether relays or fun-runs or triathlons (see page 144), the sense of being with people and sharing the race with them is unique to this sport. Football fans have tailgate parties before big games; neighborhood bars send whole contingents on buses to crucial baseball rivalries. Alumni and alumnae celebrate the old school ties, and season-ticket holders at professional games create their own alma maters in the stands. But on the roads of America there's

THE EVIDENCE FOR "RUNNER'S HIGH"

Hormones: "There have been some interesting studies recently showing such things as the metabolism of thyroid glands is different in a person who is exercising."—Dr. Ken Cooper

According to studies by a British medical team headed by Dr. Malcolm Carruthers, norepinephrine, one of the hormones from the adrenal glands, is doubled in the body after as little as ten minutes of vigorous exercise. The effect is long lasting and is associated with "happy feelings."

Muscular relaxation: "The deepest relaxation, as measured by electrodes inserted in the muscles, follows a period of voluntarily *increased* muscular tension."—Dr. Paul Issel and Dr. Walton Roth

Mellowing of the nervous system: "Fatigue is the most common symptom of low-blood sugar . . . and zinc is another mineral which can have a mellowing effect on the nervous system."—Dr. Michael Lesser, commenting on the effects of running on change in diet toward blood-sugar balance and increases in minerals.

Anthropology: "This need to run is programmed genetically into our brains."—Dr. William Glasser (Dr. Thaddeus Kostrubala, James F. Fixx, Joe Henderson say the same thing in their own way; See "Selection," page 37).

Meditation: "We should allow for time off, some leeway, some slack in the day."—Dr. William Glasser. "The time spent running is mind-cleansing."—Joe Henderson. And he offers a possible reason: "Since modern living offers much tension and so few chances for socially acceptable fights, man gets his release by fleeing." Comments like these are hardly scientific, but the overwhelming testimony of long-distance runners is that a mild euphoria, a feeling of acceptance of the world and of control over one's affairs, commonly occurs after about 30 minutes of running. Since these effects are frequently observed in only one other type of human activity—meditation—it's reasonable to assume that the repetitive motions of running induce a form of meditation. Dr. Kostrubala compares the repetitiveness of bodily motions in running with the chanting of a mantra or the praying of "Hail Marys" in saying a rosary.

The thrill of winning is most of all a personal thing.

another kind of brotherhood or sisterhood (let's call it runnerhood) that's getting something basic out of life: a dimension of people, not easily structured by class, age, ability, sex, social position, or the accidents of life, all taking part in a good thing.

All of us run at one time or another to be alone, merely to be able to have an uninterrupted moment. Or we run to see what we can do alone. May I also suggest the sociability of the long-distance runner?

Fred Rohé, *The Zen of Running*, (Random House—Bookworks, New York, 1974)

A little too much of Jonathan Livingston Seagull in this book for me, but, as the author never lets you forget, "whatever turns you on." The format is reminiscent of the love-poetry picture books so popular a few years ago (yes, it comes from Berkeley). The large black-and-white photographs of the author and friends running in the San Francisco Bay Area are impressive. Yet they're neither unusual enough to stand on their own nor instructive enough to serve a utilitarian purpose. I even have to quibble with the calligraphy and the page makeup: the text isn't poetical enough to justify this pretense.

When the author finally accepts that it's OK to give advice, he has good things to say. Run as erect as possible; run until you sweat and pant;

THE NUMBERS OF RUNNING

As you read and reread books on running, certain key numbers will become fixed in your mind. If you dislike numbers, read them here once and for all and then go your own way:

Six seconds: The way to take your pulse during exercise. Count your heartbeats for six seconds and multiply by ten for your pulse rate (expressed always in beats per minute—normal is 72, runners usually go below 60, Ron Wayne is below 30!). The six-second method is better than the ten-second for two reasons: the pulse rate declines rapidly even between six and ten seconds, and it's easier to multiply by ten than by six. Helpful tip from exercise physiologist Ellen Collins: the easiest place to get a strong pulse is on your carotid artery. Place three fingers of your right hand just to the left and above your Adam's apple. Much stronger than wrist pulse. If there's no watch available, have a friend count 1001, 1002, etc.

Seventy-five per cent maximum output: When you take a fitness (stress) test, your maximum heart rate before exhaustion is determined; you should then exercise at 75% of that to (1) avoid danger and (2) get results. Using the above pulse-taking procedure, you can monitor your exercise heart rate as follows: if your maximum is 200, then don't go over 150, or 15 beats per six seconds. If it's 160, then don't go over 120, or 12 beats per six seconds.

(Hint: Use the numbers religiously only if you tend to be a Type A person—the type who pushes himself beyond capacity.)

Thirty-minute barrier: "The first 20-30 minutes are enough to make a person fit, but the second 20-30 make running worth doing," says Joe Henderson. Beyond the barrier lies Dr. Sheehan's "third wind"—the world of runner's high. But that only comes when you can run effortlessly for that period of time.

Thirty-second stretch: In spite of what you may have read, stretching isn't effective unless prolonged for about half a minute. After the commonly recommended ten seconds, the reflex guard of the muscles hasn't been overcome. Hold your fully stretched position (wall push-up, toe-touch, legs-over or "plow") for 20 to 40 seconds, according to your flexibility.

Forty-mile week: Something of a rule of thumb nowadays for preparation for a marathon. Sheehan says six miles a day, six days a week may be enough. Many others want to do a hundred miles a week. It all depends on whether you want to finish or whether you want to meet a certain standard.

Hour-a-day-keeps-the-doctor-away: Joe Henderson's prescription for himself. Thaddeus Kostrubala, the psychiatrist, finds an hour a day, three times a week enough. Sheehan leans now to two good long runs a week. An hour a day is a comfortable period for the runner who has arrived.

Eight-minute mile: A common pace, which will result in a three-hour, 30-minute marathon, to qualify you for the Boston Marathon if you are over 40 or a woman, the marathon being 26.2 miles. Under 40, your time must be three hours or better. It takes slightly better than a seven-minute mile to break three hours. Women *world-class* runners do it at six minutes per mile; men at five minutes plus.

SELECTION:
WHY ONE MAN RUNS

I am thinking of something that happened during the day and wondering how I could have been so upset about it. I no longer touch the ground; I am moving through the air, floating. The incline is not a hill, it is just air that is a little thicker, and I can breathe deeply and draw myself up without effort. My body is producing draughts of a hormone called epinephrine, which researchers have linked with feelings of euphoria. This, combined with the alpha waves and the repetitive motion of running, which acts as a sort of mantra, makes me higher than is legally possible in any other way. . . .

In the eighth mile "things" happen. Not mental things, easily ascribed to alpha waves or hormones. Emotional things. Spiritual things. Things that it is more than a little embarrassing to speak of afterward. I feel myself reaching out to all those around me. I feel a tremendous warmth toward the six million Americans who run, the 100,000 Finns, the million and a half in Peking. I begin to believe in the dignity and brotherhood of man. I am incapable of anger now, ignorant of frustration. Hope is my watchword as I climb the incline and come across the top of the square, and though I know I am tiring I feel great strength. I pass the pole for the fifteenth time and pour the power on. My chest is straining to suck in air, my heart rate climbs to 160. I go into the final half-mile, glorying in the freedom to spend everything, to blow it all. I am finished for the night, but I know that some day, perhaps some day soon, I will reach this point and go on and on. I am moving quickly now, by my standards, and everything is working as it should. My feet come down *right.* My legs drive *right.* I power up the incline, pouring it on in the last quarter-mile. I let it all go. The wind whistles in my ears, slaps gently at my skin. I make the last turn and drive on down past the pole, and, even as I slow gasping, I wish that I could run on forever.

—David Bradley, *The Village Voice,*
reprinted in *The Jogger,* May, 1977

run within your breath, not ahead of your breath; above all, make it fun. He advocates running as unencumbered as possible, barefoot along the beach ideally. He loses me when he adds the reason for going barefoot: "electrical equilibrium is established between you and the planet." But then, I don't understand what storing a surplus of prana has to do with it. On matters of zen, Ian Jackson reaches me more cleanly (see his articles in *The Complete Runner*).

One good thought from a book is enough to make it worthwhile. You may even find the earthy approach here inspirational enough without anything new or newly said in it. For my money, Rohé justifies the whole effort with observations like this: if running can be a meditation, then it teaches us that all life can be a meditation, too. Or, simply, "running is one more way for you to discover you." For some people, this is the only sensible reason for running.

ANOTHER REASON FOR "COED" RUNNING

The Exercise Physiology Division of the U.S. Army conducted a series of tests in the basic training of male and female recruits at Fort Jackson in 1975. First the men and women were put through basic training in segregated groups. Extensive examinations before and after showed significant improvement for the men, but the women exhibited "no change in muscular strength, aerobic capacity, psychological well-being or mental health." The chief noticeable change in them was "an increase in body weight, mostly fat." Then another, similar group of recruits went through basic training with men and women integrated. This time there was no difference in male and female improvement: both improved as much as the first groups.

The study concludes, "Integrated training works," primarily because of motivation to exert to the edge of one's limits.

The presence of women running on streets, tracks, and backroads seems to me to mean more than statistics about the job market or the number of women in law schools. In open races, men outnumber women fun-runners at least ten to one. It doesn't matter. The women are *there.* They haven't simply broken into a male enclave—they've turned the whole sexist attitude of society upside down. There are enough women who do run to demonstrate how wrong our assumptions about physical ability have been.

A NEW VISION OF FEMININE POWER

"If we are to survive as a species, we need a new paradigm. We need to tap our female energy— the nurturing, supporting, intuitive energy in all of us, men and women. Society's whole competitive yang energy has to relinquish to a more sensitive, delicate balance of nature in harmony. And that's what we're beginning to see."

Dyveke Spino leads a running class near her home at the foot of Mount Tamalpais in Marin County, north of San Francisco. "If I don't run that mountain every day," she said in the course of an interview from which the above thoughts were taken, "I'm no good for anything." One of her students is George Leonard; his debt to her was acknowledged by the fact that she was the only woman featured in his provocative book, *The Ultimate Athlete.* Dyveke's credentials on the subject of the creative aspects of running are impressive. In her childhood she was considered a musical prodigy, and was torn between the piano, tennis, and swimming. Her parents moved in a circle which included Jack London and Isadora Duncan. She never gave up her love for the piano, but she turned her energies to more practical concerns: first working as a clinical

psychologist, then with disturbed children in an experimental program involving art and athletics, then in an artists' commune. With her former husband Mike she founded the Esalen Sports Center, and developed a seminar called "Women in Motion" to demonstrate how strenuous movement can become effortless in the proper focus.

The influence of Mike Spino (or perhaps it's the opposite) is obvious. Dyveke's routine includes high kicks, shake-ups, shuffles, swings, and saunters. In downtown Mill Valley her class is often seen snaking around cars lined up at parking meters and tip-toeing along crowded sidewalks. And she is the master of the psych-up: She imagines (and asks her followers to imagine) hooks dropping down from the sky and connecting with their heads, lifting them from the pull of gravity. She has "soft eyes" that turn her knees into pools of water, making them soft and fluid, and puffs of clouds gather under her feet. I think they do.

TRICKS TO PLAY ON YOUR PSYCHE

Sometime soon the psychology department of a major university is going to measure the speed of runners before and after the theme from "Rocky" is played within their hearing. At the Brass Pole Run in Oakland, California (a benefit for burn victims sponsored by the Fire Department), the sirens of fire trucks signal the last mile of the race—one has to be hardhearted indeed not to leap at the sound.

When the physiological and psychological *benefits* of running aren't enough to turn you on, try the tricks. Bill Bowerman and his friends in Eugene started the "ten miles west of Dubuque" trick: you plot your mileage on a map and chart where you have gone each day. The average jogger can make it across the country in about three or four years.

I like to point to a "victory lap" in some stadium or track. In the fall, I time a Saturday afternoon run to finish at Memorial Stadium an hour after the football game is over. I burst into the stadium through the south tunnel and circle the abandoned field; the only sound is the tinkle of empty plastic cups being blown down the concrete aisles in the breezes of the dusk.

RUNNING FOR THE HIGH: PSYCHOLOGY OR NUTRITION?

There are numerous therapies based on physical activities: dance, theatre, art. Running is perhaps the only activity thought to be therapeutically helpful *purely* for its physical effects. It doesn't demand personal expression, creativity, or "acting out."

Two important books have appeared recently on the psychological benefits of running: *Positive Addiction* by William Glasser (Harper & Row, New York, 1976) and *The Joy of Running* by Thaddeus Kostrubala (J.B. Lippincott, Philadelphia, 1976). Both have been commented on extensively in running magazines—largely, in my opinion, because they tend to glorify the benefits of running. Dr. Kostrubala's case histories are impressive; he was able to find new ways of reaching depressed patients and even of opening up his own vistas. ". . . As I ran along with my patients, my own subconscious was stimulated. And as we explored the meanings and the stimuli for both the patient and therapist, it became quite evident that I could no longer adhere to any stereotyped rules as a therapist." Dr. Glasser didn't have the benefit of having lost 55 pounds in running, as did Kostrubala, but he has compared a variety of what he calls addictions, and has found running one of the best. The issue turns on the definition of a positive as against a negative addiction. Running is a positive addiction. Is playing golf? Or gambling?

Others, such as Dr. Michael Lesser, President of the American Orthomolecular Medical Society, would stress the nutritional needs of runners. It might be called the "tag-along" effect. Running causes us to change our diets. We need to replace lost minerals. The same foods which deliver those lost minerals give us the other ones we need. "Orthomolecular" medicine is a big word for treating medical (including psychological) problems through diet. Its founder is Dr. Linus Pauling, although he is mostly remembered for his case on Vitamin C and the common cold.

But Lesser and Pauling maintain that depression and even psychoses of various kinds are curable in a very high percentage of the cases by megavitamin and mineral therapy.

For more information on orthomolecular medicine, send a stamped, self-addressed envelope and note to that effect to Dr. Lesser at 2340 Parker Sreet, Berkeley, California 94704.

SELECTION: JOE HENDERSON'S SIX COMMANDMENTS

Don't think about it any longer. Do it.

Don't check with your doctor to see if it's okay. By the time he says it is, it may be too late.

Don't take time to plan what you'll do. Just plan to start, now, and let what happens happen.

Don't pay any attention to the advisors on exercise who say, "Be cautious." Jump into it with both feet.

Don't go out first and buy new shoes and clothes. The urge to exercise may die before you get back home, and the $25 striped green shoes and $40 stretch nylon warmups will remain to haunt you.

Don't wait. Run while you feel like it, in the way you think you should. Do it on the track or on the street. Sprint or jog or combine the two. Race the clock, or race an imaginary opponent, or try to finish a distance you've set for youself. Do whatever you want, but do it.

—Joe Henderson, *Jog, Run, Race*
(World Publications, Mountain View, Calif., 1977)

SELECTION:
RUNNING AND TIME

After 30 minutes, the slow crawl of time passes away and a new phase begins. This altered perception of time, at least of mechanical time, appears both faster and slower. Long involved thoughts can occur in minutes, and at other times whole chunks of clock time disappear. . . .

This alteration of the sensation of time can be used to examine our own rhythms of work, sleep, play, and so forth. Too often we become the programmed slaves to the passage of time, and our lives seem to disappear into a dwindling infinity, like two railroad tracks that meet way ahead. As we get older, we begin to see people complain, in an amazed way, that time passes so quickly. Before they know it, their children are grown. They are gray and their friends old. They are able to recall with nostalgia the utterly languid feeling of the endless time of childhood, either as a misery to live through a dull day at school, or with joy in anticipation of the time of summer vacation from June to Labor Day.

One of the subtle attractions of long-distance running is the change of this dwindling of subjective time. . . . Often the longest moment of a whole day occurs during some fragment of a morning run. It can remain there all day, towering above all of that day's time. It is like a small, very precious jewel tucked away in my pocket.

—Thaddeus Kostrubala, M.D.,
The Joy of Running
(Lippincott, Philadelphia, 1976)

"If it's physical, it's therapy" reads the tee-shirt, as premier Northern California runner Judy Gumbs Leydig hands off in the annual Lake Merced relays, San Francisco.

PRIME MOVER IN THE WORLD OF RUNNERS

Joe Henderson has been searching for new ways to cajole people into running all his life. He is the joggers' Hidden Persuader, the man in the gray flannel sweatsuit. He conducts dialogues with himself as consulting editor of *Runner's World* magazine, wrestling over the meaning of running as Socrates was addicted to wrestle over the meaning of "the good." His writing is an exigesis of the scripture according to Sheehan and Van Aaken and Glasser. But Joe can take his text from the unlikeliest places and move us to his way of thinking with the unlikeliest ploys.

His Six Commandments (in his book, *Jog, Run, Race*) fly in the face of all conventional running wisdom. Don't check. Don't take time. Don't think. Don't pay any attention. Don't buy new shoes and clothes. Don't wait. He is saying, "But the first and the greatest of all the commandments is—Do it!" (I particularly approve of "Don't check with your doctor to see if it's okay." Unless your doctor has a Human Performance Laboratory at hand, or hasn't told you, for some reason of his own, that you have a serious heart condition, about all he can tell you is "Yes, but start slowly.")

It's no accident that two of the many books Henderson has written contain "Run" and "Long" in the title and a third "Long Slow Distance." Once a competitive runner, he now sees the rewards of running coming mostly in the second half of the daily hour he hopes you set aside for running. Distance doesn't count; distance divided by time doesn't count. Only time counts—not in the sense of "What's your time for the mile?" but "How long did you run today?"

Henderson modestly describes himself as neither a great writer nor a great runner. He tells stories about himself that are so honestly revealing they could come only from the pen of a true artist. People sneer at him for being a "bubbler." Yes, he is. People very often pay compliments only through jealousy.

If a person is going to make an impact on a whole generation of running readers, it's nice to know he's a person like Joe. His nutshell summation of the benefits of running for the soul goes like this:

Once each day, at about the same time and for about the same length of time each day, I quietly go out of my mind. I leave my rational mind behind for an hour and "spin out."

It's brain-washing in a positive sense—in the sense of cleaning and clearing gummed-up thinking by intentionally not concentrating on any thoughts for a while.

The way I handle most problems is not to worry about them but to run away from them. Running at a gentle, "meditative" pace for an hour or so is literally a pursuit of happiness.

THE ROAD TO HUMILITY

First and last, running past the 30-minute barrier, into the third wind, is humbling. Pride no longer matters. I remember confiding to a friend on a long run that in high school I thought "Ibid." was one of the most prolific writers of all time. What would St. Augustine or John Henry Newman have been capable of if they had also been runners? I raise that facetious question only to introduce a modern-day writer who bares his soul to perhaps a wider audience than either of those did. Listen:

The true loneliness, then, is me seeing that nothing I do is true. Me and this inner emptiness, me and the abyss, me and the false me I am with other people, me being what I do, what I accomplish, the clever things I say. Me and that living of a lie, a long lonely lifetime lie.

When I'm about overwhelmed by all this I take this loneliness out on the roads, there to find my true self, to hear my own message, to decide for myself on my life.

That is, of course, George Sheehan (in *The Physician and Sportsmedicine*).

For every runner who tours the world running marathons, there are thousands who run to hear the leaves and listen to the rain, and look to the day when it is suddenly as easy as a bird in flight. For them sport is not a test but a therapy, not a trial but a reward, not a question but an answer.

The lucky ones are those who can run to work and back at least some days of every week. Veteran runner Ted Corbitt, indefatigable editor of the newsletter of the New York Road Runner's Club, does it. Hal Higdon says, "Even on his easy workout days, he runs to catch the subway. One morning he ran past a corner where two men stood. 'Man,' one of them said, 'that cat's late for work every morning!'"

REVIEWS

Awareness books:

The Joy of Running, Thaddeus Kostrubala (Lippincott, 1976, $8.95; Pocket Books, 1977, $1.75).

Beyond Jogging, Mike Spino (Berkeley, 1976, $1.25).

Running Home, Mike Spino (Celestial Arts, 1977, $3.95).

Positive Addiction, William Glasser, M.D. (Harper & Row, 1976, $8.95).

Keep Your Heart Running, Paul J. Kiell, M.D., and Joseph S. Frelinghuysen (Winchester Press, 1976, $8.95).

I have already staked out the boundaries within which these books fall by suggesting *Dr. Sheehan on Running* as the best work in the field of psychology and running, and *The Zen of Running* as the epitome of the other extreme of "have good vibes and little else matters." In one way or another, the above five books tackle the question, in a serious way, of what running does for the soul (call it spirit, mind, psyche).

This area of writing is full of extravagant promises. The beginning jogger is not likely to feel any "jogger's high": he hurts too much. Indeed, some joggers can speak of a "jogger's low." Answering one such person, Dr. Sheehan writes, "Almost daily we see articles on the effect of exercise and diet on the emotions and metabolism, the significance of low-blood sugar and the role of exhaustion. Unfortunately, those results will not stand

scientific analysis, and we are left as experiments of one to try megavitamins, macrobiotic diets, etc., etc. . . . Overextended, we go to the edges of our personality and beyond to depression, paranoia, or schizophrenia. I can see this in myself. Sleep, naps, running only Tuesdays, Thursdays, and Sundays, and occasionally some Vitamin B-12 make things look brighter."

Many writers, like Dr. Kostrubala, come to the subject with a glorious "experiment of one" behind them. As we open his book, he is fat, depressed, taking to drink, spoiling his marriage, and cruising for a heart attack. At the end he has lost 55 pounds, is running marathons, has new insights into his profession, and enjoys a better sex life than ever before. He is at his best in the sort of courageous self-analysis that psychiatrists do so naturally. Unfortunately, the reader has to wade through a lot of Kostrubala's analysis of The Course of Western Civilization and psychoanalytical theory to get to the point: What is the joy of running? Like other "joy" books, there is little here about it. A better title would have been "The Fear of Heart Attacks," for this is his preoccupation. It is easy to run to conclusions from his discussion of depression, but he doesn't claim that running is a therapy. He sees it merely as another way of making a psychoanalytical approach to a patient; instead of the Freudian couch and the Jungian face-off, Kostrubala tries jogging

---

In this new therapeutic role, I was doing something markedly different. I was directly participating in the action with the patient—we were both running. And we experienced similar phenomena—pain, the high, the altered states after 40 minutes. If I compare this technique of therapy with dream analysis, it's like dreaming the same dream as the patient at the same time. The therapy was immediate. . . .

I began to believe, in a shy way at first, that somehow we had discovered a new form of therapy. It was biologically based. . . . The term "paleoanalytic psychology" seemed to fit it best of all, or "paleoanalysis."

—Thaddeus Kostrubala, M.D., *The Joy of Running* (Lippincott, Philadelphia, 1977)

Irrepressible Clive Davies always draws runners with halos. Draw your own conclusion.

along side by side. He points to some possible physical causes of "runner's high": the demonstrated fact that the brain receives about 20% more blood during a vigorous run, or the speculation that the repetitive motions of long-distance running exhaust the left, or more rational, cortex of the brain, thus allowing the creative right cortex to come to the fore. And he has some interesting psych-up ideas, such as "focusing" on pain to make it go away. I think it would have been truer to the title of the book to develop such subjects, instead of plodding through yet another account of how to start and what to wear. Many would find his discussion of carbohydrate loading, stretching exercises, preparation for a marathon, and diet to be misleading. But at least he has opened the question of therapeutical running.

Mike Spino is the rare charismatic individual who can push ahead into the thickets of mysticism without leaving his more conventional sightseers behind. A cofounder of a running program at Esalen, he has also been funded under a federal program to study the effects of exercise and he is currently conducting vacation/seminars on running, in what appears to be a commercially successful promotion. More power to him. Mike eschews theoretical speculation and jumps right in to telling what running does for the psyche. He's convincing on such usually slippery subjects as meditating during exercise and learning what love is all about through communal running. He's well known for his psych-up ideas (press the button with your thumbs and varoom off). And he's good on the reality of finding time and place for running (don't forget the stairwells and corridors of hotels). Be prepared for poetry: it's throughout *Beyond Jogging* and in the last part of *Running Home.*

Finally, a veteran runner and a psychiatrist have collaborated on an excellent book, *Keep Your Heart Running*. Ostensibly about the heart, it delves more deeply into the practical aspects of the "joy of running" than any of the above. Frelinghuysen and Kiell wisely limit their conclusions to the demonstrable; their theme is that the routine of running smoothes out the bumps of life before they become roadblocks. The medical benefits of running are nicely balanced with the psychological by this writing team, without the scare or fear the subject often arouses. You may order directly from the nonmedical half of the team: Joseph Frelinghuysen, P.O. Box 608, Somerville, New Jersey 08876. $8.95 plus 35¢ postage.

With books like these we can now speak confidently of "running therapy":

More rational but less successful, in my opinion, is Dr. Glasser's *Positive Addiction*. The author of *Reality Therapy* writes for a wide audience, but he's still engaged in scuffling with his professional colleagues over what constitutes the best form of therapy. He has nice things to say about running: It fits the classic definition of addiction in its self-induced motivational cycle. The more you run, the more you are rewarded by results—weight loss, sense of accomplishment, muscle development. And these in turn make the next level of running easier. "A positive addiction increases your mental strength," he theorizes, while the bad kind saps that strength, and more. Yet it seems to me that Dr. Glasser has simply attached a nice-sounding adjective ("positive") to an admirable activity (running), without explaining the mechanism whereby one addiction is substituted for another. The psychologists pay lip service to the idea that body and mind are one entity, and then they go about their business of drawing diagrams to show how the mind influences the body. In a literal sense, you think with your entire body; your brain is not coextensive with your mind. So if running causes you to change what you do to your body (vegetarian-like diet, tearing down and building up), it changes your mind *ipso facto*. If depression is often just a symptom of low blood-sugar, then the mitigation of depression by running is due to the corrective effect that running has on blood-sugar imbalance. Similarly, it is well known that allergic response is the key to much of what we think of as addiction. Dr. Roger Williams, among others, has proposed that many alcoholics, for example, are allergic to alcohol and try to mask the allergy by ingesting larger and larger quantities of it. My experience with runners is that the single most prominent change in their lifestyles is in diet. Consider also the recent finding that a certain type of "good" cholesterol—high-density lipoprotein, or HDL—is associated with regular running; testing for HDL is now considered more significant than for total cholesterol level. It's my guess that advances in understanding the therapeutic effects of running will come more from now on in the study of metabolism than from the study of the traditional psychological models.

three

the feet
what you need
to know about shoes

Everyone now knows that the feet have more bones than the rest of the body combined. Everyone has heard of Morton's foot. The use of "orthotics" (personally fitted devices to correct foot abnormalities) is commonplace. Podiatrists, and especially sports podiatrists, are first-class citizens in the medical profession. There's scarcely a magazine or newsletter in the running world that doesn't have its medical consultant—and he or she is frequently a podiatrist.

Exercises of the whole leg form part of the foot doctor's expertise. For the foot is a sensitive indicator of imbalances or even disease throughout the body. The hamstring stretch shown here, preparatory to raising the other leg over the head, is an exercise often used to correct sciatica and other lower back problems, which in turn may cause pain and numbness right down to the toes. And the foot doctor's approach is primarily preventive—not only of foot problems but of resulting pains and injuries throughout the body.

MORTON'S FOOT

In March of 1974 Dr. George Sheehan changed the course of sportsmedicine with an article in *The Physician and Sportsmedicine* entitled "Let's Hear It for Morton's Foot." This was the beginning of a shift in emphasis from the drug or surgical approach to foot and leg problems to the biomechanical approach. All of a sudden runners were examining their second toe and big toe to see if they had the syndrome: a shorter big toe.

In 1975 a Mill Valley, California, podiatrist, Harry F. Hlavac, founded the Sports Medicine Clinic at the California College of Podiatric Medicine in San Francisco. Since that time, through his column in *Nor-Cal Running Review* and elsewhere, Harry has been putting into practice what Sheehan threw up in the air for speculation. He has treated hundreds of runners with leg and hip problems by correcting nature's design of their feet. Among his long list of satisfied customers is Dr. Joan Ullyot, at 37 one of the country's top marathoners.

"I've heard more about Dr. Morton from athletes in the last three years than I did throughout my years of training in podiatry," Hlavac says. "Apparently there are two kinds of runners in the world today: those that have Morton's foot, and those that think they have."

Hlavac advises joggers not to panic if their big toe looks shorter than their first toe. The syndrome is a *bone* length pattern, not *toe* length. Only an X-ray can determine for sure if the first metatarsal, the big toe, really contains a shorter bone. "When you see a case of Morton's foot, you'll know it," he says.

What's so bad about a short big-toe bone? Dudley J. Morton, one of three Dr. Mortons who wrote about the foot, described, in 1935, how the

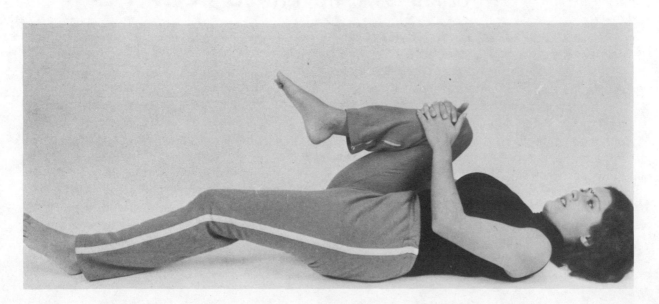

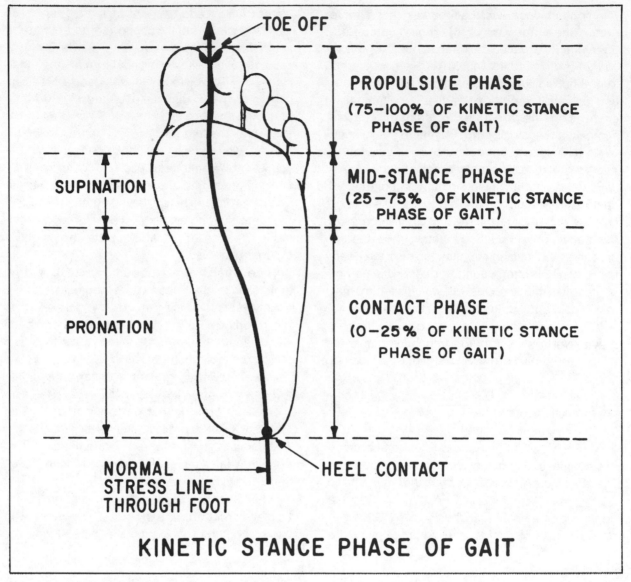

TOE OFF

PROPULSIVE PHASE
(75–100% OF KINETIC STANCE
PHASE OF GAIT)

MID-STANCE PHASE
(25–75% OF KINETIC STANCE
PHASE OF GAIT)

SUPINATION

PRONATION

CONTACT PHASE
(0–25% OF KINETIC STANCE
PHASE OF GAIT)

NORMAL
STRESS LINE
THROUGH FOOT

HEEL CONTACT

KINETIC STANCE PHASE OF GAIT

How weight is transferred along the foot in a normal foot strike

five toe bones, the metatarsals, support the foot. The big toe and second toe take half the load. If the big toe is too short, it can't provide the full one-third of the foot's support that it should. So the arch flattens out as the foot pronates, turns down and in, away from a parallel plane to the ground. The foot is said to supinate if its plane tilts down at the outside of the ankle.

Now it's normal for the foot to pronate and supinate during a stride. The heel lands usually toward the outside, accounting for the typical pattern of shoe wear. That is, the foot is in a supi-nated, outward-tilting position at strike. If it were in the pronated, flat-footed position at strike—because of the conditioning of Morton's foot or for whatever other reason—the foot and ankle bones would be somewhat rigid and the supporting musculature would not be able to help cushion the impact. The normal foot pronates as weight shifts to the forefoot (see diagram), allowing the toe-off to take most of the weight between the big and second toe. At push-off the foot is again beginning to supinate, a position it will maintain through the glide "stroke."

Sheehan once wrote, "Morton's foot (visible) occurs in about 33% of the general population. However, in a patient population of 1,000 studied by Dr. Richard Shuster, 80% of the patients had the short first toe/long second configuration. No X-ray studies were done to determine how many of the other 20% had occult forms of Morton's foot. Probably all of them." This rather pessimistic view depends on Sheehan's idea of how short is short. According to many podiatrists, the big toe must be considerably shorter in its bone structure to cause the Morton symptoms.

Hlavac and others treat foot imbalance problems with "orthotics." Casts are made of the feet and from these are fashioned rigid supports that allow the feet to move through a normal gait cycle. For Morton's foot, for example, an orthotic would fill the void under the big toe so that the foot would supinate properly on toe-off.

Hlavac points out that there are two other Dr. Mortons in podiatric literature, one of whom has given his name to another foot problem. In Morton's neuroma (T. J. Morton, 1876), the nerve which passes under the ball of the foot is compressed by the third and fourth metatarsals. A tingling or numbness often results; protective support is usually enough to relieve the irritation.

A well-diagnosed foot problem can sometimes be corrected simply by changing to a different brand of shoe. Hlavac has prepared a chart to indicate which shoes are best, neutral, or worst for each ailment. (See "Selecting Shoes," page 55.) For some time, New Balance and Lydiard have been best for width problems, but now other manufacturers are offering a range of shoe widths. According to Hlavac's chart, Achilles tendinitis may be aggravated by the Nike Cortez shoe, but it's one of the best for bottom heel problems. Pumas are great for flat feet but poor for heels. But remember that shoes, as well as theories, are subject to change from year to year.

HOW TO TREAT BLISTERS

"Blisters, undoubtedly the most common of all foot problems, are the separation of layers of epidermis (the superficial layers of the skin) one from another. When the separation occurs, fluid in the area fills the empty space created. This may be blood or a clear serous fluid. The separation of layers occurs because of friction, either linear or twisting, or skin tightly adhered to underlying structures. . . .

"If the blister has already formed, prompt first aid will hasten an early recovery. Cleanse the

---

SELECTION: MUSCLE PROBLEMS

The main muscles of concern to the athlete which are located around the knee are the hamstring and quadriceps groups. Any muscle of the body can be injured, but those that cross two joints (bi-articular muscles) are especially subject to injury. . . .

Any inherited structural imbalance, or muscle imbalance acquired through extensive training without total conditioning, will cause strain and fatigue of the imbalanced or overused muscles. That is, if an athlete trains for one specific sport and does not develop strength and flexibility in *all*

muscle groups, then a muscle imbalance will be acquired. . . .

For example, muscle pains on the inside of the thigh, in the area of the vastus medialis or sartorius muscles, often are associated with excessive mobility or excessive pronation of the foot, and the reverse is true. Treatment through the use of an artificial support will eliminate this structural or functional imbalance.

Muscle problems of the lower extremity or even around the hips and low back often relate to imbalance which can be corrected with proper foot support.
—Harry Hlavac, *The Foot Book*
(World Publications, Mountain
View, Calif., 1977)

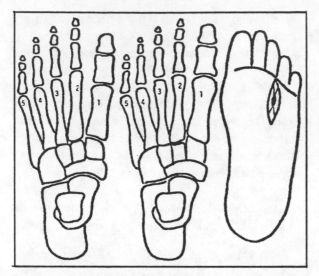

Left: Morton's Foot. Note numbering of metatarsal bones. Center: normal foot bone lengths. Right: Morton's Neuroma.

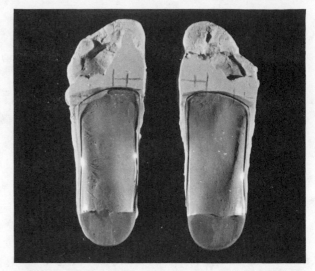

The critical area from the arch to the heel of the foot shows corrections for each foot.

Making a plaster cast preparatory to preparing an orthonic device

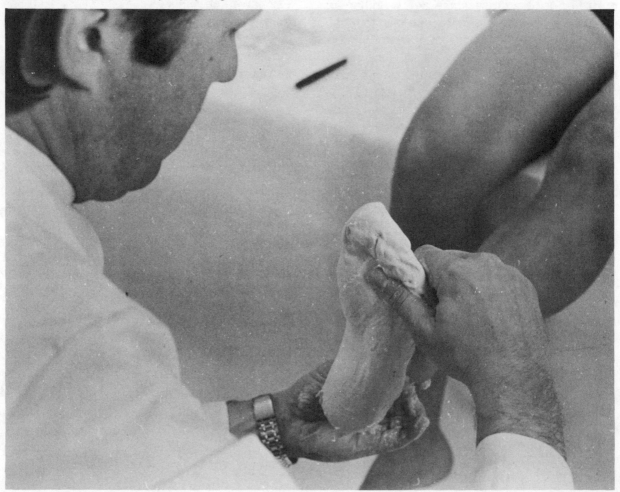

blistered area with alcohol or soap and water, and gently apply pressure on top of the blister so that the fluid will disperse to the sides. If it is small (less than one-half inch) and there is no pain, leave it alone. But if it is larger or painful or if there is deep bleeding, carefully penetrate the side of the blister with a sterile needle and remove the fluid with continued pressure. The fluid removal will greatly decrease the level of pain. Leave the overlying skin intact. An antiseptic solution or first aid cream can be applied over the entire blister. Apply a bandage or accommodative pad to prevent further irritation. If left intact, the blister should be covered and protected with a Band-Aid, or it will break and become contaminated. . . .

"To prevent blisters, first look to your shoes. If blisters are on the sides or tops of your toes, your shoes are either too small in the forefoot, or at foot impact your foot is jamming into the toebox of the shoe. . . .

"Socks must fit properly. Poorly fitting socks may roll up in wet weather or during vigorous participation. To absorb the maximum amount of perspiration (perspiration increases friction and the likelihood of blister formation), socks should contain natural fabrics like cotton or a blend of cotton and wool. Avoid the "stretch" or tube-type socks. Foot powders are also helpful in decreasing the amount of foot perspiration.

"Many runners prefer to go without socks . . . It's usually a good idea to break in new shoes with socks for the first few times and then go without after that time if you prefer.

"Many runners use Vaseline to reduce shoe friction. . . . If you have buckled (hammer) toes that make blisters inevitable, buy the best accommodating shoe you can find and tape your toes."

—Harry F. Hlavac, *The Foot Book* (World Publications, Mountain View, Calif. 1977)

REVIEW

Harry F. Hlavac, M.Ed., D.P.M., *The Foot Book* (World Publications, Mountain View, Calif., 1977)

Dr. Hlavac (silent "H," accent on last syllable) is a bright, young podiatrist who typifies the new breed of sports doctors. His comprehensive treatise on the foot, subtitled "Advice for Athletes," is at first glance a book for doctors, and it's not something to be read at one or several sittings. Yet for completeness and objectivity this work speaks for itself. Dr. Hlavac has assembled the contributions of six other podiatrists, organized his voluminous material logically, and illustrated the text thoroughly. If the writing is a little wooden and heavy, it is perhaps because the lay reader was not meant to be the audience. The book starts by saying that its goal is to help athletes help themselves, but sometimes the text appears to tell doctors how to treat patients.

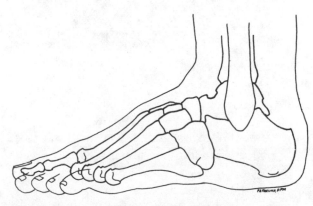

Position of bones with respect to the visible foot

This laudable work was many years in the making and should remain a necessary reference for many years to come. A bonus: the role of the foot in the whole range of sports activities is dealt with.

SHOES IN GENERAL

You're going to buy shoes at the rate of once a year at first, then twice, and pretty soon have a closet full of them. It's a reasonable expense, certainly if compared to the outlays of skiers, tennis players, golfers, or football fans. The first rule of

The Etonic Street Fighter

thumb is, don't sweat it: changing shoes is almost as good as wearing the supposedly best shoes every time.

Be a little self-indulgent at the start. Cultivate your local sports shoestore, even if there are ads for shoes several dollars less at some shopping center miles away. You may well find that this local store is your key to many other things: a local club, news of upcoming events, convenient source for books, gift ideas. Don't worry if your local store specializes only in a few major lines. The second rule of thumb is, it's hard to go wrong with any major line.

If you start evaluating shoes as if you are *Runner's World* magazine, you'll soon psych yourself out. "Loose in the toe, snug in the heel" is generally the best advice. Some runners, especially men, need more toe room. The foresole must flex, but if you're a 200-pound man, you'll want more cushion regardless of sole flexibility. A good salesman will tell you this. So the third rule of thumb is, take all your idiosyncrasies into account.

It used to be that shoes from certain manufacturers provided well-known problems and virtues. New Balance used to have a heel counter that was so low it irritated some people with Achilles tendonitis symptoms. Podiatrists could make up charts that rated shoes for each potential problem. With the 1978 models, however, most of the unique characteristics of shoes have been minimized. Most of the manufacturers offer sizes suitable for women (generally narrower). Some positive qualities still stand out: Tigers have that well-made look of well-tailored shirts; Nikes are always in the forefront of new ideas in support; Brooks gives excellent value. For winter running, Adidas Country is often mentioned. Marathoners sing the praises of Nike Elite—especially runners who want good cushion for the weight. Many experienced runners wish that companies would stick with a proven line longer, so that when a favorite of theirs wears out it can be replaced. But the final rule of thumb for the beginner and medium-distance runner is to avoid fashion and stay with a solid training shoe, even for races.

SELECTING SHOES

Give a man more than two variables and he'll make a chart of them. Time was when you could go into a shoestore, even a sporting goods store, ask the man what he had for gym shoes, try on a pair, and walk out well shod. Then came specialization sport by sport: shoes for tennis, basketball, wrestling, soccer (football and baseball always had their own cleats and spikes). And for running, the field is divided between sprinters and runners—spikes and flats. And flats in turn are divided into training flats and racing flats.

So far so good: the public demanded shoes to fit its needs, and got them. But in the last few years, shoe manufacturers have been vying like automobile companies. Each has several models, and yearly model changes. Some of the changes in shoes have become as ridiculous as changes in hood ornaments on cars. Yes, one can see fins sprouting on some. And some track meets have come to resemble the Daytona 500, as the winner holds aloft the shoes of his sponsor.

Far from bringing down prices, this sort of competition has pushed some models over $40 and made $20 a bargain. The bible of the serious runner and aspiring jogger, *Runner's World*, began to rate shoes on performance in 1975—to bring some sort of reason into this chaotic marketplace. Unfortunately, the power of the magazine with shoe buyers created a sweepstakes effect among the manufacturers. To be rated number one in training flats gave a company a significant edge in promotion; we are a nation that believes in winners and number ones. Although *RW* insisted "they're all good shoes in the top twenty-five—but some are even better than others," the numbers game began.

By the time of the "Third Annual Special Shoe Issue" in October of 1977, there were 60 pages of charts, graphs, diagrams, analyses of testing labs, profiles of a panel of experts, and even a countdown, complete with calendar, of the year-long preparation for the final judging. No one can deny it was a scientific, painstaking effort. The Penn State University Biomechanics Laboratory twisted, pummeled, wrenched, and ripped apart samples entered by the shoe companies. Their results were weighted at one half the opinions of the panel of experts. The judging was completed a month before the magazines were to be shipped out, and the results were "placed under security."

In the most important category for the average runner—and therefore for the manufacturer—Brooks Vantage edged the Adidas Runner and the Nike Waffle Trainer. Unfortunately, a single point separated the three: 247, 248, 249. The panelists gave Number Three their first-place vote by a wide margin. What would a statistician say? Perhaps the three should have been

Four models by New Balance

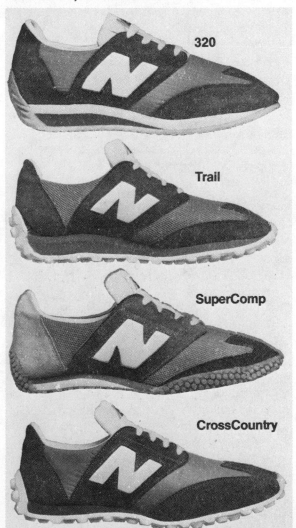

320

Trail

SuperComp

CrossCountry

awarded first place "ex aequo," under the circumstances, since the ratings mean so much economically to the manufacturers.

"Which One?" says the perplexed jogger on the magazine's cover. There's honesty. If you can slice the foresole of your shoe to improve flexibility, and trade off price with wear and tear, then the only objective factors left are heel and forefoot impact. On this basis, the top ten shoes would come out something like this:

1.	New Balance Trail	2	$26.95
2.	Brooks Vantage	6	28.95
3.	Nike LD-1000-V	6	39.95
4.	Brooks Vanguard	14	28.95
5.	New Balance 320	19	27.95
6.	Brooks Victor	20	24.95
7.	Brooks Delta	20	24.95
8.	Pony California	26	23.95
9.	Pony Road Runner	31	25.95
10.	Adidas Formula 1	34	37.95

Remember, the number after the name of the shoes refers to the total of the two rankings in impact, so that 2 is the best possible score. How about the racing flats? Here the winner, Nike Elite at $33.95 and a low weight of 224 grams, wins hands down also in impact (as well as wear and tear). Two fairly heavy shoes (Puma Whirlwind and Adidas Marathon) come in second and third. It's a difference of 2-3 ounces. For the average runner weight is a secondary factor. After that, it's just another guessing game.

Now the good news: You can still buy a high-rated shoe for under $20. A lightweight racing flat ranked fifth by *RW*, Adidas Arrow, sells for $18.95. The sixth-ranked training flat Brooks Villanova is only $19.95. Find a store that offers a variety of choice. Go to several stores. Trade shoes with your friends. (Hint: In some parts of the country, clubs have shoe exchanges.) Don't try to be the kid with the new football all the time. And don't get sucked in by lists.

In spite of all the numbers, and numbers are my personal nemesis in running, we owe this to *Runner's World*: an effort to get something down on paper so you and I can have something to talk about.

WHERE TO FIND RUNNING SHOES

Imported shoes account for 60% of the American market. The leaders are Adidas and Puma, headquartered in West Germany, and Nike. With U.S. headquarters in the West, Nike has challenged Adidas for first place in sales because of its network of exclusive stores and the relatively higher proportion of runners in Western states. Country of manufacture overseas is of little importance; the three major imports maintain good quality control and consistency.

Certain lines are identified with chains of shoe-stores, although a store rarely handles one line to the exclusion of all others. Nike is associated with "The Athletic Department" stores.

Brooks distributes through "The Athletic Attic." Tiger has five geographically dispersed distributors and one in Canada, from whom you can get information about outlets. (See box.) New Balance sells through regular outlets and is also distributed by Spiridon. Etonic is featured in "Athlete's Foot" stores, among others.

Should you buy directly from an ad or an exclusive store? Should you go to a general shoestore, a family shoestore? How about mail order, from Starting Line Sports or the many small distributors who advertise in *Runner's World* and other running magazines?

Ordering by mail is usually no problem as regards size—if you send a tracing of your feet (both). But there are quite a few other factors that should convince you to get your first good pair, at least, in person. Shoe width is important, for men and women; many lines do not have shoes narrow enough for a snug fit for women. Toe room is often overlooked; it's a mistake to try to increase toe comfort by getting a size too large. Most stores specializing in runners' shoes have a long-distance runner on the staff. Take your time and take his advice.

For literature on shoes you have heard about or seen advertised, write the manufacturer or the nearest distributor:

Adidas:
  East: Libco, 1 Silver Court, Springfield, N.J. 07081
  Midwest: Vanco, 5133 West Grand River Avenue, Box 870, Lansing, Mich. 48901
  Southwest: Hughesco, Inc., 2830 Merrell Road, Dallas, Tex. 75229
  West: Clossco, Inc., 2200 Martin Avenue, Box 299, Santa Clara, Calif. 95050
  Canada: Adidas, Ltd., 550 Oakdale Road, Downsview, Ontario M3N 1W6

Brooks: Factory Street, Hanover, Penn. 17331
Converse: 55 Fordham Road, Wilmington, Mass. 01887
Etonic: Eaton, 147 Centre Street, Brockton, Mass. 02403
Econo-Jet: 1501 College Avenue, S.E., Grand Rapids, Mich. 49502
Jackar: P.O. Box 383, Stoughton, Mass. 02072

Karhu: Carlsen Imports, 524 Broadway, New York, N.Y. 10012
Mitre: 3042 Miller Road, Lithonia, Ga. 30058
Lydiard: E. B. Sport International, 6117 Reseda Blvd., Reseda, Calif. 91335

UPSTAIRS, DOWNSTAIRS IN SHOES

First, downstairs. You won't find this brand entered in the *Runner's World* annual shoe derby. Pro-Gym Footwear, Inc. offers an unbelievable bargain: the Mach I (blue) for $7.90 a pair (not each), and the Mach IV (white) for $9.90 a pair. Add $1 for shipping and it still looks impossible. Sizes from 2½ to 12. Nylon uppers (heavy-duty 200 denier) reinforced with leather counter and leather toe. I talked with the sales manager about quality. He made points on two counts: first, repeat business is quite strong, and second, the Mach I was patterned after the Adidas SL–72. (That's the Mach I, the cheaper of the two!) Sure, they're made in Korea, but so are a lot of major brands. They're guaranteed without strings attached against defects in materials or workmanship—they're not seconds.

What's the catch? The sales manager says they're offered just above cost as part of a special sales program for schools. The main business of the company is the Sprinter Treadmill ($1800–$2000) and the Universal Weight Lifter, a machine which allows 10 to 12 people to simulate weight lifting at the same time. The company sells shoes to schools at this low price, allowing the schools to resell them at a profit and so raise money for gym equipment (such as the Sprinter). It's a matter of good will. In the few retail outlets where Pro-Gym shoes are sold, the price is about twice the above. If it makes sense to you, order from:

Pro-Gym Footwear, Inc.
P.O. Box 188
(807 Cherokee)
Marshall, Mo. 65340
(816) 886-8302

Now, upstairs. How about a pair of shoes custom-made by leading English craftsmen—to your personal measurements, of course? Get complete details by mail (and also information on other English running gear) from:

Goodair Sports
7 Rayner Street
Horbury, West Yorks
England

DOCTORING YOUR SHOES

Shoes are to a runner what a glove is to a shortstop. You've got to make them part of yourself. The manufacturer has given you a slate to write on, not a bound book.

Some simple things to prolong wear: Build up the outside edges of the heels with hot glue or any of the tube glues—long before the wear becomes pronounced. Put a protective layer of glue around the toe area (especially important if you ever play tennis in your running shoes and drag your foot in serving). Interesting variation: John Cates of Montgomery, Alabama, reports in the Hagerstown, Maryland, *Run for Fun* newsletter that aluminum ducting tape works even better than hot glue for preventing wear. Just apply a patch where wear is likely to occur—no need to wrap it over the top of the shoe. It scuffs away its slickness after a few blocks, and reportedly does not wear through for several runs.

Ron Daws has a whole chapter in his book, *The Self-Made Olympian* (World Publications, 1977), on modifying and repairing shoes. His advice on contact cement is that it should be applied in two medium coats instead of one in repairing shoes. "If the first coat is allowed to dry 10–15 minutes and the second about five minutes, the bond will be stronger."

Don't be afraid to take a razor blade to your soles. A well-known shoe sported a sole, in 1977, which extended well beyond the upper; many runners had to shave it off on the inside edge to keep it from hitting the other leg! A little greater precision is required to loosen up a stiff sole. Take a steel straightedge and carefully slice a line directly across the widest part of the sole. Test the shoe for flexibility in your hands. Open the slice up a little more, as necessary. You can always correct a mistake with glue. Well-made shoes will not tear or separate even after being sliced along a single line. Why is a sole made so stiff it has to be sliced? It may not be that inflexible for the needs of *other* runners.

Inside the shoe, you can do quite a bit more to customize. You can improve cushioning with an insole, but Ron Daws claims that some shoes have too much interior cushioning already, and allow the foot to move around too much. The simplest corrective measure is to improve the arch support with a "cookie." You can find cookies in varying shapes and sponginess (foam rubber to leather) in five-and-ten and shoestores, for $2–3. Find a comfortable position with the shoe on, then adhere to insole with contact cement. For slightly more money you can avoid having to glue the cookie in place: Dr. Scholl's Flexo comes in shoe sizes and fills the shoe up to the forefoot. For more information about advanced foot correctives, see page 49.

Don't attempt to open up the top of the shoe to provide more room for toes. You need support of the bundle of bones, known as metatarsals, in your forefoot. Remember the rule in selecting shoes: loose in the toe, snug in the heel. Loose, that is, but not flopping around.

If you've had problems with heel bruises, spurs, or inflammation, you might try a heel protector, such as offered by M–F Athletic Company, Inc., P.O. Box 8188, Cranston, Rhode Island 02920. These are simple cuplike devices, at $10.50 per dozen (they wear out fairly fast).

New Balance: 38–42 Everett Street, Boston, Mass. 02135

Nike: 8285 Southwest Nimbus Avenue, Beaverton, Ore. 97005

Canada: Pacific Athletic Suppliers, Ltd., 2433 Beta Avenue, Burnaby, British Columbia VC5 5N1

Osaga: 2620 West 10th Place, Eugene, Ore. 97402

Patrick: Action and Leisure, Inc., 45 East 30th Street, New York, N.Y. 10016

Pony: Pony Sports and Leisure, Inc., 251 Park Avenue South, New York, N.Y. 10010

Puma: Beconta, Inc., 50 Executive Boulevard, Elmsford, N.Y. 10523

West: 340 Oyster Point Boulevard, South San Francisco, Calif. 94080

6759 East 50th Avenue, Commerce City, Calif. 90022

Reebok: Bradford Distributors Corporation, Box 356, Huntingdon Valley, Penn. 19006

Saucony: 12 Peach Street, Kutztown, Penn. 19530

Spot-Bilt: 432 Columbia Street, Cambridge, Mass. 02141

Tiger:

East: Pete Buckley & Co., 650 Great Southwest Parkway, Atlanta, Ga. 30336
George A. Davis, Inc., 7205 Hibbs Lane, Levittown, Penn. 19057
Midwest: General Sports Corporation, 5121 North Ravenswood Avenue, Chicago, Ill. 60640
Southwest: Olympic Sports, 2607 National Circle, Garland, Tex. 75041
West: Curley-Bates Co., 860 Stanton Road, Burlingame, Calif. 94010
Canada: Vikski Canada, Ltd., 2058 Trans Canada Highway, Dorval, Quebec H9P 2N4

Mail Order: Shoes, Accessories, Books

Sale items, wide range of shoes, timing devices, discounts on books and subscriptions, quantity discounts, etc. Will accept person-to-person collect calls or send for catalog:

Mark Bauman
1704 Ridgecliffe Drive
Flint, Mich. 48504
(313) 234-9072

Insoles

Profoot Insoles (advertised as built into top models of Adidas) are available for $3.45, including postage, per pair (specify men's or women's size) from:

Comfort Products, Inc.
7100 Broadway Building
Denver, Colo. 80221
(303) 428-6700

Spenco Insoles are available (at about $3) by mail from:

Starting Line Sports
Box 8
Mountain View, Calif. 94042

WHAT ABOUT "CHEAP IMPORTS"?

From time to time, reports appear in magazines and books about the "same as" models merchandised in supermarkets and department stores. The price is so right for the most part that these imitations can't be ignored. Indeed, writers in *Runner's World* and elsewhere have put in a good word for their quality.

Here's Theresa Burger's evaluation: (1) The models change so fast no recommendation can be made in a book. As soon as a store runs out, a buyer brings in another model, quite probably from a different source, with entirely different features. Here today, gone tomorrow. A strong point in favor of established brands.

(2) Buy a good pair of shoes first and then experiment—you'll know what flexibility, toe-box, and heel-counter mean. You might well find a good make for everyday running. Here are some recent offerings from five-and-tens and national retailers:

—at $8.99: flashy-looking, no cushioning, ridge at heel would cause tendon troubles and blisters.

—at $11.99 and $13.99: not bad, with well-cushioned soles and smooth finishing around the insides of the heels. Remember, you can put your own Nike waffle treads on these for about $1 a pair. (See "Shoe Repair" page 60).

Some manufacturers are catching on to the new developments pioneered by leading shoe companies, such as the flare heel. A "Superwide" is offered for $16.95 (or $13.95 plus $1 shipping for "coaches") as equivalent to the Nike LD 1000 (at about $40.00):

Econo-Jet Sport Shoe Co.
1501 College Avenue, S.E.
Grand Rapids, Mich. 49502
(616) 243-3821

The same company offers "Econo-Sweats" in 30 colors and six sizes at $18.50; and nylon rainsuits in five colors for $20.85. These items are obviously aimed at the quantity buyer—schools, clubs, etc.—and good quantity discounts are offered, as well as "coaches' sample" prices. No collect phone calls accepted; write for further information.

SHOE REPAIR

There are three general levels of running-shoe repair: professional resoling, resoling at home, and patching with various compounds. For resoling, first check your local shoestore; often it will have a connection with a local resoler and will save you postage and time. Otherwise mail your shoes to such firms as:

EAST:	Fresh Tracks 27 West Rayburn Road Millington, N.J. 07946	$11.95
	Power-Soler 1065 West Broad Street Falls Church, Va. 22046	$11.50
	Scarfo Athletic Shoe Repair 787 Boston Road Billerica, Mass. 01866	$8.50, $1.25 postage = $9.75
MIDWEST:	Shurtuff 130 South Ritter Indianapolis, Ind. 46219	from $6.95
WEST:	Fleet Feet Co. 612 Emery Longmont, Colo. 80501	$8.00
	Power-Soler West 4330 West Desert Inn Road Las Vegas, Nev. 89102	$11.50
	Nike Shoe Recycling Center 10565 S.E. Washington Street Portland, Ore. 97216	$11.95
	Lloyd Center Shoe Repair 1239 Lloyd Center Portland, Ore. 97232	$10.95
	Tred 2 2510 Channing Avenue San Jose, Calif. 95131	$13.45 to $15.45 for "rebuilding," which includes new inners.

New Balance Resoling Service
(Adidas, Head, Nike, Puma, Tiger, and Tretorn also welcome):

Midwest:
Spare Pair
825 Chicago Avenue
Evanston, Ill. 60202

West:
Loeschorn's
1525 Mesa Verde East
Costa Mesa, Calif. 92626

East:
Spare Pair Service—New Balance
38-42 Everett Street
Boston, Mass. 02135

In general, the above prices include repair of cracks and tears, broken stitching, missing eyelets, worn laces. Some resolers add "bumper" toes on training shoes. The above prices include return postage. Most, but not all, shoes are resolable. Ask locally first.

You can resole your own shoes with "waffle tread," a large sheet of sole material available in shoestores. A $5 sheet will do many shoes. This is especially economical for kids' "cheapo" shoes. (See box, page 59.)

Finally, you can postpone the inevitable wearing out at the heels with various glues, available in shoestores (Sole Repair Kit, Shoe Goo, Shoe Patch, etc.). The second-generation repair kits use pellets and a gun for hot application. A nonglue system to replace worn-away material is available for $3 from:

The Heeler
5 Margate Road
Nashua, N.H. 03060

Important! Don't send your shoes—just the $3! A mail order source for Shoe Goo is:

Eclectic Products, Inc.
753 Basin Street
San Pedro, Calif. 90731

Profoot, Spenco, and other similar insoles are intended to add extra cushioning to your shoes or to replace worn-out insoles. They are not orthotics.

How to Resole Shoes Yourself

Buy a sheet of Nike waffles (about $5 at Nike outlets and elsewhere, or write Nike). This should do two normal pairs of shoes. Remove old soles with Acetone or by heating in a frying pan. (The inventor of the resoling method started out by using his mother's oven.) Use Shoe Goo to adhere new sole, which you have cut to the latest style. You can run in them in 24 hours. If you're unsure of yourself, try the process first on a cheap or older pair of shoes.

SHOE OUTLETS:
WIDE SELECTION, EAST COAST AND SOUTH

For Adidas, Brooks, New Balance, Nike, Puma, Tiger

Mail Order: Athletic Attic
Home Office
1135–E N.W. 23rd Avenue
Gainesville, Fla.

CONNECTICUT:
Charter Oak Mall
East Hartford

FLORIDA:
Altamonte Mall
Altamonte Springs
512 Cleveland Street
Clearwater
3411 W. University Avenue
Gainesville
Regency Square
Jacksonville
Lake City Plaza
Lake City
Santa Rosa Mall Shopping Center
Mary Esther
Merritt Square Shopping Center
Merritt Island
Orange Park Mall
Orange Park
Orlando Fashion Square
Orlando
Panama City Mall
Panama City
5 Flags Bazaar

The Nike Elite

The Adidas SL72

Cordova Mall
Pensacola

815 South Dixie Highway
Pompano Beach

Tyrone Square
St. Petersburg

Tallahassee Mall
Tallahassee

Westshore Plaza
Tampa

Winter Haven Mall
Winter Haven

GEORGIA:

1006 Perimeter Mall
Atlanta

Brunswick Mall
Brunswick

The Adidas TRX

120 South Dekalb Mall
Decatur

Macon Mall
Macon

NEW JERSEY:

2602 Willowbrook Mall
Wayne

NORTH CAROLINA:

173 E. Franklin Street
Chapel Hill

1609 East Boulevard
The New Dilworth Co-op
Charlotte

2520 Hillsborough Street
Raleigh

PENNSYLVANIA:

142 Montgomery Mall
North Wales

2150 Northway Mall
Pittsburgh

233 South Allen Street
State College

Berkshire Mall
Wyomissing

SOUTH CAROLINA:

Anderson Mall
Anderson

Columbia Mall
Columbia

Greer Plaza
Greer

Myrtle Square Mall
Myrtle Beach

364 Russell Street
Orangeburg

Summerville Plaza
Summerville

TENNESSEE:

Eastgate Mall
Chattanooga

TEXAS:

522 Sharpstown Center
Houston

224 Memorial City Shopping Center
Houston

VIRGINIA:

9124 A. Mathis Avenue
Manassas

George Sheehan lecturing on foot and leg problems

PODIATRISTS

Running magnifies minor foot problems encountered in walking, but this doesn't mean running should be avoided if you encounter foot problems. In a sense, running is a diagnostic tool. And the jogging boom has created a new sort of diagnostician: the sports medic.

It's still relatively difficult to find a doctor, let alone a podiatrist, who understands the special demands of the runner. There is only one clinic-school in the country devoted to podiatry: The California College of Podiatric Medicine, in San Francisco. But there are one-year, two-year, and three-year residencies at hospitals in major cities where podiatrists get their training. They are accordingly a good place to start in looking for foot help.

On the following pages are two lists: (1) some 100 hospitals where podiatry is taught, and (2) podiatrists listed by the National Jogging Association as being conversant with runners' needs. They are arranged alphabetically by state and by city within each state for ease of reference.

Community Hospital of Phoenix
6501 North 19th Avenue
Phoenix, Ariz. 85015

Mesa General Hospital
515 North Mesa Drive
Mesa, Ariz. 85201

Memorial Hospital of Hawthorne
13300 Hawthorne Boulevard
Hawthorne, Calif. 90250

Kaiser Foundation Hospital
27400 Hesperian Boulevard
Hayward, Calif. 94545

Good Samaritan Hospital
1025 Anaheim Boulevard
Anaheim, Calif. 92806

Circle City Hospital
730 Old Magnolia Avenue
Corona, Calif. 91720

Cerritos Gardens &
 Paramont General Hospitals
21530 Pioneer Boulevard
Hawaiian Gardens, Calif. 90716

Hillside and Heartland
 Community Hospitals
1940 El Cajon Boulevard
San Diego, Calif. 92140

Kaiser Foundation Hospital
975 Sereno Drive
Vallejo, Calif. 94590

Bellwood General Hospital
10250 East Artesia Boulevard
Bellflower, Calif. 90706

California Surgery Center
 and Hospital
390 40th Street
Oakland, Calif. 94609

Beverly Glen Hospital
10361 West Pico Boulevard
Los Angeles, Calif. 90064

California College of Podiatric
 Medicine
P.O. Box 7855, Rincon Annex
San Francisco, Calif. 94120

Beach Community Hospital
5742 Beach Boulevard
Buena Park, Calif. 90621

Levine Hospital of Hayward
22455 Maple Court
Hayward, Calif. 94541

Riviera Hospital
4025 West 226th Street
Torrance, Calif. 90505

Van Nuys Community Hospital
14433 Emelita Street
Van Nuys, Calif. 91401

Westside Community Hospital
2101 Magnolia Avenue
Long Beach, Calif. 90806

Southern California Podiatric
 Medical Center
1407 South Hope Street
Los Angeles, Calif. 90015

Highlands Center Hospital
1920 High Street
Denver, Colo. 80218

Orlando General Hospital
7727 Lake Underhill Drive
Orlando, Fla. 32807

Osteopathic General Hospital
1750 N.E. 167th Street
North Miami Beach, Fla. 33162

Jacksonville General Hospital
4901 Richard Street
Jacksonville, Fla. 32207

Las Olas General Hospital
1516 East Las Olas Boulevard
Fort Lauderdale, Fla. 33301

Westchester General Hospital
2500 S.W. 75th Avenue
Miami, Fla. 33155

Doctors Hospital
2160 Idelwood Road
Tucker, Ga. 30084

Atlanta Hospital
705 Juniper Street, N.E.
Atlanta, Ga. 30308

Hugar Foot Clinic and Surgery
 Center
1614 North Harlem
Elmwood Park, Ill. 60635

Henrotin Hospital
111 West Oak Street
Chicago, Ill. 60610

Northlake Community Hospital
365 East North Avenue
Northlake, Ill. 60164

St. Bernard Hospital
6337 South Harvard Avenue
Chicago, Ill. 60621

Tabernacle Community Hospital
5421 South Morgan
Chicago, Ill. 60609

Central Community Hospital
335 East 5th Street
Clifton, Ill. 60927

Franklin Boulevard Community
 Hospital
3240 West Franklin Boulevard
Chicago, Ill. 60624

Thorek Medical Center
850 West Irving Park Road
Chicago, Ill. 60613

Veterans Administration Center
Leavenworth, Kans. 66048

Huntington General Hospital
222 South Huntington Avenue
Jamaica Plain, Mass. 02130

New England Deaconess Hospital
185 Pilgrim Road
Boston, Mass. 02215

Central New England Podiatry
  Residency Program
Winchendon Hospital
Hospital Drive
Winchendon, Mass. 01475

Lutheran Hospital
730 Ashburton Street
Baltimore, Md. 21216

Maryland Podiatry Residency
  Program
c/o Rosewood Center
Owings Mills, Md. 21117

Flint General Hospital
765 East Hamilton Avenue
Flint, Mich. 48505

Kirwood General Hospital
4059 West Davison Avenue
Detroit, Mich. 48238

McNamara Community Hospital
4050 East Twelve-Mile Road
Warren, Mich. 48092

Park Community Hospital
801 Virginia Park
Detroit, Mich. 48202

Dearborn Medical Centre Hospital
10151 Michigan Avenue
Dearborn, Mich. 48124

Harrison Community Hospital
26755 Ballard Road
Mt. Clemens, Mich. 48043

Straith Memorial Hospital
23901 Lahser Road
Southfield, Mich. 48075

Kern Hospital
21230 Dequindre Road
Warren, Mich. 48091

Brent General Hospital
16260 Dexter Boulevard
Detroit, Mich. 48221

St. Francis Hospital
325 West Fifth Avenue
Shakopee, Minn. 55379

Lindell Memorial Hospital
4930 Lindell Boulevard
St. Louis, Mo. 63108

Coney Island Hospital
Ocean and Shore Parkways
Brooklyn, N.Y. 11235

New York College of
  Podiatric Medicine
53 East 124th Street
New York, N.Y. 10035

Jewish Memorial Hospital
Broadway and 196th Street
New York, N.Y. 10040

Parkchester General Hospital
Zerega & Westchester Avenues
Bronx, N.Y. 10462

Maimonides Medical Center
4802 Tenth Avenue
Brooklyn, N.Y. 11219

Samaritan Hospital of Brooklyn
759 President Street
Brooklyn, N.Y. 11215

Rockland Psychiatric Center
Orangeburg, N.Y. 19062

St. Michael's Medical Center
306 High Street
Newark, N.J. 07102

Washington Memorial Hospital
Hurfville-Cross Keys Road
Turnersville, N.J. 08012

John F. Kennedy Memorial Hospital
18 East Laurel Road
Stratford, N.J. 08084

The Nike LD1000V

Adidas Marathon

Adidas Dragon

Cherry Hill Medical Center
Chapel Avenue & Cooper
  Landing Road
Cherry Hill, N.J. 08034

Cleveland Foot Clinic
Ohio College of Podiatric
  Medicine
10515 Carnegie Avenue
Cleveland, Ohio 44106

Foot Clinic of Youngstown
2312 Hillman Street
Youngstown, Ohio 44507

Oxford Hospital
623 Unruh Avenue
Philadelphia, Pa. 19111

Metropolitan Hospital
201 North Eighth Street
Philadelphia, Pa. 19106

Moss Rehabilitation Hospital
12th & Tabor Streets
Philadelphia, Pa. 19141

Lawndale Community Hospital
Devereauz Avenue & Palmetto Street
Philadelphia, Pa. 19111

Kensington Hospital
136 West Diamond Street
Philadelphia, Pa. 19122

John F. Kennedy Memorial
  Hospital
Cheltenham & Langdon Avenues
Philadelphia, Pa. 19125

St. Mary Hospital
Frankford Avenue & Palmer Street
Philadelphia, Pa. 19125

West Allegheny Hospital
7777 Steubenville Pike
Oakdale, Pa. 15071

Valley Forge Medical Center
1033 West Germantown Pike
Norristown, Pa. 19401

St. Luke's & Children's Medical
  Center
Girard Avenue & Eighth Street
Philadelphia, Pa. 19122

Pennsylvania College of Podiatric
  Medicine
Eighth and Race Streets
Philadelphia, Pa. 19107

Rolling Hill Hospital
60 Township Line Road
Elkins Park, Pa. 19117

Metropolitan Hospital
201 North Eighth Street
Philadelphia, Pa. 19106

Center City Hospital
1829 Pine Street
Philadelphia, Pa. 19103

Podiatry Hospital of Pittsburgh
215 South Negley Avenue
Pittsburgh, Pa. 15206

Delaware Valley Hospital
Wilson Avenue & Pond Street
Bristol, Pa. 19007

Hospital of Philadelphia College
  of Osteopathic Medicine
4150 City Line Avenue
Philadelphia, Pa. 19131

Parkview Hospital
1311 East Wyoming Avenue
Philadelphia, Pa. 19124

Naval Hospital
Beaufort, S.C. 29902

Memphis Eye & Ear Hospital
1060 Madison Avenue
Memphis, Tenn. 38104

University of Texas Health
  Science Center (San Antonio)
San Antonio, Tex. 78284

Rutherford General Hospital
1527 Gus Thomasson Road
Mesquite, Tex. 75149

Kessler Hospital
203 East Colorado Boulevard
Dallas, Tex. 75208

Harris County Podiatry Residency
6565 DeMoss #103
Houston, Tex. 77074

Eastern State Hospital
Drawer A
Williamsburg, Va. 23185

Norfolk Community Hospital
2539 Corprew Avenue
Norfolk, Va. 23504

Walde General Hospital
10560 Fifth Avenue, N.E.
Seattle, Wash. 98125

New Berlin Memorial Hospital
13750 West National Avenue
New Berlin, Wisc. 53151

Weirton Osteopathic Hospital
3045 Pennsylvania Avenue
Weirton, W.Va. 26062

Fairmont Clinic
P.O. Box 1112
Fairmont, W.Va. 26554

PODIATRISTS AND DOCTORS CONVERSANT WITH NEEDS OF RUNNERS

(A National Survey Compiled by the National Jogging Association)

ALABAMA

Stanford Rosen, DPM
Alabama Foot Clinic
1900 Kentucky Avenue
Birmingham 35216

ARIZONA

Alexander T. Borgeas, DPM
129 W. Catalina Drive
Phoenix, 85013

Dr. Gerald L. Campbell, DPM
2210 S. Mill Avenue No. 2
Tempe 85282

M. R. Davidson, DPM
1028 East McDowell Road
Phoenix 85066
(602) 252-1110

Dr. Richard Jacoby
3100 E. Bell Road
Phoenix 85032
(602) 992-0440

Lester R. Klebe, DPM
550 W. Thomas Road
Suite 228-C
Phoenix 85013
(602) 264-2656

Dr. Arthur J. Mollen, DO
1625 E. Camelback, Suite F
Phoenix 85016

Dr. J. Watchman
Biltmore Medical Center
1625 E. Camelback Road
Suite 1
Phoenix 85013
(602) 266-4945

CALIFORNIA

Dr. Thomas Amberry, DPM
2454 Atlantic Avenue
Long Beach 90806

Bernard C. Berger, MD
1063 San Pablo Ave.
Pinole 94564
758-2511

Charles R. Brantingham, DPM
3791 Katella
Los Alamitos 90720
(213) 430-1084

Dr. Robert M. Barnes
1130 W. Olive Avenue
Burbank 91506
(213) 848-1202

Robert L. Brennan, DPM
4201 Wilshire Boulevard
Los Angeles 90010

Earl W. Brooken, DPM
6949 Brookford Drive
Palos Verdes 90274

Harmon Brown, MD
Student Health Services
California State College—Hayward
Hayward 94542

Paul J. Califano, DPM
7170 University Avenue
LaMesa 92041

Eric M. Dash, DPM
18050 Chatsworth Suite 233
Granada Hills 91344

Dr. Richard S. Gilbert, DPM
M.C.R.D. Podiatry Clinic
3363 Fourth Avenue
San Diego 92103

Mel Barev, MD
237 Estudillo Avenue
San Leandro 94577

Dr. Robert Basinger, DPM
27171 Calaroga Avenue, No. 4
Hayward 94545

Thomas Bassler, MD
Little Co. of Mary's Hospital (A)
Dept. of Path.
4101 Torrance Blvd.
Torrance

Dr. John M. Connolly, DPM
4200-18th St.
Suite 101
San Francisco 94114
(415) 756-1631

Dr. Kenneth Charp
528 B Street
Santa Rosa 95401
(707) 545-0570

Dr. Wesley J. Endo, DPM
2832 Summit Street
Oakland 94609
(415) 832-4197

Frank C. Fields, DPM
No. 10 Eastmont Mall
Suite 316
Oakland 94605

Jack E. Fisher, DPM
7933-B Wren Avenue
Gilroy 95020

R. Bruce Franz, DPM
509 W. 18th Street
Antioch 94509
(415) 757-1028

Frederico R. Hernandez, DPM
509 S. 8th Street
P.O. Box 318
El Centro 92243

Harry F. Hlavac, DPM
36 Tiburon Boulevard
Mill Valley 94941

Jon A. Hultman, DPM
10921 Wilshire Boulevard
No. 806
Los Angeles 90021

Dr. Temple E. Jackson
P.O. Box 4654
Compton 90224
(213) 774-5750

Charles H. Johnson, DPM
4009 Brockton Avenue (Med. Sq.)
Riverside 92501
(714) 686-6798

Warren N. Johnson, DPM
3200 Mowry Avenue Suite B
Fremont 94538
(415) 794-6633

William Jurman DPM
3503 Lexington Avenue
El Monte 91731

The Nike Lady Waffle Trainer

Dr. Dennis N. Kiper
407 Grace Avenue
Inglewood 90301
(213) 674-8877

Charles J. Kopcinski
470 Nautilus No. 302
LaJolla 92037

Harold M. Kuritz, DPM
1042 Yurrieta Boulevard
Livermore 94550

Dr. Francis A. Lantz, DPM
136 E. Artesia
Pomona 91767
(714) 622-3394

Gary Lepow, DPM
166 Rishell Drive
Oakland 94619

Howard J. Marshall, DPM
6900 Foothill Boulevard
Tujunga 91042

Thomas Newman, DPM
201 So. Lasky Drive
Beverly Hills 90212
(213) 553-7371

Glen A. Ocker, DPM
5285 Diamond Hts. Boulevard
No. 305
San Francisco 94131

Maurice J. Papier, DPM
4944 B. Newport Avenue
San Diego 92107

Dr. John W. Pagliano, DPM
4301 Atlantic Boulevard
Long Beach 90807
(213) 426-0376

Dr. S. E. Pryharsk
3600 Atlantic Avenue
Long Beach 90807
(213) 426-2577

Dr. George Reedy
20406 Redwood Road
Castro Valley 94546

Dr. V. George Rhoden
SE Medical Center
286 Euclid Avenue, Suite 309
San Diego 92114

R. Denis Russell, DPM
Fountain Valley Medical Building
111000 Warner Avenue, Suite 306
Fountain Valley 92708

Randall J. Sarte, DPM
2322 Bulano Drive No. 224
Sacramento 95821

Paul Scherer, DPM MS CCPM
1770 Eddy Street
San Francisco 94115

Tilden Sokoloff, DPM MS
433 Estudillo No. 104
San Leandro 94577

Dr. Jon M. Shook
Circle City Hospital
720 Old Magnoa Avenue
Corona 91720

William E. Stahl, DPM
1419 B Street
Hayward 94541

Dr. Jeffrey A. Stone
2932 N. Fresno Street
Fresno 93703
(209) 226-4595

Dr. Steven Subotnick, DPM
19682 Hesperian Boulevard
Hayward 94541
(415) 783-3255

Dr. Chris A. Tintocalis, DPM
1919 State Street
Suite 105
Santa Barbara 93101
(805) 962-9913

Arthur A. Walton, DPM
745 Douer Drive No. 4
Newport Beach 92660

Lyman H. Wilson, DPM
801 N. Tustin Avenue No. 500
Santa Ana 92705

Jerome A. Wisniew, DPM
625 Breadway Street No. 406
San Diego 92101

COLORADO

Dr. Stanton C. Southward
1304 N. Academy Boulevard
Colorado Springs 80907
(303) 597-5560

Dr. Gerald R. Travers, DPM
Calan Medical Building
720 N. Tejon
Colorado Springs
(303) 475-8080

Dr. William A. Wood
1304 N. Academy Boulevard
Colorado Springs 80907
(303) 597-5560

CONNECTICUT

Dr. A. J. Nezlo, DPM
698 Main Street
Branford 06905
(203) 488-7864

Dr. Michael L. Sabia, Jr.
Stamford Podiatry Group
24 Third Street
Stamford 06905
(203) 323-1171

Robert R. Rinaldi, DPM
24 Third Street
Stamford 06905

Irving Yale, DPM
Jeffrey F. Yale, DPM
364 East Main Street
Ansonia 06401
(203) 734-4806

Dr. Robert F. Weiss, DPM
Colony Street
Norwalk 06851
(203) 866-3377

Kenneth L. Wichman, DPM
117 E. Center Street
Manchester 06040

DELAWARE

Jonathan P. Contompasis, DPM
2000 Baynard Boulevard
Wilmington 19802

FLORIDA

Dr. Joe Doller
211 E. New Haven Avenue
Melbourne 32901
(305) 723-2022

Dr. Jerald Fishbein
1040-71st Street
Miami Beach 33141
(305) 866-0268

Dr. Robert I. Garnet
9230 Bird Road
Miami 33165
(305) 221-9211

Robert A. Guidice, DPM
118 S.W. 4th Avenue
Gainesville 32601

Harvey A. Pearl, DPM
3809 University Boulevard W.
Jacksonville 32217

Dr. Anthony P. Tocco
420 N. Halifax, Suite 3
Daytona Beach 32018
(904) 252-4678

GEORGIA

Paul L. Bodamer, DPM
2605 Parkwood Drive
Brunswick 31520

Dr. Richard L. Freeman
Suite 203
N. DeKalb Professional Building
3510 Shallowford Road
Chanblee 30341
(404) 458-3103

Anthony J. Gatti, DPM
638 Church Street
Marietta 30060

Dr. Donald Green
2160 Idlewood Road
Tucker 30084

Dalton McGlamory, DPM
1649 Brocheet Road
Tucku 30084

G. Burnham Peterson, DPM
Medical Arts Building
615 Roswell Street N.E.
Marietta 30060

Morris Serwitz, MD
2100 Parklake Drive NE
Atlanta 30345

Alan H. Shaw, DPM
1678 Mulkey Road
Questell 30001
(404) 941-3633

Dr. Michael J. Solomon
1300 Plaza Drive No. 2
Lawrenceville 30245
(404) 963-1802

ILLINOIS

Robert A. Biel, DPM
800 Halsted Street
Chicago Heights 60411

Dr. Gordon W. Falkmor, DPM
667 N. Lake Street
Grayslake 60030
(312) BA3-5673

George B. Geppner, DPM
4016 N. Prospect Road
Peoria 61614
(309) 685-5966

Gerald Gorecki, DPM
10510 S. Bell Avenue
Chicago 60643

William Harant, DPM
430 S. Main Street
Lombard 60140

Gary L. Rippberger, DPM
4016 W. Cullom Avenue
Chicago 60641

Dr. Stephen Smith, DPM
420 Lee Street
Des Plaines 60016

Dr. Leonard Winston
6426 N. Western Avenue
Chicago 60645

INDIANA

Dr. T. H. Clarke
320 E. Taylor Street
Kokomo 46901
(317) 457-2812

Dr. Louis Endress
907 W. Second Street
Bloomington 47401
(812) 336-1185

Richard H. Lanham, Jr., DPM
1402 Blackiston Mill Road
Clarksville 47130

Edward P. Morris, DPM
705 Jackson Street
La Porte 46350

Dr. Ray E. Stidd
2250 Midway
Columbus 47201
(812) 372-2564

KANSAS

Dr. Francis Abraham Jr.
333 E. Central
Wichita

Dr. Lawrence J. Downs, DPM
Dodge City Medical Center
2020 Central Avenue
Dodge City 67001
(316) 225-1371

Don M. Miller, DPM
208 Wolcott Building
Hutchinson 67501

Dr. Richard M. Schorberg
212 Brown Building
Wichita 67202

Dr. Donald D. Yoder
3010 W. Central
Wichita

KENTUCKY

William Thomas Beasley
10901 Youngstown Road
Valley Station 40272

Dr. David Minton
450 Oak Street
Richmond 40475

MARYLAND

Ronald Footer, DPM
615 S. Frederick Suite 304
Gaithersburg 20760

Arnold R. Forman, DPM
711 W. 70th Street, Suite 410
Baltimore 21211
(301) 889-4885

Dr. Sheldon P. Konecke, DPM
5530 Wisconsin Avenue
Suite 835
Chevy Chase 20015
(301) 656-9555

Mark Edward Landry, DPM
10500 South Glen Road
Potomac 20854

Neil Scheffler, DPM
5205 E. Drive
Arbutus 21227

Dr. Paul M. Taylor
8630 Fenton Street
Silver Spring 20910
(301) 587-5666

MASSACHUSETTS

Kenneth I. Sann, DPM
103 Main Street
North Adams 01247

Arthur G. Swedelow, DPM
114 Waltham Street
Lexington 02173

MICHIGAN

Robert N. Glick, DPM PC
13500 E. Twelve Mile Road
Warren 48903

The Adidas Formula 1. The spoiler-type extension of the sole absorbs shocks before the foot gets the full weight of the body.

The Adidas Country. The rigid heel counter pillows the heel against sideway slippage.

Steven H. Glichman, DPM
5137 Rochester Road
Troy 48084

Robert L. Kahl, DPM
238 Visger Road
River Rouge 48218

Allen E. Peelen, DPM
725 Alger S.E.
Grand Rapids 49507

Dr. C. H. Wunderlich, DPM
Kirkwood Pd. Inc.
118 E. Jefferson
Kirkwood 63122

Charles R. Yound, DPM
19075 Middlebelt Road
Livonia 48152

MINNESOTA

Fred G. Albert, DPM
408 4th Avenue N.W.
Box 646
Auston 55910

Dr. Jerry Christenson
9050 Lyndale Avenue S.
Bloomington 55020
(612) 884-3532

MISSISSIPPI

Bruce Yiller, DPM
962 Courthouse Road
Apt. 5
Gulfport 39501

MISSOURI

Stanford L. Burevitz, DPM
c/o Dept. of Pod.
Ft. Wood 65473

Dr. Paul D. Glynn
9104 W. Florissant
St. Louis 63136
(314) 867-2900

Dr. Michael E. Jourdan
9 Thayer Street
Ft. Leonard Wood 65473

Robert L. Phillips, DPM
900 8th Avenue S.
Great Falls 59405

Dr. Robert R. Shenwell
Englewood Medical Building
10901 Winner Road
Independence 64052
(816) 461-2112

NEW JERSEY

Sophie L. Bakke, DPM
438 Broadway
Long Branch 07740

Dr. Charles H. Boxman
54 South Carolina Avenue
Atlantic City 08401
(609) 345-1690

Dr. John Brickley
205 Haddon Avenue
Haddonfield 08033

Guido A. LaPorta, DPM
6 Heather Drive
Marlton 08053
(609) 983-6036

Dr. Thomas M. McGuigan
1 Highgate Drive Suite B
Trenton 08618
(609) 883-1605

George A. Sheehan, MD
79 W. Front Street
Red Bank 07701

Dr. Henry N. Turner
208 Lenox Avenue
Westfield 07090
(201) 232-3346

Dr. Leonard A. Zingler, DPM
245 Diamond-Bridge Avenue
Hawthorne 07506

NEW MEXICO

Dr. Ronald E. Saye
1441 Wyoming Boulevard N.E.
Albuquerque 87112
(505) 296-1882

NEW YORK

Howard F. Baskin, DPM
263 N. Main Street
Spring Valley 10977

Dr. Edward J. Bondville
490 Titus Avenue
Rochester 14617

Dr. Marc A. Brenner
73-09 Myrtle Avenue
Glendale 11227
(212) 456-7270

Dr. David H. Conway
368 S. Goodman Street
Rochester 14607
(716) GR3-5051

Dr. Leonard Fagen
34 Vassar Street
Staten Island 10314
(212) IN2-1095

Arthur L. Stein, DPM
388 Westchester Avenue
Port Chester 10573

Dr. Harvey Strauss
2 West Fordham Road
Bronx 10468
(212) SE3-1121

Justin Wernick, DPM
3921 Merrick Road
Seaford 11783

Ronald J. Volino, DPM
385 Kimball Avenue
Yonkers 10704
(914) 237-7772

NORTH CAROLINA

Harvey G. Tilles, DPM
614 N. Hamilton
P.O. Box 5466
High Point 27262

OHIO

Dr. W. R. Bennerr, DPM
922 Blanchard Avenue
Findlay 45840

Richard J. Berkowitz, DPM
3224 Berkley Avenue
Cleveland Heights 44118

Dr. Nancy Lu Conrad
1106S Court Street
Ardeville 43114

Dr. J. Phillip Davidson
3200 Belmont Avenue
Youngstown 44505
(216) 759-1132

Dr. David D. Dull
4442 Logan Way
Youngstown 44505
(216) 759-0904

William M. Funerty, Jr., DPM
2052 E. 125th Street
Cleveland, Ohio 44106
(216) 721-3957

Dr. Charles R. Marlowe, Jr.
Beverly Hills Medical Center
Suite P
1614 South Byme Road
Toledo 43614
(419) 385-6489

Dr. Joseph I. Seder
Cleveland Clinic Foundation
9500 Euclid Avenue
Cleveland 44206
(216) 229-2200

Dr. Sheemon A. Wolfe, DPM
2422 Salem Avenue
Dayton 45405

Harry Zelwin, DPM
3237 DeSota
Cleveland Heights 44108

OKLAHOMA

Dr. Henry M. Asin
528 N.W. 12th Street
Suite 15
Oklahoma City 73103
(405) 947-8041

OREGON

Dr. Norman L. Klein
1701 N.E. 122nd Avenue
Portland 97230
(503) 252-1464

Stan James, MD
750 East 115th Avenue
Eugene 97401

PENNSYLVANIA

David L. Berman, DPM
801 Dover Road
Penfield Downs
Philadelphia 19151

Dr. Patrick R. Clune
Hickory Medical Center
10 Snyder Road
Sharon 16146
(412) 343-0110

Tom McGurgian
Philadelphia College of Podiatry
832 Spruce Street
Philadelphia

Dr. Gary Gordon, DPM
273 N. Easton Road
Glenside 19038

Augustine C. Morano, DPM
407 W. Germantown Pike
Norristown 18401

Dr. Wayne B. Wolf
3865 Mt. Royal Boulevard
Allison Park 15413
(412) 486-6722

John B. Wong, DPM
P.O. Box 229
Ardmore 19003

Dr. George A. Yarnell
20 East Baltimore Pike
Lansdowne 10950
(215) MA6-1403

TENNESSEE

Ivan N. Cooper, DPM
504 Bount Professional Bldg.
Knoxville 37926

Brian N. Kiel, DPM
803 Mt. Moreah Road
Memphis 38117

TEXAS

Gene Bartlett, DPM
1220 Josey Lane
Carrollton 75006

Alan Ettinger, DPM
5201 Camp Bowie
Fort Worth 76107

Dr. Edward J. Kent, DPM
Park Forest Foot Clinic
3798 Forest Lane
Dallas 75234

Ronald S. Lepow, DPM
4152 Bellaire Boulevard
Houston 77025

Morris M. Prigoff, DPM
2837 W. Illinois Avenue
Dallas 75223

Dr. Donald A. Rhodes
4501 Marie Drive
Corpus Christi 78411
(512) 855-3272

Dr. Chester L. Rossi
Torno Medical Center
1029 E. Thomas
Pasadena 77502
(713) 473-2843

William L. Van Pelt, DPM
1111 Gessner Road
Houston 77055

UTAH

Dr. H. Gary Morley
885 North 500 West
Provo 84601
(801) 374-6900

VIRGINIA

Dr. Myles J. Schneider
7420 Little River Turnpike
Annandale 22003
(703) 750-1124

Barry L. Swedlow, DPM
1938 Thomson Drive
Lynchburg 24501

WASHINGTON

Dr. Robert H. Armstrong
Safeco Plaza Tower
Seattle 98105
(206) 634-3344

Kurt Blau, DPM
1412 Medical Arts Building
Tacoma 98402
(206) 627-4181

Dr. James Garruck
Department of Orthopedics
University of Washington
Seattle 98185

S. Theodore Hansen, Jr., MD
Department of Orthopedics
Harborview Medical Center
325 9th Avenue
Seattle 98104

Jack Lee Morris, DPM
P.O. Box 552
Sunnyside 98944

Stan Newell, DPM
10560 A 5th Street NE
Seattle 98128

Dr. Peterson
Sports Medicine Center
5407 17 NW
Seattle 98107

Mark Uchimura, DPM
227 SW 153rd Street
Seattle 98166

Toshifumi J. Saigo, DPM
852 106th NE
Bellevue 98004

WEST VIRGINIA

Stephen R. Folickman, DPM
2917 University Avenue
Morgantown 26505
(304) 599-9000

David Gleitzman, DPM
2917 University Avenue
Morgantown 26505

WISCONSIN

Dr. W. H. Falvey
4300 West Burleigh Street
Milwaukee 53210

Edward R. Hommell, DPM
127 E. Mifflin Street
Madison 53703

Michael B. Thompson, DPM SC
3001 Washington Avenue
Racine 53405

DISTRICT OF COLUMBIA

Dr. Paul M. Taylor
Columbia Medical Building
Suite 613
1835 Eye Street

Washington, D.C. 20006
(202) 331-1151

Jerome Shapiro, DPM
5406 Connecticut Avenue NW
Washington, D.C. 20015

CANADA

James Brittain, DPM
47 Prince Street
Oshawa, Ontario L164C9
Canada

Irving H. Goldhamor, DPM
213 N. Fern Avenue
Ontario
Canada 91762

Donald H. Johnson, MD
Carleton University
Colonel By Drive
Ottawa, Ontario K15 536
Canada

Where to Obtain Dr. Scholl's Arch Supports

Dr. George Sheehan and other writers often refer runners with foot problems to Dr. Scholl's No. 610 and Athletic "A" Arch Supports. This firm advises that it carries a full line of foot and leg aids in addition to arch supports. Dr. Scholl's Foot Comfort Shops are located in most major cities, but the following stores have been designated for full-stock service and as mailing centers:

New York, N.Y.: 399 Fifth Avenue
Chicago, Ill.: 21 North Wabash Avenue
Boston, Mass.: 21-23 Temple Place
Birmingham, Ala.: 211 North 21st Street
Torrance, Calif.: 160 A Del Amo Fashion Square
Spokane, Wash.: 419 Riverside

four

the body in motion

how to run and what to wear

In 1880 a photographer at Stanford University, Eadweard Muybridge, photographed horses in a trotting gait to determine if all four feet were off the ground at any one time. It was the first successful motion picture, and it proved a point. In the 1960's, Bill Bowerman analyzed reels of film of runners to help him coach the track team at the University of Oregon. There *are* ways to improve running style, he insisted. When others were advocating a leaning forward posture, Bowerman's trademark was "running tall": an upright position with the feet tracking directly under the body. When others were stressing ways to lengthen the stride, he was showing evidence that it is more important to keep the body's weight properly supported all through the stride. "Energy is not wasted in lifting the body upward with every step, but is concentrated largely on thrusting it forward into the float (off the ground) phase of the stride."

When you're jogging on a track, you can observe a wide variety of running styles. Many younger runners lift their knees high and kick up in the back. Others point their toes forward and hit the ground with a fairly straight leg. Bowerman says, "A relatively short stride is most efficient. It is better to understride than to overstride." Sprinting requires knee lift, of course. But a relaxed swing of the leg 800 times per mile must be as efficient as possible. Bowerman lays down two rules: don't overstride and keep your knees slightly bent at all times. A plumb line dropped from your ear should fall straight down through the shoulder and the hip at every point in your stride.

Watching Bill Rodgers or Frank Shorter run (as in the film *Marathon*) is a lesson in posture. Joe Henderson says, "Watch the way a child runs to see what a natural style is." The elbows carry the

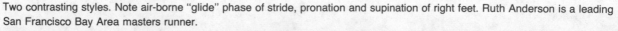

Two contrasting styles. Note air-borne "glide" phase of stride, pronation and supination of right feet. Ruth Anderson is a leading San Francisco Bay Area masters runner.

forearm at a right angle to the upperarm, not locked in a V. The arms move clear of the body, not across the chest. Everything is relaxed, from the fists to the neck.

Watch yourself in store windows as you run along the street. Have a friend watch you circle a track, or, better yet, take sideview pictures of you.

THE BODY BEFORE AND AFTER

According to a well-known theory, there are three body types to which correspond three levels of physical activity and three levels of social interaction. The ectomorph is introspective, tall, and bony. The mesomorph is muscular, aggressive. The endomorph is an extrovert, with a heavier body and an aversion to active sports. According to Dr. William Sheldon, we're born into one of the three categories, more or less. What happens when a roly-poly middle-aged man takes up jogging, goes on a severe diet, and loses 50 pounds? This is not an uncommon experience. Two women who have recently authored books on running for women say they have gone from "size 14 to 10." The accompanying photos record a typical transformation of a man in his 30's—from 208 pounds and sedentary to 158 pounds and running marathons.

The overnight appearance of some 25 million joggers on the streets (according to a recent Gallup poll) has given exercise physiologists an unprecedented opportunity to study the body in motion—all types of bodies. The world is just beginning to accept the woman as a long-distance runner. The results are in from the personal experience of thousands of women runners: terrible things don't happen to their bodies. No extra supports are needed *except for comfort*. Their endurance is theoretically superior to men's endurance. As for pregnancy, this report is typical of many: "We have a mommy-jogger in our club. She ran a mile one morning, and later in the day had a bouncing baby boy, weight 7 pounds 11 ounces. She ran three miles every day before and after. We all love her."

Other myths are vanishing equally fast. Heat is the only real danger for a heavy (in distance) run-

ner, not cold. Thousands of runners brave subfreezing temperatures, dressing for weather 25 to 30 degrees warmer. The frozen-lung myth has finally been put to rest.

One of the important lessons that has emerged from the attempt to improve running technique is that breathing from the stomach is the body's way of getting maximum oxygen. Another myth is punctured: the chest-out, stomach-in model of

Before and after: the proof is in the waistline. A forty-pound weight loss after two years of running, building to the April 1977 Seaside Marathon.

military fitness. You can practice stomach-breathing as you jog. When you inhale, let your stomach bloat out, and fill your whole body with air. One way to get used to this is to practice it while walking on all fours. Your stomach will extend down naturally. Speech teachers and yoga experts have known all about this for years; it has taken two generations for us to unlearn the antibody mechanisms of calisthenics.

Self-Tests for Runners

1. *The Bill Bowerman Talk Test:*

If you can carry on a comfortable conversation while jogging, you're not running into "oxygen debt." You're taking in enough oxygen to supply your muscles.

2. *The George Sheehan Flexibility and Strength Tests:*

You have a muscle imbalance, leading to possible sciatica or other lower back problems, if you can't:

a. Do a bent-leg sit-up slowly with your hands behind your neck.

b. Flatten the hollow of your back to a wall without leaving room to slide your hand between while the shoulder blades and buttocks are against the wall.

c. Sit upright on a table and extend your legs without hurting the backs of them.

d. Touch your toes without bending your knees.

3. *The Dave Costill Slow-Twitch, Fast-Twitch Muscle Fiber Test:*

Until recently, a biopsy was necessary to determine your percentage of the two types of muscle fiber—long-distance runners having as much

From *The Aerobics Way* by Kenneth H. Cooper, M.D.

12-MINUTE WALKING/RUNNING TEST
Distance (Miles) Covered in 12 Minutes

FITNESS CATEGORY		AGE (Years)					
		13–19	20–29	30–39	40–49	50–59	60+
I. Very poor	(men)	<1.30*	<1.22	<1.18	<1.14	<1.03	<.87
	(women)	<1.0	<.96	<.94	<.88	<.84	<.78
II. Poor	(men)	1.30–1.37	1.22–1.31	1.18–1.30	1.14–1.24	1.03–1.16	.87–1.02
	(women)	1.00–1.18	.96–1.11	.95–1.05	.88–.98	.84–.93	.78–.86
III. Fair	(men)	1.38–1.56	1.32–1.49	1.31–1.45	1.25–1.39	1.17–1.30	1.03–1.20
	(women)	1.19–1.29	1.12–1.22	1.06–1.18	.99–1.11	.94–1.05	.87–.98
IV. Good	(men)	1.57–1.72	1.50–1.64	1.46–1.56	1.40–1.53	1.31–1.44	1.21–1.32
	(women)	1.30–1.43	1.23–1.34	1.19–1.29	1.12–1.24	1.06–1.18	.99–1.09
V. Excellent	(men)	1.73–1.86	1.65–1.76	1.57–1.69	1.54–1.65	1.45–1.58	1.33–1.55
	(women)	1.44–1.51	1.35–1.45	1.30–1.39	1.25–1.34	1.19–1.30	1.10–1.18
VI. Superior	(men)	>1.87	>1.77	>1.70	>1.66	>1.59	>1.56
	(women)	>1.52	>1.46	>1.40	>1.35	>1.31	>1.19

* < Means "less than"; > means "more than."

HOW TO FIND A DOCTOR WHO UNDERSTANDS RUNNERS (MEN *OR* WOMEN)

"Call your nearby hospital. You ask for the cardiology department. You talk to the nurse on duty, and ask her if there's someone on the staff who jogs. If she says no, you hang up and call another hospital, because if there's a doctor-jogger usually everybody in the hospital knows it. Usually it's some dumb-nut doctor who nobody would ever refer anybody to. But that's the guy you want to give you your stress test.

". . . The average doctor is set up for testing middle-aged executives. If you show up in your

as 90% slow-twitch. A correlation has now been made between fast-twitch percentage and jumping ability.

  a. Place a chalk mark on the wall at 15, 20, and 24 inches above the floor.
  b. Stand next to the wall and jump as high as you can with both feet together. Have someone mark your jumping height.
  c. Twenty inches represents a fifty-fifty muscle-fiber composition. Closer to the 24-inch mark means fast-twitch predominantly; closer to the 15-inch mark means slow-twitch.

Perhaps a more accurate procedure is to reach as high as you can, mark that point on a wall, and then touch as high as you can above the mark on a jump. Measure the difference and use the same 15-, 20-, and 24-inch standards.

The physiological phenomenon of slow- and fast-twitch muscle fibers is easier to picture than explain scientifically. George Sheehan explains, "slow-twitch fibers carry the glycogen or sugar-source . . . hence, the more slow-twitch cells, the more sugar available for the long distance run." James F. Fixx says, "some muscle fibers, designated ST, contract slowly . . . virtually every top distance runner . . . has more ST than FT fibers." Bud Getchell, of Ball State University, where slow-twitch/fast-twitch was investigated, puts it this way: "The slow-twitch fiber has a higher overall capacity to use oxygen for energy than the fast-twitch fibers." Is it glycogen, contraction, or oxygen? They're all intertwined.

4. The Ken Cooper 12-minute Field Test:

As an alternative to the expensive treadmill test, aerobic fitness can be determined effectively and accurately by having the subject run as far as he or she can in 12 minutes. If you can cover more than 1¾ miles, you consumed 52 or more milliliters of oxygen, and your health is excellent. Less than a mile represents only 28 milliliters of oxygen, and poor health. These values must be adjusted for age and sex. Eighty per cent of the American population cannot do more than 1½ miles, up to 42 milliliters of oxygen.

5. The Biotonics Stamina-Strength Test:

Stamina is a function of muscle strength. To test the stamina of any muscle, apply a maximum load for six seconds. One half that load can be sustained for one minute, and one sixth of that load can be sustained indefinitely.

6. The Harvard Step Test:

If you're average height (between 5 feet 3 inches and 6 feet), get a bench or chair you can stand on (16 to 18 inches). Get a shorter or taller chair depending on your variation from normal height, or, since most chairs are 16 to 18 inches, devise an appropriate mount to step up on. Step up with both feet and down 30 times a minute for 4 minutes. A minute after you finish, count your pulse for 30 seconds; wait 30 seconds, and count for 30 seconds again; wait for another 30 seconds and take a final 30-second count. Multiply your total pulse counts by 2, and divide this into 2,400. The result above 90 is excellent; above 80 good; etc., with below 60 being poor.

(There are many variations, including the common "insurance company" test involving jogging in place. The Step Test is more accurate.)

Adidas shoes and your track shorts, he won't know what to do." —Dr. Tom Bassler
  (See also "Stress Tests," page 112.)

ASK THE DOCTOR

One of the unexpected pleasures of becoming part of the running fraternity (and sorority) is discovering a new pocket of literacy. Every avocation has its journal, its cadre of statisticians and analysts, its story tellers. But running has philosophers, psychologists, humorists, gurus, and just plain good writers. The explosion of the jogging phenomenon fortunately coincided with the spread of inexpensive lettershops and copying equipment—or there would be a lot of frustrated writer/joggers around. Hundreds of running clubs produce newsletters on a regular basis. Their content, as you can see from selections throughout this book, is generally of a high quality. Creative bent is revealed in those that have room for more than announcements of upcoming events and reports of recent races.

At the top of this heap stands *Runner's World* and at the forefront of writers in *RW* is Dr. George Sheehan. Both maintain highly professional publishing standards without losing touch with the simplicity and humanity of their subject. Together they are to jogging what the movies, let's say, and Tom Mix were to a generation of aspiring cowboys.

Sheehan is a New Jersey cardiologist, in his 50's, who runs in just about every race he can possibly get to and shares his aches and depressions with the thousands of readers of *Runner's World* and other magazines where his monthly column appears, such as *The Physician and Sportsmedicine*. He answers questions as a starting point. He replies to every letter addressed to him whether the answer appears in the column or not. He doesn't hesitate to quote Thomas Aquinas to answer critics who say that all joggers' faces show boredom (it's contemplation). He says if he had it all to do over again he would be a podiatrist. I think he would be just what he is: a generalist, a thinker, a writer.

Sheehan's contribution to the knowledge of the art of running is evident in any book touching on the subject and certainly throughout this one. He is a master of the common-sense rule. He quotes Gandhi on restraint of our palates to answer a complex question about the advisability of fasting. He was the first to insist that "runner's knee" starts with a foot problem. Occasionally he is taken to task—as when once he insisted that the body cannot take a sizable amount of food just before a race. But he never waffles.

The debate is just beginning over the effects of jogging on heart disease. Conferences are being

---

SELECTION:
UP AND AWAY

Some hills are, of course, worse than others. On the east coast, we have some well-known monsters. Heartbreak Hill in the Boston Marathon, Cemetery Hill at the four-mile mark of the five-mile course at Van Cortlandt Park. There is hardly a major race that doesn't have a strategic hill to make the event memorable for the runner. I have run all of these, and on them reached areas of pain unmatched at any other time in racing—even in flat-out finishes or in marathons where I had to quit from exhaustion.

But the worst hill of all was in a 15-mile race one August. The heat and the mileage had taken a toll, and I was nearing the finish line when I reached this hill, which seemed the longest and steepest I have ever had to climb in a race. Going into the hill, I was some ten yards behind another competitor and well ahead of any pursuer.

Up on top of the hill, a teammate yelled encouragingly to me, "Go get him, you can get him." Twenty yards up the hill I had slowed perceptibly. The runner in front began to pull away.

"Pick it up, pick it up," came the cry from the top. By now, I was leaning forward, making groping movements with my hands but very little forward progress. My friend would not give up.

"Keep moving," he yelled. "Keep moving." It was no use. And now the others behind me were catching and passing me. The runner who was ahead of me had reached the crest and disappeared.

Then from the top of the hill came the best advice of the day. "Walk fast," he shouted. "Walk fast." I did and I passed two men who were running.

—"Straining Up Hills," from *The Physician and Sportsmedicine*

Children seem to have a naturally good running style.

held regularly to bring together specialists to exchange papers on the issue. Epidemiological studies are springing up everywhere. And ten years from now, when all the evidence is in, we will look back on what Sheehan had to say about it in one of his columns, and nod our heads: "Exercise that is drudgery, labor, something done only for the final result, is a waste of time."

REVIEW

Bud Getchell, *Physical Fitness: A Way of Life,* (John Wiley & Sons, Inc., New York, 1976)

"The ability to sit all day without getting fat has not been bred into the human being."

"Look at yourself naked in a full-length mirror. If you look fat, you are fat."

"The jog-walk-jog technique of conditioning represents perhaps the simplest approach to cardiorespiratory fitness."

Plain statements of exercise theory like these make an otherwise academic treatise an enjoyable experience to read. Getchell is, after all, at the Human Performance Laboratory at Ball State University in Muncie, Indiana—where researcher Dave Costill has conducted exercise and diet studies well known to runners. The variety of tests, measurements, and anatomical explanations in this book can overwhelm you—going as they do beyond the more empirical approach of Ken Cooper. But the experts in this field I have

SELECTION:
HEAT TOLERANCE: THE KEY TO THE
PUZZLE?

An intriguing question arises when we realize that there are great physiological similarities among individuals of a particular competitive class. For example, virtually all world class distance runners will have a maximum oxygen consumption rate of over 70 ml./kg./min. They will all be of approximately the same stature with the same low percentage of body fat (usually 6% or less). In addition, many other factors normally associated with superior distance running performance will be found to be uniformly high (sustained cardiac output, vital capacity of lungs, etc.) *within* a competitive class. . . .

Various theories have evolved to answer this question. The most popular thinking on this topic centers around individual differences in certain cellular factors. Costill (1972) has discovered that marathoners tend to differ in the aerobic effort which they can *sustain* for long periods of time. Derek Clayton, world record holder for the marathon, had a relatively low aerobic capacity (69.7 ml./kg./min.) but could sustain a high percentage of this value (86%) for long periods of time. These and other data have led to the conclusion that performance capacity in the marathon seems to depend on the ability to use a large portion of one's aerobic capacity for sustained periods of time. Indeed there is much variation between individuals in the percentage of their maximum aerobic capacity which they can sustain for long duration. And there seems to be a correlation between this percentage and performance in the marathon.

Another interesting trend emerges when we carefully observe the measurement of maximum oxygen consumption rate. These rates are the best measurement of an individual's aerobic capacity. High maximum VO_2 scores are well correlated to distance-running success.

While these measurements are made, an individual exercises on either a bicycle ergometer or a treadmill. The subject breathes into an oxygen analyzing system. Using this system, it is possible and common to measure the temperature of the air which the subject is expiring. It is often observed that the higher that a person scores on the maximum VO_2 test the higher the temperature of the expired air. Again, we find indirect support for the idea that heat tolerance is correlated with distance running superiority. . . .

talked to consider Getchell the best single source of information in sports medicine. He is understandably short on the "inner" game that is running. But he carries his research and advice out into almost every imaginable form of human activity, evaluating each on its ability to promote muscular strength, endurance, flexibility, and cardiorespiratory fitness. Three sports activities come up with absolutely zero: archery, bowling, and golf.

Getchell gives adequate attention to the needs of the female jogger, but is a little short on general advice to runners. That you can get elsewhere. Meanwhile, more "experts" should listen to his jog-walk-jog theory.

REVIEW

Laurence E. Morehouse, Ph.D., and Leonard Gross,
Total Fitness in 30 Minutes a Week
(Simon & Schuster, New York, 1975)

The popularity of this hopeful book and its successor, *Maximum Performance*, dismays most serious joggers. They know from pleasant experience that 30 minutes a *day* is often not enough—either for fitness or for enjoyment. In one sense most joggers have a blind side as bad as that of Morehouse and Gross: they neglect anything but the bare minimum of stretching exercises. But with only 30 minutes a week to

Although heat tolerance has a strong genetic and developmental component, a given individual can certainly increase his/her internal heat tolerance by heat training. It is interesting to note that many world and national class distance runners have used heat training throughout the year.

Ron Daws was known for his regular heat training. And many others, American runners such as Ed Winrow and Chuck Smead, are noted for their heat training. One wonders whether their successes (under all conditions) were not due to their heat training—to an enhanced ability to tolerate high internal temperatures.

No one can really say that heat tolerance is the key to the puzzle. It is not proven and it would be difficult to prove that such a relationship exists—that runners are superior by right of their relatively greater capacities to tolerate high internal temperatures. Nevertheless, there are many things which bear some looking into. Who knows, some day we may all be training in special suits and the ideal training location may have to be more than a high altitude site. It may have to be hot as well.

—E.C. Frederick and
Jack Welch
Running, 1974

play with, it's obvious that the Total Fitness team isn't going to get very far into aerobics.

As a matter of fact, they dismiss Ken Cooper's program in a sentence. Without confronting the issue head-on, they argue something like this: (1) Muscles *can* be developed in a regular isotonic program of as little as 30 minutes a week; (2) since every muscle helps the heart pump blood, this limited program will help the cardiovascular system too. Then they unveil the key to the system: the pulse test. This, they claim, is the best measure of physiological response to exercise. It tells you when you are working against a full load, and when you should increase it. Beyond this, the book is a tasty stew of dietary advice, exercises,

pep talks, an homey anecdotes. If *Total Fitness* is less than the total truth, at least it has spread some good advice for the completely sedentary.

In *Footnotes*, the newspaper of the Road Runners Club of America, Sy Mah accurately observes, "A program which improves flexibility, muscular strength and endurance is worthwhile. But in terms of survival, cardiovascular fitness is critical, and a total fitness program must produce improvements in blood pressure and lipid levels." Morehouse's Fifteen Fitness Myths are intriguing. His suggestions for finding time during the day to stretch and exercise muscles are excellent. And he has many provocative things to say about the whole range of sports activities, such as not using a weighted bat when warming up in the on-deck circle. Here's Morehouse's advice for people who have knee problems they haven't been able to correct with shoes:

One supplementary caution: If you jog, don't jog downhill. Not long ago, a group of members at my country club formed a jogging group. Before long they had to stop exercising entirely, because their knees were giving out. They had difficulty walking and climbing stairs. They came to me for an explanation. I told them that jogging or running downhill puts a terrific strain on the knees. The rule: Run up, walk down.

THINK TANKS FOR RUNNERS:

AMJA Newsletter, Editor, Dr. Tom Bassler; published by the American Medical Jogger's Association, P.O. Box 4704, North Hollywood, California 91607.

This is naturally a rather exclusive organization (membership fee of $25 includes the newsletter, membership in NJA, AMJA tee shirt and lapel pin, and "tax deductible travel in connection with AMJA meetings"). There was some ruckus recently over nondoctors joining, and especially over the Boston Marathon dropping its qualification standards for AMJA members. But this is a forward-looking group, filling an indispensable function, and if it's any consolation their newsletter is as corny as most and twice as dry—to the layman. Dr. Bassler is well known for his outspoken views on the immunity of long-distance run-

HANS SELYE:
EXERCISE AS A METHOD OF STRESS REDUCTION

Selye's 1956 book, *The Stress of Life,* put forward the theory that "the more we vary our actions the less any one part suffers from attrition." According to this account, the ultimate expression of illness or injury to the body is the General Adaptation Syndrome, the body's reaction to outside insults. The body reacts to stress, in Selye's analogy, like a small country reacting to an invasion. It can't send all of its troops to any one border at any one time. The trick is to cause bodily reactions (such as the stress of exercise) on a regular basis, so that no one great stress will sap all the body's "troops." In effect, whatever you cause in pain by running is a debit against other stresses. Modern theories of stress date from this landmark book.

ners from coronaries. If a marathoner ever had a heart attack, according to Bassler, it was due to a preexisting heart condition.

Laboratory of Human Performance, run by David Costill at Ball State University, Muncie, Indiana, is a major research center on exercise physiology in the United States. It was here that such things as slow-twitch, fast-twitch muscle fiber composition were first studied.

SLOW-TWITCH, FAST-TWITCH MUSCLE FIBERS

Dr. George Sheehan resigns himself to a certain level of long-distance performance because his muscle fibers aren't predominantly "slow-twitch." Marathon runners Steve Prefontaine and Frank Shorter, among other well-known long-distance runners tested by muscle biopsies, have shown extremely high percentages of slow-twitch, as against the fast-twitch of sprinters. It has been assumed that runners are therefore born to be one type or the other. All is not lost. Dorothy V. Harris reports in *WomenSports* that recent research at Indiana University indicates men and women have relatively the same percentages, and that "slow-twitch fibers can be improved"

with training, "at a moderate or slow pace over longer periods of time."

The slow-twitch concept is not meant to bring up visions of muscle fibers that actually "twitch." The word "slow" refers to the ability of the fibers to utilize oxygen. Fast-twitch fibers consume oxygen in fast gulps, and therefore are the perfect muscle fibers for sprinters. Physiologists now believe that endurance training—long, slow aerobic activity—builds stamina simply by converting fast-twitch to slow-twitch fibers, or, more accurately, by conditioning muscle fibers to use oxygen in a more regulated, long-term pattern. (To see where you stand, try the fast-fiber jump test on page 78.)

REVIEW

The Physician and Sportsmedicine

In the magazine business, *Sportsmedicine* is known as a trade journal. It is published by McGraw-Hill, Inc. for doctors specializing in athletics. It is distributed to them free (so-called

THE SPECIAL NEEDS OF WOMEN

Yet there is another side to modern physical training in women's colleges, and one that threatens danger. This is shown in the complaints of the alumnae that the spirit of athletics has crept into gymnasium work, and that muscularity is encouraged at the expense of the kind of development that is especially needed by women.

It is said, also, that girls are sometimes allowed to overdo and to injure themselves seriously. For example, cases were mentioned to me in which health is said to have been ruined for life by indiscretion in high kicking, jumping, and so on.

The girls not only vie with one another, but they also have even the idea of coming as nearly as possible to the standards set by men. It is one more futile effort to ignore differences of sex. The degree to which women can and ought to go in for athletics is not known, nor does it seem to be carefully enough studied from the standpoint of sex.

—Edith Rickert,
The Ladies' Home Journal, January, 1912

INTERVIEW: DR. JOAN ULLYOT

The Institute of Health Research is housed in a three-story Victorian, gingerbread San Francisco-style, in the shadow of the concrete mass of the Pacific Medical Center, of which it is a part. Here Director George Williams, M.D., and Joan Ullyot, M.D., preside over a health-maintenance program that is unique in the country. The word "Research" in the title is accurate but woefully undescriptive. The Institute monitors the health of its clients—currently 2,000 or more—through a comprehensive series of blood tests over a period of years. Twenty-three determinants of good health are sifted from individual to individual and from one "participant's" base period to his second and third years, or more. The goal of the computer-assisted program is to detect potential illness before it reaches the sickness threshold—to preserve maximum health instead of treat obvious disease. Harvard-educated Dr. Ullyot moved away from her specialty of pathology to direct the exercise physiology phase of the program.

Dr. Ullyot talks as she writes—quickly, precisely, openly. She recalls thinking of herself as a "klutz who wasn't good at anything" until the innocent sport of running proved something to her. Now she has gone back to tennis with confidence—and with a vengeance. Women are conditioned to approach sports quite differently from men, she points out. "Men have the pain ethic. If it's not hurting, you're not doing it right. I say *have fun, make running enjoyable or forget it*."

The previous day she had run a marathon in Sacramento. "You won't believe the map they handed out," she said. "I probably ran 27 or 28 miles, and others knocked 30 minutes off their best times." The map was a maze on paper and must have been untraceable on foot. There were more switchbacks than the hike from Half Dome to Yosemite Valley.

"I tried out my new Nike Elites," she said less wearily, "and I'm going to wear them at the Women's Nationals in Minneapolis next month. Good cushion and plenty of toe room."

She was wearing New Balances and a stylish warmup suit, great for bouncing up and down the steep, creaky staircase to and from her office. But that was just the most convenient thing to put on that morning in the Monday rush. When she runs to work, a neat five miles, she wears shorts and a tee shirt and showers at the office. She runs home, too, so that adds up to a nice ten-mile day.

Dr. Ullyot's work is inextricably intertwined with Joan Ullyot's avocation. Even before a complete computer analysis is made, she develops broad conclusions from following the health histories of the Institute's clients. The 23 determinants in the blood samples form a "bodyprint" that's as unique as a fingerprint. A person can have a "gray area bodyprint"—be in a borderline health condition—for years without exciting the interest of a doctor who is trained only to combat obvious illness. Dr. Ullyot sees evidence that runners have a favorable ratio of two types of cholesterol—high-density and low-density. Aerobic exercise seems to have an effect on lowering dangerous triglycerides. She deals with these broad conclusions in chemical analysis and simultaneously watches them at work in her own body.

She's aware she's now a celebrity in the running world. She received the Road Runners Club of America award for journalistic excellence in 1976. She gets to, and finishes high in, about 30 long-distance races a year. She runs sub-three-hour marathons when trying (best, 2:51) and runs them at about 3:15 for training. But she seems to enjoy herself most when talking about her foibles. "I'm just another refugee from housewife's syndrome," she says. When *Sports Illustrated* interviewed her in 1977 on the subject of an athlete's diet, she pointed out that in her studies of cholesterol and triglycerides the best-protected people were runners who were vegetarians, then non-running vegetarians. "Are you a vegetarian, then?" she was asked. "I won't pass up a good piece of meat," she replied.

Most authorities recommend keeping elbows at about waist level and hands fairly loose while running.

PATTERNS FOR WARMUP SUITS—SEW YOUR OWN

Patterns available in chain stores and by mail offer you an inexpensive way to get a quality cold-weather suit. The advantage: you choose your own materials. You can get a fabric which won't droop after several machine washings and will give you the weather protection you want. Note that wherever cotton is specified a cotton blend is probably better. Dark materials naturally absorb more sun. Add pockets to the top if it only has one or none; it's better than never knowing whether you'll need mittens or not.

Simplicity Pattern 8080 ($2): standard suit with zipper top and elastic waist and ankles, for men or women.

Simplicity Pattern 8272 ($2): as above, except hooded jacket, tab on ankles, skirt (!) if you want one. Misses sizes.

Butterick Pattern 5199, 5200 ($1.50 each): one for women, one for men—similar to Simplicity 8080 except stripes for sleeves and legs.

Very Easy Vogue Pattern 9830 ($3.50): stylish woman's suit intended for stretchable knit. Pants are straight-legged, elasticized at ankles and waist; top is pullover blouson with kangaroo pocket.

controlled circulation), but others may subscribe for $24 per year of 12 issues.

The average jogger would hardly find enough here to justify that expense, but anyone researching an article or interested in a specific medical problem of his own could do worse than checking a few back issues at the library or a doctor-friend's office. Important work is reported here many months before it reaches laymen's magazines. In July, 1977, for example, *Sportsmedicine* reported on an important six-year study by Dr. Kenneth Cooper at his Institute of Aerobics Research: Out of 2,276 runners studied over that period only two suffered any cardiovascular complications, and they recovered and resumed running. The same issue contained an impressive and optimistic article on the effects of running on depression.

Women runners would perhaps benefit most from the magazine, as research on the sex-specific needs of the woman athlete has begun in earnest in recent years. And there are plenty of trivia and unintentional humor here. In a report on the effects of long-distance running on menstruation, the Sepember, 1977, issue quotes a study in which "a female long-distance runner who was unable to become pregnant while in training became pregnant immediately when she quit running."

Dr. George Sheehan writes a column for *Sportsmedicine* under the nicely descriptive title

"Running Wild." He lets himself go here in a way that *Runner's World* readers might not expect—and here he is talking to his colleagues. Since Sheehan has said, in print, "I've kind of given up on doctors," he is watched very carefully by his

---

SELECTION:
BABY ENJOYS MOTHER'S EXERCISE

A brisk breeze blows in from Mission Bay as Patti Hurl gets her jogging companion ready.

First, she puts the baby in the stroller, then fastens the mini-seatbelt across her lap and adjusts the tiny sunbonnet. Bright-eyed Robin Hurl, all of five months old, is ready for the first lap of the about ten miles weekly she logs in the stroller pushed by her jogging mother.

Patti, 29, has been running all her life, she said, even up to six months ago when she stopped jogging a month before Robin was born. She has been "running seriously," Patti added, since 1968 when she took an exercise physiology class from Dr. Bill Phillips, a runner himself, at San Diego State University.

"That was the stepping-stone that led to my involvement in an exercise physiology lab and the adult fitness program," said Patti, who now is an instructor in the adult fitness department of the university.

"Today I jog about 35 miles a week. Robin goes with me for about ten. I push her in the stroller on concrete usually and I've never had any leg problems.

"I love to run because it's fun, but my primary reason is to burn calories. And it's fun to socialize, run with friends.

"I thought that maybe when I had my first baby that my life would be changed. Kellie, now three, is my first child and I jogged with her in a stroller, too. But it hasn't. My friends just wouldn't let me sit at home and the babies go right along."

Patti said she pushed Robin in the recent Fourth of July Coronado half marathon, a distance of 13.1 miles, at a pace averaging 7:30 to

7:45 a mile. She competed in the Mission Bay half marathon, the same distance, the month before Robin was born at a pace of 7:35. And all this, she added, with her doctor's heartiest approval.

In addition to taking Robin jogging, Patti and her husband, a fire fighter for the city who jogs half an hour a day five days a week, recently took the baby on a 15-mile hike up and down a canyon in Baja California. And the baby goes along swimming and cycling with her parents.

She also goes along while her mother teaches aerobic dancing classes at the university and at San Carlos Country Club, as Kellie did when she was tiny.

"When you live in an exercising atmosphere," said Patti, who was graduated from San Diego State University with a degree in Physical Education, "you don't let children tie you down. And I've seen other pregnant women and women with babies jogging now. I saw one man pushing a baby buggy.

"We get a lot of different reactions when we're out running. A child psychologist told us that it was very stimulating for Robin. People sometimes say, 'Oh, that poor baby,' when they see her.

"Then there was one fellow who saw Robin sleeping in her stroller and had his own ideas. 'Why don't you let her get out and run?' he called, and that was funny. But as long as the stroller's in motion, Robin's asleep. It's when we stop that the trouble sometimes starts."

—Lucretia Steiger
San Diego Track Club News

DO-IT-YOURSELF WARMUPS

Remember those kits for backpackers—from Frostline in Denver? Now there's another Colorado firm with kits for runners: a sew-it-yourself warmup suit. There's more here than just the savings (50% or more) and the pride of accomplishment. In addition you can get a better fit and embellish your suit with extra pockets or emblems. For a free color brochure of what's available, write:

Colorado Sunkits, Inc.
Box 3288
Boulder, Colo. 80307

---

peers, lest he slip. Letters to the magazine frequently take him to task for his emphatic dictum, "runner's knee starts at the foot."

You might be doing your personal doctor a favor by asking him to add this magazine to his list of "throw aways," as they call the nonprofessional journals. The address:

The Physician and Sportsmedicine
4530 West 77th Street
Minneapolis, Minn. 55435

REVIEW

Running is literally "the magazine for thinking runners." It publishes no schedules, results, local

---

**COMBINATION RUNNING JACKET:
NIGHT, BRIGHT SUN, SOLAR HEAT**

A good combination of qualities important to runners: bright at night, cool in hot sun, warm in winter sun . . . in a jacket. An aluminum skin is bonded to nylon in the Apollo jacket, so the reflective qualities are good at night and in hot sun, and the heat-absorbing qualities are good in cold weather. Tuck-away hood for rain protection. Underarm circulation of air. Men's and women's sizes. Only 10 ounces. $34.00 ($3.00 additional for XXL). From:

Norm Thompson
N.W. 18th and Thurman
Portland International Airport, Main Terminal
Portland, Ore.
(503) 249-0170

---

news. It concentrates on the broad issues of health, technique, physiology—but it is far from dry and dusty. Published by avid runner/writer Jack Welch, it comes out four times a year ($5). You'll find things here before they filter down to the more well-known publications.

Running
P.O. Box 350
Salem, Ore. 97308

REVIEW

**Joan Ullyot, M.D. *Women's Running*
(World Publications, Mountain View, Calif., 1976)**

Books are often packaged and titled to sell the merchandise before it's sampled. Sometimes the publishers misfire and discover that the faddish come-ons only put the serious buyers off. There's an initial suspicion in glancing through this book that "Women's" is the wrong word in the title. It's too good as *anybody's* introduction to running. After closer reading, though, it becomes obvious that quite a subtle attitude pervades the book—a very womanly attitude.

Poetic, emotional, breathless? Wrong. Feisty, whining, argumentative? Wrong again. Chatty, hip, gossipy? Still wrong. I can think of a dozen male writers whose style is better characterized by those adjectives. Joan Ullyot writes like the scientist she is and the realist she is. She surveys the subject of running from cover to cover, from the first painful aversion to exercise to the thrill of a marathon in Central Park. It's terse, soundly supported, clear, entertaining. Although it pays suitable attention to such things as support of breasts and how to avoid rape (shouldn't any book on the subject?), this is a book about women's running primarily because its author is very much a woman and a runner.

A book this complete is liable to open questions without being able to handle all their ramifications. Many would disagree with Ullyot on her quick dismissal of megavitamin therapy. Her theory about the ultimate dominance of women in ultralong-distance runs has been challanged as

SELECTION:
YOU HAVE JUST BEEN PASSED BY A
WOMAN

Recently I have been practicing maintaining bursts of speed over increasing distances. Once when I was experimenting with pace along the Golden Gate Promenade I came upon a person who could truly classify as a jogger. So slowly was he moving that I felt like Apollo as I overtook him and moved easily forward. Suddenly I heard the sound of thrusting feet on gravel and realized that the jogger had taken my pass as a dare. His footsteps grated louder and faster behind me and suddenly my elation turned to fear. I felt as though I were being chased. I was too afraid to look around. I could no longer remember what the man had looked like, only could hear the sound of him after me, chasing me. Faster and faster we went, faster than racing as I tried to maintain my edge to the Gate and freedom from this terror. Later, while comfortably crossing Arguello Boulevard, I was to realize that this person was not chasing me, of course, but his pride.

Gestures and comments between runners are as much a part of the action as the course. Comments in passing are often amusing, sometimes maddening. I try to keep my cool when feeling hot under the tank top, however, by reminding myself that any utterance shows much more about the describer than the described.

I love the man at races who, if I should pass, cheers "You're looking good!" This man, I think, is a free man. But what about the man who passes me with "You're looking good!" I debate whether to try so complimenting the next man I overtake. "Hey you're looking great! Way to go!" I shout over my imagined shoulder. Somehow it doesn't work.

For some reason, many running men love to call women "girls." At the Avenue of the Giants I could surely have lopped an hour off my time had I not been so preoccupied with assuring everyone who called me "girl" that I was a "woman." They probably all thought I had some kind of hangup or something. I do. Slaves, servants, and idiots have traditionally been called "boy" by their English-speaking masters. Is it coincidence that secretaries are frequently referred to as "my girl" by their unenlightened male bosses?

Sometimes we women are our own worst enemies. Two heavy, giggling middle-aged matrons in the Presidio laughed loudly to see me running behind my husband. When I assured them that I was actually faster than he and asked them to stop laughing, they practically went into spasms.

A few weeks ago my distance partner and I were taking a practice cruise along the Great Highway. Up ahead I could see a road crew of about six men and inwardly groaned, bracing myself for the catcalls. But only one huge smiling face beamed from beneath his hardhat. "Alllriiight!" he cheered.

Now, *that* is progress.

—Elaine Miller, in *Soonar Soundings,*
San Francisco Pamakids

---

statistically unsupportable. And just when an important national address is given, the typographer lets us down by omitting the city! I personally am annoyed by charts and find too many here.

But these are the limits of my quibbles. This is one of the best buys as an all-around book on running.

FOR WOMEN

Clothing Designed for Women

Valerie Nye and Ellen Wersel are runners in the Washington, D.C., area, who say they "got tired of wearing clothes cut for men." They offer shorts, tops, and warmups and will design team

The neckline is in contrasting color

Ideal for cool weather and marathons

In soft cotton blend. Choose yellow, blue, red (white neckline) and white (with blue neckline).
S-M-L

The waistband is gently elasticized to ride loosely above your hips.

Short Tank Top
— cut just below the waist, it comes in the same absorbant cotton blend as our other tank top.
— available in yellow, blue, red and white. S-M-L

Styles in women's tops and shorts. Comments from Moving Comfort.

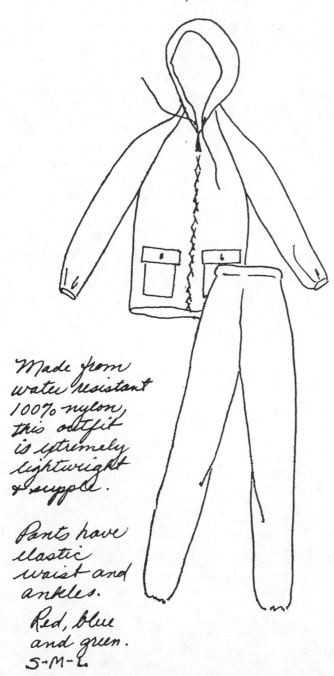

Made from water resistant 100% nylon, this outfit is extremely lightweight & supple.

Pants have elastic waist and ankles.

Red, blue and green.

S-M-L

A water-repellant, all-weather windbreaker suit from Moving Comfort.

uniforms for men and women runners. Write for a current catalog:

Moving Comfort
5792 Dunster Court No. 272
Alexandria, Va. 22311
(703) 998-5467

Running Shorts "For Women Only"

Six different styles of running shorts, from "shimmery, satiny" boxer short to competition types, are available from Gobelle, P.O. Box 986, Del Mar, California 92041. Prices are in the range of $9-$12; emphasis is on proper fit, good design, "airy" fabrics, some machine washable. Send for catalog/order form.

FASHION IN JOGGING?

Most books advise you to wear whatever's comfortable: loose-fitting bluejeans, shorts, old tee shirts. That's fine for the everyday jog. But even when nobody's looking at you, you'll feel more confident and psyched-up if you're wearing something you would *like* to be seen in.

Create your own outfit, if you must. But here are some hints about what others are doing and wearing:

Along the beaches in Southern California, swimming suits are *de rigueur* for running. No

Jogging attire along the beaches in Southern California is strictly catch-as-catch-can. Swimsuits predominate.

shoes, of course. A few fantasizing souls don the John Garfield outfit, complete with towel wrapped around neck (in the East this is known as the "Rocky"). By all means flex your shoulders and shadow box. On long runs there's another bonus: it's not uncommon to stumble onto a nude beach, unreachable by any other convenient means.

A pleasant custom of exchanging tee shirts has spread from such sports as crew. You may not want to give up your Boston Marathon shirt—it may not be fair, for this is the ultimate badge of personal accomplishment. But if you meet someone from afar, offer your club shirt or the one from your local charity run. In a short time you'll develop a collection of university shirts, Heart Association shirts, and shirts with provocative gag lines.

Barbra Minty and Oleg Cassini wearing the Oleg Cassini for Osaga warm-up suit

There's nothing wrong with the old-fashioned cotton shorts, but for a little extra money you can have a lot more comfort. The European-cut, nylon shorts are available with built-in liners for men, not as supporting as athletic supports but quite adequate for running. Many men prefer stretch briefs or Speedo swimsuits under an unlined short. But no matter how comfortable the shorts, or how highcut and tight, you'll develop rashes on long runs unless you use a lotion or Vaseline between your upper legs. On very long runs, sweating can also cause rubbing problems where the seam of the shirt meets the underarm (and across the chest, men). After a year of suffering, many a man laments, "Why didn't anyone tell me to use Vaseline?" This is also one reason why singlets with deep armholes were invented.

Men's competition-style shirts are usually a poor fit for women who are well developed at all. Yet clubs continue to order them willy-nilly for everyone in the membership. V-necked shirts with trim shoulders and short-short sleeves are widely available in sports stores, and many women's track teams and club members are designing and making their own shirts.

The relatively small Portland, Oregon, shoe manufacturer Osaga has announced a line of sportswear, including running outfits, designed by Oleg Cassini. The showroom for this firm is:

Osaga Actionwear, Inc.
498 Seventh Avenue, 2nd floor
New York, N.Y. 10018
(212) 279-5330

Clothes as well as shoes by Osaga are available in many family shoestores, as opposed to department stores, according to the manufacturer. Company stores are located on the West and East Coasts as follows:

Mr. Joey Salazar
Osaga
132 Coronado Mall
Albuquerque, N.M. 87110
(505) 293-6670

Mr. Allen Denson
Osaga of Oregon
1226 Jantzen Beach Center
Portland, Ore. 97217

Rodney & Phyllis Bobbins
Osaga
163 La Mirada Mall
La Mirada, Calif. 90638
(714) 522-0813

Mr. Al Schuckert
F-3 Moorestown Mall
Moorestown, N.J. 08057
(609) 235-7277

Mr. Eldon Sorenson
Osaga of Oregon
7-K Northtowne Shopping Center
Spokane, Wash. 99207
(509) 489-8832

Mr. Mark Fizer, Manager
261 Valley River Center
Eugene, Ore. 97401
(503) 484-1714

A variety of tops and shorts (mini-mesh, natural shoulder, V-neck shells, crew-neck shells, scoop neck tops, and boy-leg or soft-skin running and racing shorts and briefs) are available from:

Starting Line Sports
Box 8
Mountain View, Calif. 94042

A reasonably priced line of jogging suits ($18.95) and shorts and shirts is offered by:

The Aerobics Mart
12100 Preston Road
Dallas, Tex. 75230

A line of shorts and tops designed by marathener Ron Hill is available from

Total Environment Sports
P.O. Box 7394
Ann Arbor, Mich.

Ron Hill Freedom Shorts and Action Vests. The shorts incorporate a wrap-over to conceal a unique side slit that allows for complete freedom of leg movement when running and helps prevent chafing. The vests have narrow shoulder straps and deep armholes for freedom and ventilation.

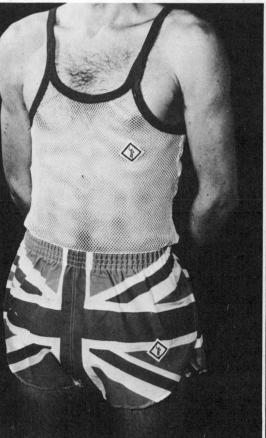

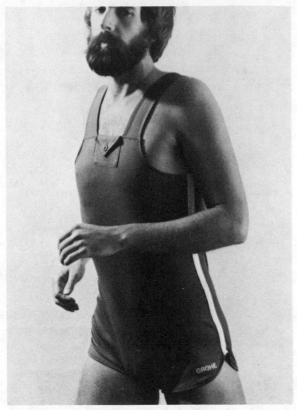

A one-piece cotton and polyester racing and training suit is available in men's sizes S, M, and L, and women's sizes XS, S, M, and L, from Grohe, 1420 Warren Avenue N., Suite D., Seattle, Washington 98109.

First Quality Shorts, Shirts, Sweats

Unisex style, stretch nylon shorts; 100% cotton shirts—at $9.95 and $4.95 respectively (plus 50¢ postage for mail orders). Acrylic/polyester sweats at $39.95 plus $1.00 postage. Dealers throughout the country, or order from:

Sub-4
Attn. Tom Steiner
17972 Sky Park Circle
Irvine, Calif. 92713
(714) 754-0491

THE NEW GENERATION OF RUNNING GEAR

All you have to do is look at the ads and you'll know it's come: fashion, style, sophistication, and not a little know-how in warmup suits, singlets, tops, shorts. Gone are the formless figures and antiseptic poses; here are the "in" people, clutching, posing, laughing the "arrived" laugh, enjoying themselves. It's a repeat of what happened to the ski-wear market some 20 years ago.

It's good. As sportsman Oleg Cassini says, "Anyone performs better when he looks the part." Cassini has designed a line of running gear to fit the body better, look smarter, perform up to the demands of the sport. A daily runner as well as competitive tennis player, he has investigated new materials and blends to achieve the "towel effect" in warmup suits without sacrificing breathability. His velour suit (65% cotton) is the only one on the market that's washable; his terrycloth suit and fleece suit of 100% cotton breathe well. New materials with a shiny, windbreaker effect are coming. His assistant Carol Bain, former track coach in Texas, emphasizes these outfits are antisag and definitely not unisex—and, most important, are meant to be *used*. (For catalog see page 92, Osaga.)

"The Line" has introduced new names to match the new feeling in jogging suits. Listen: Just Shell, Second Skin, Bare Feeling, Faye, Sylvester, Winged Audacity. And new combinations: jacket-shorts, rain suits, silk-mesh singlets and silk shorts. They're color-crazy. Free brochures from: The Line, 907 East 62nd Avenue, Denver, Colorado 80216.

Other places to explore new gear: Spiridon (the distributor for New Balance Shoes), P.O. Box 170, Allston, Massachusetts, 02134, (617) 782-4210: Beautiful, full-color catalog of running gear, featuring "super shorts" and singlets. Dolfin Corporation, Shillington, Pennsylvania 19607: "Clothing systems," in nylon tricot with support briefs. Sub-4, 17972 Sky Park Circle, Irvine, California 92714, (714) 754-0491: Stretch nylon with the "hidden pocket" in shorts—but only one pocket in warmup tops. Also check out Nike's line (see page 58 for address). And Adidas (see page 57) for their "horizontal stretch" made of Keyrolan®—flashy outside, soft inside. And how about this: not a tote bag, not hand-held bottle—a canteen velcro-attached to your running gear to contain four ounces of liquid. $3 from RWC, Box 56, Moultrie, Georgia 31768.

OTHER SOURCES

Other sports have their special shoes, clothing, accessories, but there's never a clear-cut division between the demands of one activity and the other. Skiing is a good example. You may be interested in:

Akers Ski, Inc.
Andover, Me. 04216

Their 1977 24-page catalog includes many items imported from Finland and Norway that would interest runners in cold weather country. One is a "fishnet" tee shirt, $5.50 or two for $9.95, which promises "natural insulation against cold or heat" along with moisture evaporation. And they have a shoe which "the Akers family all wear": Karhu Trampas, $29.95, designed for people who are on their feet a lot—well-elevated heel, heavy padding, built to withstand wear and abuse. (Sizes are in English, not American markings, so send foot tracing for best fit.)

Karhu shoes were ranked high in the *Runner's World* 1976 shoe issue. See page 57 to obtain a catalog of the complete Karhu line. Runners' shoes are excellent for wearing around the house!

PROTECTION FROM THE ELEMENTS

Damart Thermawear
Knitted fabric called "thermolactyl" lets perspiration out, keeps you warm down to 10°F. or colder when you run. Free catalog on underwear:

Damart, Inc.
1811 Woodbury Avenue
Portsmouth, N.H. 03801

Visors
It's in now to wear caps and visors from heavy-equipment companies and "cold country" manufacturers. Some sort of protection from the sun is advisable in strenuous running. One-size-fits-all visors are available by Puma ($1.95) and Adidas ($2.75) from Starting Line Sports, P.O. Box 5, Mountain View, California 94042.

The same source also offers:
Anti-fog for glasses: Contact lenses may be the only long-term solution! 14cc bottle . . . $1.50.
Frost, Sun, Toxic, Insect, Wind Guards: Outdoor creams each formulated for a specific use (Toxicguards against poison oak and ivy); 2-ounce bottle . . . $1.95 each.
Wristbands: Various color combinations, terry cloth . . . $1.90 per pair.

A POTPOURRI OF COLD WEATHER TIPS

"It's smarter to go out overdressed than underdressed"—Dr. Noel Dr. Nequin, Medical Director, Cardiac Rehabilitation Center, Swedish Covenant Hospital, Chicago, co-chairman of the Mayor's Marathon. (You will quickly learn how little you need for warmth—quite a bit more for protection against wind.) In wet weather he advises keeping your feet dry by using leather shoes and putting plastic bags over your socks, if necessary. (Even the best running shoes aren't going to last long if constantly wet—the uppers tend to separate along the outside of the forefoot. Protect leather shoes with silicone agents.)

Keep your feet warm with all-wool socks and add a pair of lighter socks if necessary, advises Richard Jones, manager of Eddie Bauer sporting goods store, downtown Chicago.

"The ideal costume for either men or women is the warmup suit such as those worn by athletes; easy fitting stretch pants with matching zippered turtle-neck jacket."—Bill Bowerman, who adds the reason why: "A bit of style consciousness, providing it doesn't become competitive, is all right."

"When it's cold you'll see a lot of warmup suits. They look nice, but they seem to me an unconscionably expensive way to keep warm when there are so many cheaper ways," is James F. Fixx's opinion, with the more experienced runner in mind.

"Feet cold? Put on a hat!"—Rory Donaldson quotes this old saying to underline the basic maxim that the head, then the neck and hands are the places where the body loses most of its heat. Get a stocking cap (wool), wear a turtle-neck sweater under your top, and keep mittens handy in freezing temperatures. (Mittens are more heat efficient than gloves.)

"The absolutely best insulator when it's wet is wool."—Donaldson again, adding the thought that an old wool pullover from a thrift store is the best bargain for people who like to run in the rain.

"Dress in many light layers rather than one heavy layer."—Rory Donaldson.

"I have an old wool sweater that I put on over my tee shirt when it gets really cold. With a sweatshirt on top and my nylon outershirt over that, I have on four layers, each with its cushion of warm air."—James F. Fixx.

"If you're right handed, you'll find that your left hand gets cold first and tends to stay colder, and vice versa if you're left handed."—Jim Sexton, Saskatchewan runner.

"A ski mask made of either wool or orlon is far superior to anything else I have tried."—Jim Sexton. Experienced cold-weather runners say follow the lead of skiers: use face masks only in wind or subzero temperatures.

"Don't toss out those old pantyhose or tights

Even when the weather is very cold, many runners find themselves pulling off their hats and gloves to cool down a bit. Note that the jogger on the right has pulled off only his right glove; chances are he's right handed.

just because they have a run. Layer them under your running outfit and they'll help fight the wind."—Judy Moore, Fashion Editor, *Chicago Sun-Times*. Black leotards under the usual running shorts are the simplest protection for the legs against cold. Bill Bowerman says, "Long-johns in cold weather."

"Nylon is good in a windbreaker or rain jacket, but it doesn't breathe. Only wear nylon when you can take it off when the wind or rain dies down."—Ellen Collins, Vital Fitness Evaluation Center. Nylon *blends*, however, are now being used in warmup suits because they keep their shape after washing, dry fast, and breathe fairly well.

MORE WEARING APPAREL

Race or Club Shirts
Orders of 15 or more a specialty:

Finish Line Sports
212 N. Parkerson
Crowley, La. 70526

Funny Lines on Shirts
Things like "I'm not fast, but I'm ahead of you":

Blair's T-Shirts
1162 Dorset
Costa Mesa, Calif. 92626

English Style Shirts and Shorts
Union jacks, stripes, sunburst designs; also mesh vests, rainsuits and raintops, women's attire, British club shirts:
Send stamped, self-addressed envelope for list to:

Total Environmental Sports
424 West Fourth
Rochester, Mich. 48063

License Plate Tops
The "in" license plate design popularized by "California Swimin" decals and tee shirts, now available with "California Runnin":

Hauner Aquatics
425 N. Fairmont
Lodi, Calif. 95240

One-Piece Racing Suits
The Grohe cotton-dacron sleeveless, short-leg leotard-type, at about $15, sized for men and women:

Grohe
1420 Warren Avenue North
Seattle, Wash. 98109

European Cuts
Lowcut singlets (tops), highcut shorts, light-weight:

New Balance
38-42 Everett Street
Boston, Mass. 02134

Olympic Athletic Sales
13400 Burbank Boulevard
Van Nuys, Calif. 91401

(Rainsuits and all-weather suits also available from both of the above. More European styles:)

Aspen
8000 East 40th
Denver, Colo.

International Sports
P.O. Box 2095
Boulder, Colo.

Protective Items
For running in extreme cold, Frost-guard cream is claimed to keep all exposed skin comfortable without excessive clothing:

Reyco-Reynes Products, Inc.
P.O. Box 1203
Sonoma, Calif. 95476

NIGHT RUNNING

Fluorescent-reflective materials on legbands, headbands, and vests are available from:

Jog-a-Lite
Box 125
Silver Lake, N.H. 03875

Prices range from $2.49 for legbands, $2.95 for headbands, $12.95 for vests, postpaid.
Another method of night protection is to wear a reflective band on one wrist and the opposite

ankle. For $2.75 postpaid you can order a set (Scotchlite® on 2-inch-wide nylon backing secured with Velcro® fasteners) from:

A couple running in the dark is protected by Jog-a-Lite headbands, vests, and legbands.

Ell
Box 12857
New Beighton, Minn. 55112

Glo-Bands®

Circlets—1½-inch-wide, yellow by day and reflective by night, available in bands from sizes 6 to 10 inches ($2.25 per pair) to 41 to 49 inches ($4.25 each), from:

Jads Company
P.O. Box 217
Wakefield, Mass. 01880

Add 50¢ for postage and handling and 20¢ for each additional item; 10% discount on items over $7.00 list. 5% tax for Massachusetts delivery.

The Reflexite sashband

Sashbands

1⅜ x 52-inch vinyl, washable band, in fluorescent colors: $1.50 plus 50¢ handling:

Reflexite Corporation
P.O. Box 306
New Britain, Conn. 06050

Volume discounts available to clubs—inquire.

Digital Pedometer

Clips on waistband, measures up to 100 miles according to stride you set. $14.95 plus 50¢ handling:

Misty Mountain Gifts
Walton Mountain Road
R.D. No. 3
Box 100
Walton, N.Y. 13856

THE AEROBICS CENTER

Several phases of aerobics activity are headquartered here. Dr. Ken Cooper can be reached directly at:

The Cooper Clinic
12100 Preston Road
Dallas, Tex. 75230
(214) 239-7223

five

compensating

tests, exercises, and diets to keep you running well

Every muscle in the body is balanced by an "antagonist," and every metabolic function is regulated by a gland. If either a muscle or a function somehow gets out of control, the body pays for it in pain. Unfortunately, it takes some time for this fact to sink into the beginning runner's head. "I'm exercising—I'm in good shape," goes the argument.

Dr. J. E. Schmidt of Charlestown, Indiana, created a stir in early 1976 by announcing in a national magazine "Jogging Can Kill You!" He adduced all sorts of internal problems, supposedly caused by the bobbing up and down of the body in motion. After the initial stir there has been an embarrassed silence, as one authority after another has asked for and been denied further explanation of the imagined ills of the runner. But Dr. Schmidt could have changed his story slightly and had a real message for the public: Jogging can injure you and cause you pain.

Dr. George Sheehan has written, "When you run, three things happen to your body, and two of them are bad." What's good is that you're developing your cardiovascular system. What's bad is that you're (1) overdeveloping and tightening your calf and hamstring muscles, and (2) underdeveloping your muscles which are the antagonists to these: the shin and thigh and abdomen muscles. Dr. Sheehan's "Basic Six" exercises to compensate for what you are doing bad by running are simple and direct:

(1) You stretch three muscles to reduce what you have overbuilt: the calves, the hamstrings, the lower back.

(2) You build three muscles you have neglected: shin, thigh (quadriceps or quads), and abdomen.

Sheehan also has something important to say about *how* you do his exercises:

(1) Do them slowly and deliberately.

(2) Stretch as far as possible until a tight and burning sensation is felt.

(3) Hold the stretch position for at least ten seconds. (See also p. 103 on thirty seconds as the ideal time.)

(4) Repeat them eight or ten times.

All of this may sound like just another list of meaningless rules, until you see what's behind them. As Dr. Rex Wiederanders has thoroughly explained in *Biotonics,* the strengthening of a muscle does not automatically occur unless the muscle is fully flexed. When you run, your shin and thigh muscles may seem to be taking a load, but they are hardly flexed. And the full flexing need last only eight seconds or so to attain its full potential for development. That's why "stretching as far as possible" and holding is so important.

When the Basic Six are explained to a jogger, he immediately masters the first one—the wall push-ups. But I have yet to see anyone actually get a paint can or other weight out and do the shin and thigh exercises. It reminds me of the old story of the bug-poison salesman explaining to the farmer how to use his product. "First you get the bug down on his back, and second you put a drop of the poison on his belly." "Why don't I just step on him when I have him down?" asked the farmer. "That," answered the salesman, "is also a good way."

There are indeed many good ways to do those three stretches and those three strengtheners— as long as you understand what you're trying to accomplish.

The Basic Six are illustrated on the following pages. It's truly amazing how books and articles on exercise can confuse even these simple steps. One recent and otherwise excellent book says, "First test for trouble. Stand up straight, then try to bend over and touch the ground with your fingertips. That's the minimum standard for flexibility." Many adequately flexible people can't touch their toes—and repeatedly testing yourself to try to do it can hurt your back. It goes on, "Now lie down, make a bridge with your knees and try to do a bent-leg sit-up. Doing one without having anyone or anything hold your feet in place is the minimum standard of abdominal strength." Not one person in ten can do a bent-leg sit-up slowly, holding his back a few inches from the floor, without having his legs hooked under something. The upper body simply weighs more than the legs. But just about everyone can do this exercise improperly, that is, bouncing the back up off the floor and bringing the body quickly to an upright position. There is no minimum standard for flexibility and no minimum for abdominal strength.

The Basic Six stretching and strengthening Exercises:

3) The legs-over hamstring and lower back stretch

1) The wall push-up or push-away

2) The back-of-the-chair hamstring stretch

4) The paint-can shin strengthener

5) The paint-can thigh strengthener

6) The bent-leg sit-up

It's also inadvisable, according to current thinking, to place your hands behind your head in doing a sit-up since you may bend your neck forward excessively and injure your spine. What Dr. Laurence Morehouse calls the "sit-back" is a good way to strengthen the abdomen: hook your bent legs under something for balance, and slowly let yourself down until your straightened back is just off the floor—and hold it there until your muscles quiver. The "back-curl," as described in Chapter One, is perhaps best of all: with your hands behind your *neck* curl up as far as you can without letting your lower back leave the floor. Try it—it's tough!

The leaning-against-the-wall exercise, intended to stretch your calf muscles, can also be done by standing with your toes up on a curb or against a hillside—very good to know when you can't find anything to lean on. And you can do the shin and thigh strengtheners without weights, as long as you exert your leg muscles and hold them fully flexed. For example, as long as you're down on the floor (like the bug), why not do the split-leg toe-touch (as pictured)? Ted Corbitt recommends

an excellent hamstring and lower-back stretch, equivalent to the legs-over:

After you've done your wall push-ups, bend over and touch your fingers to the floor by bending your knees sufficiently. Now keep your fingers there and slowly straighten your knees. Roll your back into a straightened position, and begin again.

TWO-FERS

Dr. Morehouse recommends his wall push-ups to strengthen the arms; Dr. Sheehan recommends them to stretch the calves. Why not combine the two? In fact, you can help yourself hold for 30 seconds, as recommended by exercise physiologists, by counting out 30 very short push-ups while your legs are in the stretched position.

Similarly, you can get two exercises in at the same time by wiggling your shoulders or revolving your head during other exercises. When you're doing sit-backs, extend your arms and roll

A typical parcourse, a sort of miniature golf course for runners. Parcourses are now being franchised throughout the country.

them around in their sockets. When you're raising paint cans with your toes or leg, count by making ten revolutions with your head—Jack LaLanne's special. Invent your own combinations. Very few are incompatible, unless they're forced.

An exceptional two-fer, which massages the back as it stretches the hamstring, is the combination legs-over and leg-grabber. Lying on your back, pull one leg tightly against your chest. Now swing the other leg, fully extended, slowly back over your head. This has cured more sciatica for more people than all the spas in Europe. (Caution: If you go to a nonrunning doctor with a sciatica problem, characteristically he will pound his two closed fists together to demonstrate what happens to your lower back when you run. And he'll tell you your running days are over. Believe Dr. Sheehan: Sciatica is most often a problem of

tight hamstrings and weak abdominal muscles—a "swayback" from way back.)

When I suggested these two-fers to exercise physiologist Ellen Collins, she said, "Aha! So you're a Type-A person!" Then she said, "Why not do your wallpush-ups with your *fingertips,* and exercise your fingers at the same time?"

PARCOURS

The Swiss started it, so we should perhaps allow them to name it: *parcours,* or *Vita Parcours*—a fixed course of exercises, usually located near a running area, where athletes can measure their level of fitness. The British have had similar programs for schools since World War II. In the U.S., courses have sprung up mainly on college cam-

SELECTION:
STRETCH IT OUT

Think of this. Animals are healthier, more active, and more supple for a far greater percentage of their lifetime than human beings. A cat, for example, is muscularly supple and lithe for almost seven eighths of its life. A human being, on the other hand, is only considered in "prime condition" for about half his life.

Why is that? The answer is simple, if you've spent time watching a cat. See how often he stretches. See him wake from a nap and stretch every muscle and work every joint in his body. Stretching his paws and hind legs, arching his back and curving his spine . . . a lithe, healthy creature able to perform amazing feats of physical activity for seven eighths of his life. And you? How often have you taken just a minute to touch your toes a few times? (Can't? Then go as far as you *can*!) How often do you flex your biceps, your forearms, wriggle your wrists and ankles, bend over backward to compress those vertebrae, do a deep knee-bend or two? How long does it take?

How long will seven eighths of *your* life be?

—Rex Wiederanders, M.D.,
with Edmond G. Addeo,
Biotonics,
(Funk & Wagnalls, New York, 1977)

puses; but I have seen them along such popular running routes as the Marina Green in San Francisco and South Shore, Lake Tahoe, in Northern California, and throughout the running meccas of Oregon. The Swiss regimen of mainly isometric exercises is usually followed, but an explanatory "e" is added to the name: parcourse.

I said "measure" rather than "improve" one's level of fitness, because most runners will find it more convenient to do their important exercises elsewhere. That means the stretching exercises and the muscle builders for the legs and abdomen (see Sheehan's Basic Six exercises, page 101). If nothing else, however, parcourses are visual reminders that runners often overlook the rest of their bodies because their legs feel so firm.

Most high school tracks are equipped with a set of bars, which are adequate for most of the parcourse exercises—if you use them. A friend of mine, Joe Harrington, likes to remind me, "Always run somewhere where you can be sure to find bars. Parallel or otherwise."

The well-constructed parcourse at Skyline College, San Mateo, California, is self-explanatory.

At position 8, shown here, "the isometric squat," runners lower themselves with back to pole and hold for a count of from 15 to 60 depending on fitness level.

An update on parcourses: The two circuits in San Francisco (long before the European name was imported, exercise physiologists referred to

The two most basic strengthening exercises are push-ups and sit-ups. The abbreviated push-up shown here, using the knees, is a good way to start. After you have mastered a dozen of these, you can try the straight-leg version.

Bent-leg sit-ups can be combined with a torso twist at the top.

The basic stretching exercise for legs and back: bring knees to chest and hold 30 seconds.

Two stretches for the back and waist.

A stretch for the inner thigh.

A thigh and hip stretch. An excellent book on stretching is Bob and Jean Anderson's *Running Stretches* (1976), $7.00. Write P.O. Box 2734, Fullerton, California 92633.

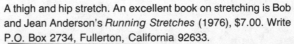

them as "circuits") were established by the Parcourse Company in San Francisco. At last count it had 110 courses that were in operation nationwide.

Exercise

Dance Your Way to Better Breathing, Flexibility, Muscle Tone. One good way to make sure you compensate sufficiently for the muscle imbalance of daily running is to enroll in a regular dance or exercise class: yoga, ballet, even tap. In some parts of the country dance studios are aiming their message at runners. For example, Feet First, Inc., in Bethesda, Maryland (7244 Wisconsin Avenue) offers a class it calls the "Jogger's Workshop." And "Aerobic Dancing" is now franchised nationally.

Exercise Physiology

Dorothy Harris writes a regular column in *Womensports* magazine on all phases of dieting, exercise, fitness. I have found this column to be the most helpful *factual* survey of anything in this field—and that includes the running magazines and the medical journals. No attempt at inspiration here, but if you are inspired by solid information presented with no nonsense style, don't miss this column. It has not come to my attention that Harris is specifically interested in the woman's point of view; so much the better.

Dorothy Harris
Penn State University
White Building
University Park, Pa. 16802

Runners lose great quantities of body fluid while running, especially in warm weather. Here volunteers hand cups of Body Punch to marathon participants.

SELECTION:
A NEW PAR FOR THE COURSE FOR BUSINESSMEN

Looming larger by the day on the U.S. health and fitness horizon is a Swiss concept called *parcours,* an outdoor obstacle course for joggers that is designed to benefit practically every set of muscles in the body.

In city parks, beside hotels and resorts, these training trails have begun to attract converts of all ages who seek to supplement periodic jogging workouts with more strenuous all-round exercise. The idea is to run from one exercise station to the next, stopping long enough to perform, on special apparatus, light gymnastics, hand-stands, pull-ups, sit-ups, and the like.

In Switzerland, where the idea had its roots in the 1960's, *parcours* has become something of a national institution and spread to all Europe. The Vita life insurance company of Zurich launched the first *parcourses* to raise the national fitness level, and today there are some 450 courses installed in 100 towns.

Sven Wiik, a noted Swedish cross-country skiing coach, laid out an early *parcours* in Steamboat Springs, Colorado. "Jogging," he says, "takes care of the legs, so the point of these exercise stations is to concentrate on building the upper body while giving the runner a little breathing spell along the way." Wiik points out that there is nothing formal or obligatory about running the course: You stop and exercise as lightly or strenuously as you wish.

On some courses, however, there are boards and charts posted at the exercise stations advising technique and number of repetitions. In the Marina district of San Francisco there is a notably scenic and well-designed *parcours* with more than a dozen stations, and each is posted with recommended repetitions for three levels of difficulty.

Chicago has a popular new version of the *parcours* system strung out through Lincoln Park between Diversey Parkway and Fullerton. There are balance beams, climbing logs, parallel bars, and a horizontal ladder set up along the trail, with time limits to work against.

Sea Pines Association of Hilton Head, South Carolina, established a *parcours* at Big Canoe, a development outside Atlanta. There is another on the University of Florida campus and many others either already in use or on the boards.

In less than a year, the Recreational Development Corp. of Charlotte, North Carolina, has established more than 50 courses, which the company calls Fit-Trails, across the U.S. Among the new sites, Seattle; Ossining, New York; the Wintergreen ski area in Virginia; and Fort Lauderdale.

—*The American Express*, July, 1977

RECIPES FOR REPLACEMENT DRINKS: WHY USE THEM, HOW TO MAKE THEM

Replacement drinks have been variously dubbed "bottled sweat" and "running water." The purpose of using them is clear: to replace what you lose in sweat.

Gone are the days when salt tablets were the prescription for sweaty exercise. Sweat is salty, but mainly because of the minerals and chemicals it contains known as electrolytes—chiefly sodium, potassium, amino acids plus ascorbic acid and some glucose. Salt without water is actually dangerous; the idea now is to duplicate the lost electrolytes in a drinkable solution.

George Sheehan, skeptical as ever, says, "Most commercial replacement fluids contain inadequate amounts of ... electrolytes...." Bill Gookin, the developer of the popular ERG (Electrolyte Replacement with Glucose), claims that the highly promoted Gatorade contains about five times as much sodium as potassium, whereas more recent research indicates sweat contains somewhat more of the latter than the former.

SELECTION:
ALCOHOL, PRO & CON

. . . The use of alcohol in athletics is nothing new. According to Dr. Max Novich (*Drugs in Sport,* 1970), European athletes at the turn of the century used alcohol extensively. There were reports of cyclists in 24-hour races drinking rum and champagne throughout the race, and of marathon runners consuming considerable quantities of cognac or beer during competition.

When competition is over, alcohol takes on a new value. Frank Shorter has called his daily beer consumption a good way to relax. Recently, an Oregon doctor visited the Sierra Madre Occidental of northwestern Mexico, home of the legendary Tarahumara Indians (*RW,* "The Super Runners," May, 1972; "The Tarahumaras," May, 1975), and found that they employed alcohol quite liberally as a relaxant. Noted for their all-day runs and 200-mile kickball games, they spent most of their time while he was there lying in the shade, drinking a homemade concoction.

Not only has there been a severe lack of agreement about the effects of alcohol, there has been great difficulty just in defining what alcohol is. One author writes (Shelton, *Health for the Millions*), "It is neither a food, thirst-quencher, nor medicine. It is a poison pure and simple." Yet Dr. Sheehan says, "First we must understand that alcohol is not only a drug but also a food."

Accepting that we are far from understanding alcohol, yet closer than we've ever been, the most important distinction would seem to be between use and abuse. It has been shown that, on occasion, abuse may have no adverse effects whatsoever.

"I can recall a teammate in college," Dr. Sheehan relates, "who was carried home after a nightlong beer blast and rose the next day to win the intercollegiate two-mile championship. I have heard much the same story of a well-known runner who was poured into bed the early morning of a national championship and later that day won going away."

But a more familiar memory, of the late Steve Prefontaine, stands as an illustration of how abuse can be devastating.

The distance between this extreme and that of the exhausted Boston runner who was revitalized by vodka is extremely great, and represents the spectrum of effects alcohol can have. A more common effect was experienced by Dr. Sheehan when he decided to test the merits of alcohol on himself. On a Saturday night he drank six beers, near Shorter's consumption on the eve of his Olympic victory. The next day he ran a good six-mile race.

"After a day off," Sheehan said, "I again drank six beers the following night. The next day I thought about running, but went home and took a three-hour nap instead."

—Jim Lilliefors, *Runner's World,* March, 1977

ERG not only matches this proportion, but also approximates the over-all concentration of body fluids. Gookin points out that water, which is more dilute than body fluids, is absorbed more slowly into the body (recall that stomachful of water sloshing around after that drink you took in the middle of a long, hot hike?). So Gookin insists on a concentrated solution—isotonic, or on a level with that of body fluids.

I hear that this minute physiological point caused a falling out between Gookin and his one-time distributor, Starting Line Sports. The latter firm now markets Body Punch, whose more dilute concentration is advertised as speeding electrolytes faster into the blood stream.

Drinks containing higher levels of glucose than these two competitors typically employ citric flavors to improve their taste. Citric acids have the disadvantage for runners, however, of masking the body's real liquid needs. (Body Ammo 1 and 2 are not part of this debate, since they are strictly protein and glucose tablets, respectively.)

One more (Perrier) for the road

The bottom line on replacement drinks is that (1) you don't need them unless you run long enough, in hot enough weather, to sweat for 20 or 30 minutes, and (2) when you do need them you can concoct your own at a fraction of the commercial cost. (Beer, a good electrolyte replacement, is not much more expensive than the products named above.)

Mike Souza, an ultramarathoner in the Sacramento, California, area, suggests tomato juice diluted with water. Fellow ultramarathoner Jonathon Brown says, "It seems to maintain an energy level and unlike Body Punch it seems to be absorbed in your system on a continuous basis."

E. C. Frederick, editor of *Running*, has written extensively on the subject and offers a simple recipe and a simple guideline:

To a quart of warm water add 1/3 teaspoon of salt (preferably Morton's Lite Salt) and 4 to 6 tablespoons of brown sugar.

Drink it cold, keep the sugar content low, and dilute further rather than concentrate.

(Frederick has also proposed complex formulas containing *all* the electrolytes and vitamins present in sweat.)

George Sheehan's recipe is orange juice with a weak salt solution. He claims this contains adequate amounts of sodium and potassium (as well as the fructose needed to develop glucose). Frederick and others would add a little baking soda as a buffering agent and for additional sodium.

Along lines of natural-food theories, Frances Sheridan Goulart, author of *Bum Steers* and other vegetarian books, suggests a variety of blended drinks. How about blackstrap molasses and raw honey in boiling water? Or raw grains liquefied in orange or pineapple juice? You can make a simple broth with fermented soybean paste (miso) without a blender. Mrs. Goulart also points out that the occasional craving runners have for a tossed salad or juicy peach is likely due to the potassium which those foods contain in abundance.

The story of Body Ammo's development, incidentally, is a typical example of progress in the new field of sportsmedicine. Practical results usually leapfrog ahead of physiological theory. Marathoners reported observable improvement in endurance and recovery with Body Ammo long before it was understood that the protein and fructose in those supplements were simply in a form that the body could metabolize faster. Eating an orange or a steak before a race does little good because the digesting mechanism turns off when exercise begins. But the Body Ammo supplements are metabolized without going through the usual "preliminaries." Body Ammo 1 is a complete amino acid supplement; Body Ammo 2 is a combination of the sugars glucose and fructose. Each is available at $4.50 for a bottle of 60 tablets from Protein Research Laboratories, Order Department, Room 500, 274 Brannan Street, San Francisco, California 94107. Another popular and apparently successful supplement used by runners is based on potassium-magnesium aspartate. "Second Wind" Jogger Tablets, which contain this and many other minerals and vitamins, are available in health food stores or from the manufacturer: Alacer Corp., Buena Park, California 90622 (100 tablets, $9.95).

Formulas for Runners' Drinks

Six recipes (two each for training, replacement, recovery) offered for $2 total. Send stamped, self-addressed envelope to:

> A. Schreiber
> 7205 Brompton 336-A
> Houston, Tex. 77025

COMPENSATING FOR YOUR CONDITION: STRESS TESTS AND FITNESS PROGRAMS

You were born with certain physical limitations, and if you're normal you've put further burdens on your body through neglect. You may think you're healthy—if you define health as the absence of obvious illness. But all of us live with "illness"—to redefine the word—which lurks under the threshold of symptoms. The single most common and dangerous of these unseen enemies is high blood pressure, but there are many less dramatic examples. Any sort of unusual stress put on the body—such as jogging—can exacerbate these limitations. And you are especially likely to have undetected problems as you grow older.

Common-sense advice for a potential jogger, accordingly, is to have a physical examination if you are over 35. Why 35? That's the experience of physical fitness experts: some men and women will maintain conditioning into their 60's, others will be old at 30, but most of us will be slowing down and putting on weight *in a regular pattern* by that age.

A physical examination can mean a whole range of tests. The bare minimum is a doctor's examination, which includes weight, blood pres-

Stretching it out

sure, and personal background. If you add to this blood tests to determine serum triglycerides and cholesterol, you can be rated for coronary risk, according to a Heart Association evaluation called Risko. Some "multiphasic" examinations—the annual checkup—also include recovery pulse rate tests (which are commonly given when you apply for life insurance) and vital capacity (ability to take in air) tests.

Very few people see the need, or are told by their doctors, to go beyond these tests. Who should have a stress test, and why, is a clouded question. Some specialists maintain that a runner who drops dead suddenly from an apparent heart attack probably would have died from the same heart defect even earlier—if he hadn't been a runner. But it is always disquieting when runners die *on the run.* In recent years at least, one experienced runner has died in the Boston Marathon of an apparent heart attack. Two runners whom I knew casually died after long runs (the full story of one of these cases is told with care in Hal Higdon's *Fitness After Forty*). A well-known dictum in running circles is Dr. Tom Bassler's claim that a marathoner is immune to heart attacks. Since Dr. Bassler speaks for the American Medical Jogger's Association (see page 83), his thoughts on the subject are not to be taken lightly. His key point is that a preexisting heart defect should be looked for in any case of a runner dying from an apparent heart attack; and running can't cause heart defects.

So the obvious goal of a stress test is to uncover preexisting heart defects. This is why most stress testing is done in the cardiology unit of hospitals. Two manufacturers of treadmills—by which most testing is done—have told me that more than 90% of all hospitals in metropolitan areas now do stress tests. If you're not a postcardiac patient, you will probably never be told of the availability of such tests. But you *can* call your hospital, or any cardiologist in group practice, and arrange for one (at a cost of from $75 to $125). (The National Jogging Association periodically publishes a list of places to take stress tests, mainly hospitals. *The Aerobics Way* by Ken Cooper contains the 1977 list. Many of these locations, such as YMCA's, will refer you to hospi-

Most distance runners have a lean look—and a correspondingly low percentage of body fat.

tals. The current list would include virtually every major hospital in the country.) But the problem of going to a cardiologist or hospital is that you'll get a yes-no evaluation on the question of a heart defect, and little more. Unless you get a cardiologist who is also a runner (as Dr. Bassler advises), you might be made to feel a little out of place among patients who are known to have heart problems.

A treadmill has meaning for the runner, however, far beyond discovering defects. Many cardiologists feel that they can get a clear enough picture of defects of the heart from a step test, such as the modified Masters. Resting ECG's (electrocardiograms) and ECG's taken immediately after various levels of exercise are analyzed in the doctor's office, or are transmitted by telephone to a computer for analysis. (The latter system makes it feasible to analyze as many as 12 leads quickly, which results in a slightly better chance of detecting heart problems than with a single or three-lead system.) The only drawback of a step test as against a treadmill is that it's difficult to regulate the amount of energy the patient is exerting—so the step test can't be easily graduated or repeated for comparison at a later date. It's the capability of the treadmill to increase the workload at a *gradual, known rate* which greatly adds to its value to the runner.

At a "human performance laboratory" at a university you are more likely to get the benefits of this feature of a treadmill than at the "cardiopulmonary" center of a hospital. At each increasing speed and angle of grade of the treadmill, blood pressure and oxygen uptake are monitored. A training heart rate and exercise program are prescribed on the basis of maximum aerobic capacity, maximum heart rate, and recovery time. In addition, most "fitness" analyses include testing of muscle groups and determination of body composition, such as per cent body fat.

How do you locate a fitness evaluation center? First, try your hospital and find out if a cardiologist there is interested in the problems of a runner who is not a postcardiac patient. Next, inquire for the nearest location of Vital:

5508 East 16th Street
Indianapolis, Ind. 46218
(317) 353-9307

At present, this firm has a full "fitness evaluation center" only in San Francisco, but its other "cardio rehabilitation centers" are rapidly getting into sportsmedicine.

Finally, if you are near such places as Ball State University in Muncie, Indiana, or Cardio-Metrics in New York, or the University of California at Davis, or Vital in San Francisco, or The Cooper Clinic in Dallas, or the National Athletic Health Institute at 575 East Hardy, Inglewood, California 90301, telephone (213) 674-1600, or any of the following universities which have stress test programs as of this writing, that's where to go.

University of Alabama
University Station
Birmingham, Ala. 35294

University of Arkansas
Fayetteville, Ark. 72701
(501) 575-2859

Harding College
Searcy, Ark. 72143

Stanford Medical School
730 Welch Road
Palo Alto, Calif. 94034

San Diego State University
San Diego, Calif. 92182

Southern Illinois University
Carbondale, Ill. 62801

Drake University
Des Moines, Iowa 50311

University of Kansas
Lawrence, Kan. 66044

University of Maryland
College Park, Md. 20742

Central Michigan University
Mount Pleasant, Mich. 48858

University of Nebraska/Omaha
Omaha, Neb. 68601

University of New Mexico
Albuquerque, N.M. 87131

State University College
Cortland, N.Y. 13045

Wake Forest University
Winston-Salem, N.C. 27109

Kent State University
Kent, Ohio 44242

Portland State University
Portland, Ore. 97207

East Stroudsburg State College
East Stroudsburg, Pa. 18301

University of Pittsburgh
Pittsburgh, Pa. 15261

Pennsylvania State University
University Park, Pa. 16802

University of South Carolina
Columbia, S.C. 29205

University of Wisconsin/LaCrosse
LaCrosse, Wisc. 54601

University of Wisconsin
Madison, Wisc. 53706

Ball State University
Muncie, Ind.

University of California at Davis
Davis, Calif. 95616

FOUR IMPORTANT CENTERS:

Vital Fitness Evaluation Center
1 Embarcadero Plaza
San Francisco, Calif. 94111
(415) 433-3286

Institute for Aerobics Research
12100 Preston Road
Dallas, Tex. 75230
(214) 239-7223

Cardio-Metrics Institute
295 Madison Avenue
New York, N.Y. 10017
(212) 889-6123

George Sheehan
Stress Testing Program
Riverview Hospital
Red Bank, N.J. 07701
(201) 741-2700

In addition to hospitals and universities, a third major source for stress tests, and one which will probably involve a more complete program for runners, is the YMCA. In New York, a full program is offered at the

West Side YMCA
5 West 63rd Street
New York, N.Y. 10023
(212) 787-4400

The YMCA has had well-established stress-testing programs in a number of major cities, such as Honolulu, San Francisco, Cleveland, and Toronto, at the most reasonable rates. Higher costs are usually associated with long-term programs.

The Vital Fitness Evaluation Center in San Francisco is perhaps the first privately operated one of its kind in the country. Unlike The Cooper Clinic, it appeals directly to the sports conscious person, with an eye to improving not only cardiovascular fitness but also the strength and stamina needed for specific leisure-time activities. It has gone a step beyond the fitness programs of certain large corporations, yet a good deal of its appeal is to business firms that want to protect the health and improve the efficiency of their key executives.

Complete fitness programs are likely to cost about double the fee for a simple stress test. The Vital program runs from $225 to $285; the program offered by the West Side YMCA in New York City is about twice that again.

Warming up

SELECTION:
AFTER WORKING THE REST IS EASY

. . . At the Olympic Marathon Trials in 1976, former 10,000-meter Olympian Jeff Galloway ran a lifetime best of 2:18:29. In the two months before that race Galloway had run 100 miles. That's not an average, that's the total!

Chuck Smead ran his PR of 2:14:39 after a summer of abbreviated training. He had been ill for a number of weeks, and unable to log his customary mileage. He didn't think he was in shape, but he was rested.

. . . Engage a group of runners in a conversation about rest, and you'll find that most of them agree that rest is important. Most will also agree that they probably don't get enough of it. Perhaps a number of them will even admit to having given it some serious thought. But, in all likelihood, only a few of them will ever have done anything about it.

Rest is a lot like stretching exercises in that respect. A lot of lip service is paid to its importance, even to its *necessity*. But few runners actually incorporate it into their training programs.

. . . Running is an exercise in destruction. Each time we run, we tear ourselves down. Muscle tissue is torn. Mitochondria, the powerhouses of the cells, swell grotesquely. Metabolic wastes accumulate. Blood-sugar levels drop. Dehydration occurs and, along with it, excessive losses of electrolytes upset the delicate balance required for efficient muscle and nerve function. We become overheated. Muscle glycogen is depleted. And as the intensity and/or duration of the workout increases, this damage becomes more pronounced.

In the period between runs, the body attempts to recover and rebuild. Torn muscle is repaired, new mitochondria are formed, metabolic wastes are flushed out of the system, blood-sugar levels are restored. We rehydrate and replace lost electrolytes. Any damage to muscles and to the nervous system due to hyperthermia (high body temperature) is repaired. Glycogen is replenished.

These two phases—destruction and regeneration—together constitute conditioning. And the two can never be separated if a conditioning program is to proceed in a positive direction.

In any program of running, then, the body is systematically broken down and rebuilt. And each rebuilding leaves the body a little stronger than before. These incremental increases amount to the development of a progressively stronger body capable of more and faster running.

. . . Workouts should be varied in intensity and duration from day to day to promote regeneration. Running hard, or long, only every 48 hours seems to be optimal. In between, workouts should be short and/or easy, and one's life should be adjusted to maximize regeneration. Plenty of sleep is certainly important, but what one does with waking hours is equally so.

This "cycling" of workouts is nothing new. Enlightened students of distance running, like Bill Bowerman and Tom Osler, have been preaching it for years. Its efficiency at producing optimal training effects has been proven time and again by the high proportion of world-class runners who have flourished on this type of program.

Rest can be divided into two types: "passive rest" and "active rest." Passive rest is what we

Other Fitness Programs

A sort of compromise is offered by Focus on Fitness, launched in 1978 by impresario Bill Graham. FOF workshops in 12 locations throughout Northern California provide, for a $125 membership fee, a five-week course in all phases of fitness, beginning with a step-test evaluation. The goal is a lifelong program: members are retested every three months, and receive a monthly newsletter for a modest annual fee. Graham says that Focus on Fitness will go next to Los Angeles, and then across the country.

normally do, or *don't* do. In short, passive rest is inactivity. We do nothing in particular to promote rest, but instead give nature time to run its course.

But there are other things we can *do* which will enhance regeneration and will multiply the effectiveness of rest.

. . . After a hard run, things like light stretching, meditation, a sauna, or a massage will cause regeneration to proceed more quickly than it would if we simply took a nap. These sorts of activities are regeneration-promoting.

. . . We can regenerate a psyche which has been damaged or overworked by a long or hard run using the same positive approach we've taken in healing the body. Do something unusual. Take a walk somewhere you've never been before, read something different, sit in a bus station and watch the world in action, catch a Walt Disney movie, take a long drive over a back road, walk in the rain, visit the ocean, go to a museum, make love—not necessarily in that order, nor one after another. In short, do something that will increase your awareness, stimulate you, generate new interests and ideas. It is just as important to have a fresh, healthy interest in your running as it is to have a sound body to do it with.

. . . Emil Puttemans, at least once a year, has a period in which he does no running at all. He overeats, gets a little sloppy, and becomes the antithesis of his normal self. Puttemans claims that these "rest" days are the most important part of his annual training pattern. . . .

—E. C. Frederick and Jack Welch,
Runner's World

Running, dancing, skipping rope, and bicycling are the major activities employed for aerobic work. For free brochure, write:

Focus on Fitness
747 Front Street
San Francisco, Calif. 94111   (415) 434-3633

Focus on Fitness advertises: "So you blew it. Start over." Why not avoid "blowing it"? Several organizations focus on getting kids started in the right directions toward lifelong physical fitness. If you're an educator, physical education specialist, or simply lover of children, you may want to know more about the programs of these people:

American Alliance for Health, Physical Education, and Recreation (AAHPER)
1201 Sixteenth Street, N.W.
Washington, D.C. 20036
(202) 833-5554

Write for Publications Catalog listing films and pamphlets aimed at promoting noncompetitive, vigorous exercise and creative play. In San Francisco, a foundation offers training programs for business firms, communities, and schools as an alternative to the competitive and largely spectator-oriented games of our culture:

New Games Foundation
P.O. Box 7901
San Francisco, Calif. 94120
(415) 824-6900

Write for current announcements of activities.

Treadmills

Running on a treadmill is like making love for the benefit of Masters and Johnson. But if you need one, you can order by mail:

MacLevy
92-21 Corona Avenue
Elmhurst, N. Y. 11373
(212) 592-6550

The "Professional Unit" is offered at $695 prepaid ($15 additional west of Mississippi). Moves up to 9½ mph.

A treadmill that can go up to 12.3 mph and up to a 15% grade is offered by:

Trotter Treadmills, Inc.
95 Marked Tree Road
Hollister, Mass. 01746
(617) 429-5821

Prices from $989, up.

Cooling down

An Alternative to Treadmills: The Exercycle

Two of the major commercial suppliers of treadmills, Quinton and Marquette, are happy to sell to the home-user, but suggest that most of the benefits of a treadmill for the average jogger can be obtained much more reasonably with an exercycle. Even a stress test can be performed with good reliability on a cycle. For descriptive literature write:

> Quinton Instruments
> 2121 Terry Ave.
> Seattle, Wash. 98121

For jogging in place:

Angled, padded board for indoor jogging without "pavement shock"—$19.95, $2.00 shipping; inquire about special school offer:

> American Sealcut
> 201 E. 66 Street Penthouse H.
> New York, N.Y. 10021

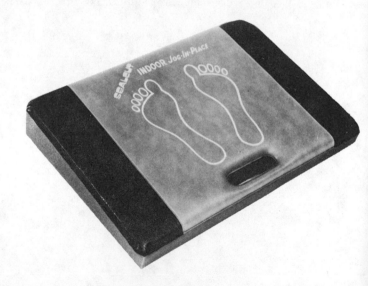

For stretching Achilles and calf muscles in place:

Adjustable wedge, cork top—$14.95 per pair, $1.95 shipping:

Flex-Wedge Co.
Box 5
Getzville, N. Y. 14068

The Best Compensation of All: Rest

When the article from which the excerpts on page 116 are taken first appeared in *Runner's World*, in October, 1976, it caused more than the usual stir among competitive runners. Ticking off one example after another, Frederick and Welch showed that ingrained assumptions about continuous training were open to question—even at worldclass levels. Joggers, take heart: the laws of conditioning are the same for all. When you feel guilty about missing a week, read this.

FOOD SUPPLEMENTS
Protein, Vitamins, Minerals?

Most nutritionists specializing in sportsmedicine are leery of claims that athletes or runners in particular need more than "a balanced diet" plus extra carbohydrates before and electrolytes after a long run. However, if you feel differently, one good source for supplements is your local Shaklee distributor. Check the white pages of your telephone book. If you try a "juice fast," too, you might want to keep your energy up with supplements. Shaklee promotes Instant Protein Energy Bars, Drink Mix, and Vita Lea (multiple vitamins) for runners.

Bee Pollen, B-15 ("The Vitamin Banned in the U.S."), B-12

Free information! Send stamped, self-addressed envelope to:

Sports Nutrition
1330 E. Dover Street
Mesa, Ariz. 85203

Cold-processed, "full-potency" bee pollen—"the largest selling pollen in the world"—also available from:

Gary Fanelli
400 Cottman Street
Jenkintown, Pa. 19046

BOOKS FOR YOUR BODY

Encyclopedia of Athletic Medicine, compiled by Dr. George Sheehan. Various aspects of health and injury in any sport involving running: leg muscle pulls, stress fractures, shin splints, Achilles tendinitis, etc., sometimes unconventional but sensitive to the special needs of runners. $1.95, World Publications.

The Running Foot Doctor, Steven I. Subotnick, D.P.M., M.S. (World Publications, 1976). A case history approach to the understanding of foot and related problems, designed to let you try to work

---

DO IT YOURSELF TO YOUR MORTON'S FOOT

 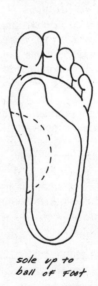

cookie in arch　　　sole up to ball of foot

Dr. George Sheehan suggests a little exercise in self-help before you run to a podiatrist with your big-second-toe problem. To keep your foot from pronating too much to a flat-footed position, build up your arch with padding of any sort, according to the two-step stage illustrated. First cut a half-moon "cookie" as shown, feathering it so it's thicker toward center of your foot (white area in drawing). Then attach this with tape, in a comfortable position, to another pad the size of your insole but cut off below the ball of your foot. A sheet of surgical felt, 21'' x 36,'' costs about $10; inquire at a surgical supply store.

THE EULA WEAVER DIET

Americans are obsessed with living longer, which is part of the "more is better" syndrome. Granting this, we can also readily sympathize with postcardiac patients or others suffering from debilitating diseases, who want to live longer only if they can improve the quality of their living. For these people, Dr. Nathan Pritikin's Longevity Research Institute in Santa Barbara is a godsend, and his book, *Live Longer Now* (Leonard, Hofer, Pritikin; Grosset & Dunlap, 1974), a bible. Pritikin's results have been spectacular, his most famous patient, at least in the running world, being 88-year-old Eula Weaver, Olympic gold medalist for her age. Perhaps Eula is a rare exception (how many others run at her age?). Perhaps Pritikin's claim to have reversed arteriosclerosis through diet and exercise is extravagant. Other researchers have questioned his analysis. Yet he is having success with a simple, spartan formula: 80% complex carbohydrates (fresh vegetables, whole grains), 10% fats, 10% protein. The surprising thing about this diet is that it rules out staples ordinarily recommended: no nuts (too much fat), limited fruits, including raisins (too much sucrose, which is not a *complex* carbohydrate), limited dairy products (again, too much fat). Coffee, tea, alcohol, salt—out! The message for those who have a severe medical problem is clear: there are other things in life besides food. For those of us who are not at death's door, Pritikin's formula at least dramatizes the content of basic food types and warns us about overuse of such things as salt and alcohol.

out your own problems before seeing a podiatrist. Concise, colloquial, witty. Dr. Subotnick teaches at the California College of Podiatry in San Francisco and practices in Hayward, California. (See page 64 for how to locate a podiatrist in your area.) 208 pages, illustrated, $6.95 hardcover, $3.95 paperback. For *The Foot Book,* Harry Hlavac, see page 53.

Food for Fitness, editors of *Bike World*. Facts and fallacies on protein requirements, weight control, carbohydrate loading, drugs, etc. A book designed to help vigorous athletic performance through better nutrition. 143 pp., illustrated. $3.50, World Publications.

Nutrition for Athletes, Ellington Darden. An athlete-nutritionist goes deeply into what to eat and not to eat if you are a competitor. 208 pp. $3.95. Athletic Publications.

The Runner's Diet, editors of *Runner's World*—a very practical guide to virtually every aspect of dietary essentials for runners, including prerace eating, role of glucose, recommended daily allowances, salt, liquids, vitamins, body weight, etc. 80 pages, illustrated. $2.50, World Publications.

Order from:

World Publications
Box 366
Mountain View, Calif. 94042

six

joining
teams,
clubs, and groups

I don't think you can get the full satisfaction of running without joining a club—and I'm a non-joiner. There's a lot that's social about jogging, in the best sense of the word. You get some of that feeling when you're in the middle of a thousand howling, leaping runners when suddenly the starting gun goes off and a yell goes up as from a chorus. Then there's the description L. Fraser Rasmussen of the Buffalo Chips Running Club in Sacramento gives: "The real reason we all run is to withstand the quarterly potlucks we schedule under the guise of club business meetings. In actuality it is simply a good ole runners' 'gorge.'"

Here are seven good reasons for going beyond this—and joining several clubs. In San Francisco, for example, the Dolphin South End Runners have at least two spinoffs: the Turk Street Runners and the Pamakids. Members of the smaller clubs belong to the parent, but have their own activities for their own interests. Why not join a club somewhere distant? This might happen:

1. You'll get good ideas for your own club activities.

2. When you travel or plan a vacation, you'll be a leg up.

3. You'll get broader news from their newsletter than from any of the national publications.

4. You'll see a lot of interesting writing and photos.

5. You'll see more that interests the fun-runner than you'll see in slick magazines.

6. You may locate old friends who have moved away from your area, or whom you knew in high school.

7. And in your heart of hearts you know they need the support.

Nothing is quite as democratic as a running club. People you read about in the bigger maga-zines are there sweating with you. Where else would you meet an Olympian, or an Olympic contender? And Olympian or not, there are people who accomplish Olympian feats who still participate on an equal footing with you, such as:

— Walt Stack, in San Francisco, at 70 an ultramarathoner

— Jim O'Neil, in Sacramento, holder of the American record for the marathon for over-50

— Abe Underwood, in Sacramento, who recently did the 72-mile run around Lake Tahoe

— Edward Mendosa, in Tucson, former Olympian

—J. A. Kelley, in Boston, major American marathoner for 20 years

— Toshika d'Elia, in New Jersey, at 47 one of the top American women marathoners

— Kenny Moore, Mike Manley, Jon Anderson, Craig Virgin, in Eugene — Olympians all

— Ken Weidcamp, in Portland, major organizer in the Northwest

— Ted Corbitt, in New York, editor of the largest club journal in the country, organizer, ultramarathoner, world record holder at 56

These are a few of the names which constantly come up in club newsletters—there are hundreds more, for running of all sports is a lifetime thing. On the following pages are several lists of clubs. It's confusing. Should you join a YMCA club, such as the prominent West Side YMCA in New York City? Should you join the AAU? It's a matter of taste, of where you live and with whom you like to associate. Off and on, there has been a conflict between the AAU as an organizing body and non-AAU clubs. This goes back to feuds on a national level, before jogging was the people's sport. (In some cases, overly eager AAU people have approached sponsors of races and discouraged them from continuing their sponsorship unless the organizing group joined the AAU.) I think you'll find there is little conflict at the member's level. Go to fun-runs organized by local clubs. See who else goes. Write for a newsletter that appeals to you by location or name. Joining a running club can be as low key as you like it, and the best way to stay motivated.

NOMINATIONS
Best Runner's Club Paper

Newsletter of the New York Road Runners Club
Published quarterly, and edited meticulously by the tireless Ted Corbitt, this has long been the leading tabloid in the country for serious runners, and should be even more important as the New York Marathon becomes the focus of attention in the public's eye. Full news coverage of important long-distance events around the country and abroad, as well as in the vicinity of New York. Thoughtful editorials and articles. Liberally festooned with race photos and sometimes cartoons. Mainly serious reporting, but also plenty of the human touch. Subscriptions ($4 per year, $2 for students) should be sent to:

> N. Y. Road Runners Club
> 226 East 53rd Street
> New York, N. Y. 10022

Regional Coverage
Newsletters and Magazines

Runner's Gazette

> 102 West Water Street
> Lansford, Pa. 18232   (717) 645-4692
> Ed Gildea, Editor

50¢ per copy, $6 for 12 issues; published quarterly. The fourth issue, dated Summer, 1977, is a 40-pager, tabloid size, completely typeset, with numerous photographs and excellent coverage of Eastern events, some national, and instructional articles. A bargain even for the casual runner.

(For *Running Times*, see page 143; *Footnotes*, page 33; *Running*, page 88. These and the above are national in scope if not in circulation.)

(A sampling of those not mentioned elsewhere)

Yankee Runner

> P.O. Box 237
> Merrimac, Mass. 01860   (617) 346-9664
> Rick Bayko, Editor

35¢ per copy, $5 for 18 issues per year; a little ragged in production (*TV Guide* size, typewritten, various odd-size inserts), but a must for the New England runner, with complete schedules, results, photos.

Running News

> P.O. Box 25113
> Kansas City, Mo. 64119
> Bob Kuhn, Editor

75¢ per copy, $7 per year of twelve issues; 12- to 16-page tabloid, typewritten, candid-quality photos and cartoons, focusing on news and events in Mid-America. Field as well as track; heavy school coverage.

The Runner

> c/o New Times
> Dept. NT3-20
> One Park Avenue
> New York, N.Y. 10016

New from *New Times* beginning in August 1978, The Runner will include articles on "the entire state of mind running expresses." $12.00 for twelve issues.

 **BUFFALO CHIPS** *RUNNING CLUB*

Good Local Newsletters
(Subscription part of membership in club)

Potomac Valley Seniors Newsletter

> 4821 Kingston Drive
> Annandale, Va. 22003

A filling meal of race reports, stories, anecdotes, humor, names, and original pieces worthy of national attention.

Baltimore Road Runners Club Newsletter

> Route 1, Box 246 Evna
> Parkton, Md. 21120

Well-produced, magazine-style publication (2,000 copies, three times a year), a pleasure to read.

Newsletter of the San Diego Track Club

> 5994 Broadmoor Drive
> La Mesa, Calif. 92041

> Jack Johnstone, Editor

Running activity is feverish in the San Diego area, and the runners have a publication to match. Somebody has a creative pastepot down there, an uncle who owns a camera store, and a gung-ho audience. A recent issue has a group photo of the membership at the Avenue of the Giants marathon—some 650 miles north of San Diego —and I count 44 runners. A nice feature is a continuing series of photographs of runners in their prejogging days: Can you identify this former fat man?

The Oregon Distance Runner

> 14230 S. W. Derby
> Beaverton, Ore. 97005
> Ken Weidcamp, Editor

Graphically the most pleasant magazine in the running field — no doubt due mainly to the efforts of advertising artist Clive Davies, a record-holding masters runner and humorous illustrator par excellence. I suspect that the care given to this publication is a big reason why the club is so well organized and active. The power of the press!

Buffalo Chips Running Club

> 6555 Riverside Boulevard
> Sacramento, Calif.

> Abe Underwood, Editor

This club's newsletter exudes a good-natured irreverence, mutual support, and fun. No long-winded reprints of interval training methods here. A pleasant feature of this and other letters is the exchange of bits of humor from one to another. The Dolphin South End Running Club in San Francisco is one in the spirit with the Chips.

Chico Running Club Newsletter

> Route 5, Box 79DA
> Chico, Calif. 95926

As the selection on the 1977 Ride-and-Tie indicates (see "Events," page 141), this letter isn't tossed off carelessly. Well thought-out features and pleasant layout distinguish this modest publication. After reading a few issues, you feel you've met some new friends.

Minnesota Distance Runner

P.O. Box 14064
University Station
Minneapolis, Minn. 55414

Jim Ferstle, Editor

A full, straightforward account of what's going on in the state, with very little picked up from other sources. The trend here as elsewhere is toward marathoning. All kinds of interesting tidbits turn up in even the most serious newsletters, such as the report here that the Italian runners at the Montreal Olympics obtained four to five% of their total calories from wine.

HTC News

8811 Edgeville Drive
Huntsville, Ala. 35802

Harold Tinsley, Sr., Editor
A compact and fact-filled journal, with schedules

SELECTION:
A WINNER'S DAY

(Tasty writing and local color in club newsletters can't be duplicated in the bigger publications. I leave to your imagination the scenario behind this report from Buffalo Chips. It was only a ten-miler in Stockton, California, but. . . .)

Local shoe magnate, Sally Edwards, an Ophir Baddie (they have her name but the Chips have her soul) *won* the women's division in a sparkling 64:28 and demolished the women's course record by nearly five minutes. Reputed to be the illegitimate offspring of Jack Sanchez, the plucky little capitalist finished far ahead of the 2nd woman finisher and received a beautiful marble and pewter plaque for her victory (that's the kind of stuff the ones who win get . . . but Sally was gracious, letting the rest of us look at it, handle it, and salivate for a few minutes). Sally, as luck would have it, also was the first name drawn in the merchandise awards and, amid gasps of disbelief, passed over two brand new pairs of Nike Waffle Trainers and selected a six pack of cheap wine from the table. Underwood's unsavory influence on this situation was all too apparent.

—Doug Rennie

Family rates are usually quite considerate in running clubs. Members of the Body Ammo Club of Berkeley, California, the Burger family poses at the start of the Bridge-to-Bridge charity run, September 1977, San Francisco. The pit crew seems disinterested.

and results from a broad area of the Southeast. Runners outside Huntsville may subscribe ($2 for six issues) without joining the club.

Hagerstown Run for Fun Club Newsletter

118 Partridge Trail
Hagerstown, Md. 21740

William M. Jackson, Sr., Editor

Lives up to its name: all the information a runner in this area needs, served up with a homey touch.

Births and birthdays are duly noted. The letter reminds members of what every runner should be aware of: you can support your club by ordering subscriptions, shoes, and drinks (some, all, or more) through the club.

The Harrier

P.O. Box 188
Eltingville Station
Staten Island, N. Y. 10312

Marc Bloom, Editor

Not really a local publication, but produced in a local style. *The Harrier* covers high school and college cross-country running two to five miles nationally, with a brief look at road running. Strictly for the young competitor. $8 per year, monthly.

Northern California Running Review

NCRR
P. O. Box 1551
San Mateo, Calif. 94401

A well-produced magazine primarily for the competitive runner on the Pacific Coast — quite professionally done, as you would expect of the sponsoring West Valley Track Club. High school runners and events are given coverage here they receive nowhere else. You won't miss any dates if you get this regularly; many photos, feature articles from top Northern California runners. Send for free sample copy, or subscribe for $6 (12 issues a year).

PEOPLE—AND LONGEVITY

A runner picked his way through one of the narrow gauntlets of humanity on the Boston Marathon route, when suddenly a hand shot out to grasp his. "Hey, do you know Ken Weidcamp?" the man said. The runner was wearing the word "Oregon" somewhere on his shirt, and in the Northwest or even the Southeast that means Ken. (See "The World's Best Running Places," page 162.)

The names in running aren't the celebrities who have made their names elsewhere and then taken up jogging. They're the people who organize clubs and races and show up at just about everything. They're the former Olympians who join the Sunday fun-runs, the Masters who are a living encouragement to beginners. Occasionally, they're the winners.

The Yankee Runner polls its readers (some 1,500 paid subscriptions) annually on their choice for athletes of the year in New England, and such names as Amby Burfoot (1968 Boston winner) and John A. Kelley (twice winner at Boston and Olympic marathoner years ago) always score high. Sig Podlozny, "epitome of the road running participant," was universally loved; his untimely death as a result of an automobile accident in 1977 inspired an outpouring of tribute from all parts of the country. *The Yankee Runner* calls Charlotte Lettis "The Grand Old Lady of New England Running," but that means old only in tireless hours of promotion of the sport.

At 71 years of age, Dr. Lou Gregory ran 5,000 meters in 21:39, a world age record. That's approximately seven minutes per mile. And that was two years ago. The Southern newsletter of the Road Runners Club of America, issued at Troy, Alabama, reported that this local boy "tries to run daily, but his 1926 injury prevents that possibility. . . . He smiles now before a race, contrasting with his scowl of yore."

In the Central California area, where runners can know real heat, two ultramarathoners are familiar figures at cross-country runs and special events. Jim O'Neil blazed to a 2:35:46 marathon in February, 1977, setting an American record for those over 50 (he *is*, just). This was just one of his many age records. Meanwhile, Abe Underwood went down to a track in Santa Monica and circled it for 6 hours, 14 minutes for a distance of 50 miles. That's 200 times around. Olympic Gold Medalist Billy Mills (10,000 meters, 1964—one of the most stirring finishes by any distance runner) maintains an interest in running, speaking to groups in the Sacramento area as well as nationally.

Sometimes you see names in a magazine or book without any idea of the locale from which these Olympians have sprung. Clive Davies is well-known in the Northwest (an art director at McCann Erickson Advertising in Portland, Oregon, he does the best illustrations of running maps and situations in any magazine I've seen). But he is known worldwide for the ten (10) records he holds in the 60 and over category (1500 meters: 4:57.9). Tom "Turtle" Osler once ran 114 miles in 24 hours to promote a charity at Glassboro (N.J.) State College, where he teaches math; he's known all over for his minor classic *The Conditioning of the Distance Runner,*

SELECTION:
MASTERS RUNNING

. . . I was in a state of happy agony nearing the finish, knowing I was the winner of my division, when I saw Rod Nichols up ahead. I had always thought of Rod as a very good runner working out his salvation in the 40-and-over group. But suddenly I noticed that Rod was getting quite bald, and it occurred to me that Rod had been around the running scene for a very long time. He began to look more and more like a very competent 50-year-old.

At considerable cost, partially paid for by the panic I felt at this thought, I caught up to him. Easing alongside, I casually gasped, "How old are you, Rod?"

"I'm 75," he replied in a tone just short of exasperation—and then added, "I'm 44."

I relaxed. I didn't have to beat him. When he gets to be 50, I thought as I cruised around the high school track to the finish, I'll be in the 60-and-over.

—George Sheehan, M.D.,
in The Physician and
Sports medicine

George Sheehan may look like he's struggling—but he's way out in the lead!

first published in 1967 (29 pp., $1.50 — order from World Publications).

Men over 40 and women over 35 are classed as "Masters" in most races, with additional age brackets (though without corresponding names) at 50, 60, etc. The growing practice is to consider 40 the dividing line between women "Open" and "Masters" runners. The AAU runs masters events in various regions of the country. The U.S. Track and Field Federation conducts its masters championships each year in Green Valley, Arizona. For further information, write Steve Myers, Box 984, Green Valley, Arizona 85614.

REVIEW

**Hal Higdon, *Fitness After Forty*
(World Publications,
Mountain View, Calif., 1977)**

Hal Higdon speaks his mind, writes entertainingly, and knows his stuff. What else can you ask of a writer writing on your favorite pastime? Hal ends his parade of charts and graphs and statistics with the score-yourself questionnaire to top them all: How to Live to Be 99. All the information, the anecdotes, the occasional pep talks don't quite add up to the promise on the cover: "How to get in shape and how to stay in shape for the best years in your life."

Nevertheless, Higdon always gives good reading value. He's been everywhere and seen everyone. He's fair, and his evidence for the value of running is balanced by respect for the sport's critics. Whether you're far from 40 or hopelessly past it, you'll enjoy this book as much as a man with an age-crisis.

Books—

Some of Running's People

CORBITT: The Story of Ted Corbitt, Long Distance Runner. The father of U.S. ultradistance racing, Corbitt has run more marathons than anyone else in history—and, incredibly, he's never failed to finish any marathon he's started! This is his biography, crafted by John Chodes. Chosen as one of the best sports books of 1974 by the *New York Times.* 160 pp. Illustrated. 1974. $3.95. Track and Field News.

FIRST FOUR MINUTES (formerly "Four Minute Mile"). Roger Bannister's stirring autobiography: the great account of the four-minute breakthrough in the mile—perhaps the most famous occurrence in track history. 252 pp. Illustrated. 1955. Hardcover. $3.00. Dodd, Mead.

RUNNING WILD. Gordon Pirie's life story. The former British distance superstar and world record holder reveals all in readable style. 224 pages. Illustrated. 1961. Hardcover. $2.50. Athletic Arena.

Order any of the above from:

Track and Field News
Box 296
Los Altos, Calif. 94022

AAU REGIONAL OFFICES

You can call or write any regional office to find out where there is a local AAU running or track and field club near you. If your region is not listed below, you can write or call the AAU National

Headquarters: AAU House, 3400 West 86th Street, Indianapolis, Indiana 46268; telephone (317) 297-2900.

ADIRONDACK

Room L105
855 Central Avenue
Albany, N.Y. 12206
(518) 489-1603

ALASKA

P.O. Box 4-1872
Anchorage, AK 99509

ALLEGHENY MOUNTAIN

507 Magee Building
Pittsburgh, PA 15222
(412) 261-3754

ARKANSAS

J.W. "Billy" Mitchell
801 Scott
Little Rock, AR 72201
(501) 376-0060

CENTRAL

205 W. Wacker Dr.
Chicago, IL 60606
(312) 782-4229

CENTRAL CALIFORNIA

P.O. Box 1020
Tulare, CA 93274
(209) 688-8744

One of the side benefits of the running explosion is that the younger generation really has something to look up to.

KEY TO MAP OF AAU REGIONS

REGION I	Maine, New England, Adirondack, Niagara, Connecticut, Metropolis, New Jersey
REGION II	Middle Atlantic, South Atlantic, Potomac Valley, Allegheny Mountain, Virginia
REGION III	North Carolina, South Carolina, Georgia, Southeastern
REGION IV	Florida, Florida Gold Coast
REGION V	Hawaiian
REGION VI	Central, Indiana, Ohio, Kentucky, Lake Erie, Michigan, West Virginia
REGION VII	Wisconsin, Minnesota, Midwestern, Iowa
REGION VIII	Missouri Valley, Ozark, Oklahoma, Arkansas
REGION IX	Gulf, Southwestern, South Texas, West Texas, Southern
REGION X	Intermountain, Rocky Mountain, New Mexico, Arizona, Border
REGION XI	North Dakota, South Dakota, Montana, Wyoming
REGION XII	Inland Empire, Oregon, Pacific Northwest
REGION XIII	Pacific, Southern Pacific, Central California, Pacific Southwest, Southern Nevada
REGION XIV	Alaska
REGION XV	Far East

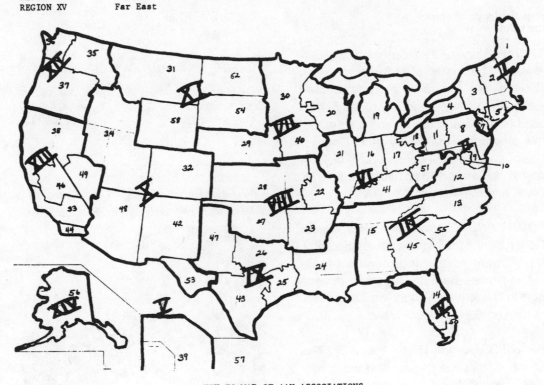

KEY TO MAP OF AAU ASSOCIATIONS

1	Maine	21	Central	41	Kentucky
2	New England	22	Ozark	42	New Mexico
3	Adirondack	23	Arkansas	43	South Texas
4	Niagara	24	Southern	44	Pacific Southwest
5	Connecticut	25	Gulf	45	Georgia
6	Metropolitan	26	Southwestern	46	Central California
7	New Jersey	27	Oklahoma	47	West Texas
8	Middle Atlantic	28	Missouri Valley	48	Arizona
9	South Atlantic	29	Midwestern	49	Southern Nevada
10	Potomac Valley	30	Minnesota	50	Florida Gold Coast
11	Allegheny Mountain	31	Montana	51	West Virginia
12	Virginia	32	Rocky Mountain	52	North Dakota
13	North Carolina	33	Southern Pacific	53	Border
14	Florida	34	Intermountain	54	South Dakota
15	Southeastern	35	Inland Empire	55	South Carolina
16	Indiana	36	Pacific Northwest	56	Alaska
17	Ohio	37	Oregon	57	Far East
18	Lake Erie	38	Pacific	58	Wyoming
19	Michigan	39	Hawaiian		
20	Wisconsin	40	Iowa		

FAR EAST

Box DN c/o Sports Dept.
Pacific Daily News
Agana, Guam 96910
(Guam) 477-9711, ext. 62

FLORIDA

1221 Lee Road
Suite 102
Orlando, Florida 32810
(305) 295-9184

GEORGIA

3670 Frey Lake Road
Kennesaw, GA 30144
(404) 427-0378

HAWAII

P.O. Box 7189
Honolulu, HI 96821

INDIANA

3959 Central Avenue
Indianapolis, IN 46205
(317) 283-5688

KENTUCKY

1515 Tyler Park Dr.
Louisville, KY 40204
(502) 458-4989

LAKE ERIE

Room 8 City Hall
Cleveland, OH 44114
(216) 241-5115

METROPOLITAN

15 Park Row
Room 321
New York, N.Y. 10038
(212) 267-7334

MICHIGAN

18100 Meyers Road
Detroit, MI 48235
(313) 864-9464

MIDDLE ATLANTIC

738 Land Title Building
Broad and Chestnut Streets
Philadelphia, PA 19110
(215) 563-6935

MIDWESTERN

Box 1522
817 W. Oklahoma
Grand Island, NE 68801

MINNESOTA

Carole Mead
9810 3rd Street
N.E. Blaine, MN 55434
(612) 786-1291

MISSOURI VALLEY

4422 Belleview
Kansas City, MO 64111
(816) 931-6277

MONTANA

923 Avenue B, N.W.
Great Falls, MT 59404
(406) 453-1561

NEW JERSEY

1670 Irving Street
Rahway, New Jersey 07065
(201) 381-4380

NEW MEXICO

P.O. Box 8606
Albuquerque, NM 87108

NIAGARA

3925 Harlem Road
Buffalo, N.Y. 14226
(716) 839-1996

NORTH DAKOTA

916 W. Central
Minot, N.D. 58701
(701) 839-1924

OREGON

P.O. Box 16129
Portland OR 97216
(503) 243-4112

PACIFIC

942 Market Street
San Francisco, CA 94102
(415) 986-6725

PACIFIC NORTHWEST

P.O. Box 5098
Kent, WA 98031
(206) 852-9550

PACIFIC SOUTHWEST

1135 Garnet Avenue
San Diego, CA 92117
(714) 275-1292

ROCKY MOUNTAIN

220 Leyden Street
Denver, CO 80220
(303) 321-2262

SOUTH CAROLINA

P.O. Box 5504
Columbia, SC 29250
(803) 799-4678

SOUTH TEXAS

523 Cave Ln.
San Antonio, TX 78209
(512) 822-7369

SOUTHERN

P.O. Box 8728
Metairie, LA 70011
(504) 885-0882

SOUTHERN PACIFIC

10911 Riverside Drive
P.O. Box 6015
North Hollywood, CA 91603
(213) 877-0256 or 985-5005

SOUTHWESTERN

215 W. Vickery Blvd.
Fort Worth, TX 76104
(817) 429-3583

VIRGINIA

Utica Bldg.
Suite 101-B
4900 Augusta Avenue
Richmond, VA 23230
(804) 353-9438

WEST TEXAS

P.O. Box 2792
1515 Avenue J
Lubbock, TX 79401
(806) 744-5207

SELECTION:
SAM BELL'S TEN COMMANDMENTS FOR COACHES (AND PARENTS!)

1. Believe in the Joy of Distance Running!
(You can't sell it to others if you don't have it yourself.)
2. Be a Recruiter!
(Don't let them come to you—go out to them.)
3. Never Use Running as a Punishment!
(Don't order young people to "do a lap" or work harder when they're not doing as well as you expect in some other area.)
4. Give Every Runner Encouragement to Run the Year Round!
(Off-season and bad-weather running should be blessed.)
5. Understand Aerobic and Anaerobic Training!
("Steady state" training and "oxygen debt" training can be blended.)
6. Teach Proper Mechanical Running Principles!
(Running is natural but fundamentals must be kept in mind.)
7. Running Is a Sport to Help People Grow!
(The goal should be secondary to the human qualities involved.)
8. Runners Differ!
(The exceptional runner shouldn't set levels expected of everyone.)
9. Don't Overtrain!
(Overwork discourages; happy work encourages.)
10. Don't Overcompete!
(Reduce pressure and you'll get better performances.)

Sam Bell is a U.S. Olympic coach, the Head Track and Cross-Country Coach at Indiana University. His Ten Commandments above are adapted from an article in *The Harrier*.

WISCONSIN

1400 N. Prospect Avenue
Milwaukee, WI 53202
(414) 276-0716

WYOMING

907 Carlson
Cheyenne, WY 82001
(307) 638-6851

**MEMBER CHAPTERS
OF THE ROAD RUNNERS
CLUB OF AMERICA**

ALABAMA

Birmingham TC (Track Club)
Versal Spalding
2405 Henrietta Road Court
Birmingham 35223

Huntsville TC
Harold Tinsley, SR.
8811 Edgehill Drive, SE
Huntsville 35802

Troy TC
Nick Costes
Department of Health,
Education, and Recreation
Troy State University
Troy 36081
(205) 566-3159

ARIZONA

Arizona RRC (Road Racers Club)
John Weldy
2524 North 69th Street
Scottsdale 85257
(602) 946-3222

Southern Arizona RRC
Joseph W. Cary
25 Goldfinch Circle
Sierra Vista 85635

CALIFORNIA

East Bay RRC
Charles NcNahon
154 Grover Lane
Walnut Creek 94596

Bay Area RRC
Bill Flodberg
12925 Foothill Avenue
San Martin 95046
(408) 683-2810

San Luis Distance Club
Stan Rosenfield
P.O. Box 1134
San Luis Obispo 93406

San Francisco DSE Runners
Walt Stack
321 Collingwood Street
San Francisco 94114
(415) 647-9459

Kids will love running—if they're not pushed too hard.

COLORADO

Denver TC
Steve Kaeuper
2263 Krameria
Denver 80207
(303) 388-8180

Colorado Masters RA
Bill and Nancy Hamaker
1525 South Lansing Street
Aurora 80012
(303) 750-9043 home
(303) 341-8032 work

Fort Collins TC
Ray Boyd
P.O. Box 1435
Fort Collins 80521
(303) 484-5076

Northern Colorado TC
Neil Gillette
P.O. Box 1744
Greeley 80631

Pikes Peak TC
Merv Bennett
Pikes Peak Y
P.O. Box 1694
Colorado Springs 80901

Rocky Mountain Road Runners
Buzz Yancey
929 Washington #5
Denver 80203
(303) 831-6129

Timber Ridge Runners
Gary Phippen
P.O. Box 1262
Evergreen 80439
(303) 674-7641

FLORIDA

Fort Lauderdale RRC
Dennis Tunks
731 Northeast 61st Street
Fort Lauderdale 33334

Gulf Winds TC
Dr. James C. Penrod
2412 Winthrop Road
Tallahassee 32303
(904) 386-6294

Northwest Florida TC
Ed Sears
174 Charles Drive
Valparaiso 32580
(904) 678-6329

Pensacola Runners Association
Stuart Towns
P.O. Box 2691
Pensacola 32503
(904) 476-8750

Valparaiso-Niceville AA
Fred Carley
177 BA, Route 1
Niceville 32578
(904) 897-2559

Walt Stack, leading organizer and runner in Northern California—ultramarathoner at 70.

INTERVIEW

Walt Stack

ThelegendaryWaltStack, a new word added to the language by a man's ability to run, turned 70 shortly after this picture was taken. It's a characteristic pose; Walt is often seen tossing beer cans over his shoulder in marathons. (Marathoners are preserved from being litterbugs by the attentiveness of fans.) It's also characteristic because, when he gave me this photo, he couldn't figure out for a long time where it was taken. You see, he runs in too many races. Finally he decided this was the eight-mile brickyard run in Martinez, California. "Look at that funny, square-shaped stick," he said; "it's not the usual tongue-depressor."

Walt dotes on women. After a race he can be seen handing out running schedules of the Dolphin South End Running Club to the best-looking women in sight. And he has the perfect cover for this new-way-to-meet-girls. He wants to maintain the club record of having the highest percentage of female membership in the country: 35%.

Whenever he describes his club—he founded it 11 years ago—he keeps coming back to this point. "Get the women out and it'll be a better club for everyone. Out on the road, I mean." And women take to the DSE easily, he explains, because it's low key. The story goes that DSE member Joan Ullyot was listening to two male

---

GEORGIA

Atlanta TC
Billy Daniel
1760 Dyson Drive, NE
Atlanta 30305

Savannah Striders
William Bakkeby
159 Traynor Avenue
Savannah 31405
(912) 354-8705

GUAM

Guam Running Club
Mike Flynn
P.O. Box 756
Agana, Guam 96910

HAWAII

Mid-Pacific RRC
Thomas Smyth
203 Ilihau Street
Kailua 96734
(808) 254-3944

IOWA

Cornbelt Running Club
John Hudetz
1115 Sixth Avenue
DeWitt 52742   (319) 659-3100

ILLINOIS

Galesburg RRC
Evan Massey
1080 Tamarind
Galesburg 61401
(309) 342-8270

competitors at the starting line of a club run. One was going to start slowly and finish strong; the other said he felt like going out fast and easing off. To this Joan replied that she was in a mood to start slowly and ease off. Since that time the official club motto has been: Start slowly and taper off.

If more clubs had this attitude, Walt maintains, it would be far easier for women and other supposedly nonathletic types to come out for races. "But we never call them races. Runs, just runs."

When a traveler asks the National Jogging Association or the Road Runners Club of America for recommendations on places to run in San Francisco, they refer him to Walt. The legendary one meets him for a run across the Golden Gate Bridge or along the Dipsea Trail. And this happens two or three times a week. He has traversed the bridge so often that the steelworkers once gave him a trophy engraved "Champeen Runner." But if you're from out of town, he says, remember it's the DSE club, not just the Dolphins. The latter is a swimming and rowing club under the same umbrella.

Walt has swum with his good friend Jack LaLanne in the icy waters of San Francisco Bay; has run marathons with Peter Strudwick, who was born without hands or feet; has jogged with Larry Lewis at least once a week while that St. Francis Hotel waiter passed his 100th birthday;

and yet he's still awed by young Patty Wilson of La Palma, California, who ran almost the length of the Pacific Coast, to Portland, Oregon, in the summer of 1977. "My biggest thrill," he says, "is to see people doing things they once thought impossible—such as just running a mile." In March of 1974 Walt Stack started out with 1,355 other runners in the John F. Kennedy Memorial Run in Boonsboro, Maryland. Subfreezing temperatures crippled the field in the Appalachians as a wind whipped along the trail—for this was a run of 50 miles. Walt finished 34th. He was 67 years old.

Today, he still gets in an hour's swim in the Bay before heading off to his job as a hod carrier. In the evenings he's at his desk for another hour or two answering mail and attending to club business. How does he keep it up? "Runners keep it up longer," he's likely to answer, with a wink. "But remember, this is a cooperative thing, this running business. We all support each other. And that reminds me: Tell them to think of the next guy and send a stamped, self-addressed envelope if they expect an answer from me or anybody running a club."

Consistency seems to be Walt Stack's secret. He moves through a marathon or a five miler at the same effortless pace. At the DSE club they say that if Walt ever fell out of an airplane he'd fall at a rate of eight minutes per mile.

Glenview RRC
Jerry Parsons
1504 Pfingsten Road
Glenview 60025
(312) 729-5507

Illinois RRC
Alan Edgecombe
P.O. Box 2976, Station A
Champaign 61820
(217) 367-7711

Illinois Valley Striders
Steve Shostrom

3018 North Bigelow
Peoria 61604
(309) 685-3654

Midwest RRC
Dick King
5600 South Drexel
Chicago 60606
(312) 643-9894

Moraine TC
Mike Beard
6826 Chelsea Road
Tinley Park 60477

Springfield RRC
Tim Bonansinga
1412 South Douglas
Springfield 62704
(217) 782-1090

INDIANA

Hoosier RRC
Steve Kearney
205 West Porter Avenue
Chesterton 46304
(219) 926-4344

Fort Wayne TC
Harry Koontz
4634 Manistee Drive
Ft. Wayne 46815
(219) 485-9124

KANSAS

Mid-America Masters
T&F (Track & Field)
Bob Creighton
111 South Sixth Street
Atwood 67730
(913) 626-3679

Wichita Running Club
Brant Wooten
3054 South Custer
Wichita 67217

LOUISIANA

Cajun TC
Don Stuckey
627 East 11th Street
Crowley 70526
(318) 783-4533

RRC of Slidell
Ray Durham
675 Dale Avenue
Slidell 70458
(504) 641-0440

New Orleans TC
President
P.O. Box 30491
New Orleans 70190

MARYLAND

Baltimore RRC
John Roemer
Route 1, Box 246
Evna Road
Parkton 21120

Federick Steeplechasers
Jim Dillon
15 Eureka Lane
Walkersville 21793

Queen City Striders
Ray Kiddy
1916 Harrow Lane
Cumberland 21502
(301) 777-7391

RASAC
Joseph Lacetera
1006 Whitaker Mill Road
Joppa 21085
(310) 877-0718

MASSACHUSETTS

Berkshire Hill Runners
Jim Dami
17 Frederick Street
North Adams 01247

Central Massachusetts Striders
Wayne Lamothe
9 Atwood Road
Cherry Valley 01611

Greater Springfield Harriers
Brian Powell
120 Oxford Road
Molyoke 01040

New England RRC
Rick Bayko
19 Grove Street
Merrimac 01860
(617) 346-9664

North Medford Club
Julian Siegal
368 Lincoln Street, Apartment 11
Waltham 02154

Poet's Seat Ridge Runners
Edward C. Porter
26 Madison Circle
Greenfield 01301

Sharon RRC
Dale Van Meter
66 Summit Avenue
Sharon 02067
(617) 784-6348

Sugarloaf Mountain AC
Ed Sandifer
P.O. Box 853
Amherst 01002

MICHIGAN

Battle Creek RRC
Robert Fischer
52½ Elm
Battle Creek 49017
(616) 963-9458

Kalamazoo TC
Tom Coyne
1584 Spruce Drive
Kalamazoo 49008

Mid Michigan TC
Gordon Schafer
4378 West Holt Road
Holt 48842

Saginaw TC
Ray Bartels
4440 Winfield
Saginaw 48603
(517) 793-0979

Upper Peninsula RRC
Dan Lori
Box 776
Iron Mountain 49801

MINNESOTA

Minnesota Distance
Running Association
P.O. Box 14064
University Station
Minneapolis 55414
(612) 484-5164

MISSISSIPPI

Mississippi TC
Walter Howell
608 Dunton Road
Clinton 39056

Ocean Springs RRC
Terry Delcluze
1207 Lodonderry Lane
Ocean Springs 39564

MONTANA

Big Sky Wind Drifters
P.O. Box 1766
Bozeman 59715

MISSOURI

Columbia TC
Joe Duncan
4004 Defoe Drive
Columbia 65201
(314) 445-2684

St. Louis TC
Jerry Kokesh
1226 Orchard Village Drive
Manchester 63011

NEVADA

Las Vegas TC
Tony Gerardi
5020 Lancaster Drive

Las Vegas 89120
(702) 451-4060

NEW YORK

Hudson-Mohawk RRC
Paul Rosenberg
124 Daytona Avenue
Albany 12203
(518) 489-6590

New York RRC
Fred Lebow
Box 881, FDR Station
New York 10022
(212) 688-6824

Greater Rochester TC
Paul Gesell
4472 Main Street
Hemlock 14466

NORTH CAROLINA

Asheville TC
Bob Wiltshire
Parish House (St. Mary's)
339 Charlotte Street
Asheville 28804
(704) 252-2752

Charlotte-Mecklenburg TC
Bob Maydole
704 Pine Road
Davidson 28036
(704) 892-3078

Cumberland County RR
Roger J. Peduzzi
USAIMA– Medical Training Branch
Fort Bragg 28307

OHIO

Cleveland RRC
Bill Bredenbeck
5916 Longano Drive
Independence 44131

Cleveland West RRC
Stephen Gladis
530 Humiston Drive
Bay Village 44140

Ohio River RRC
Felix LeBlanc
1013 Tralee Trail
Dayton 45430

Toledo RRC
Fred Fineske

4128 Hill Avenue
Toledo 43607

University of Toledo RRC
Sy Mah
2158 Sylvania Avenue
Toledo 43616

Youngstown RRC
Jack Cessna
269 Alameda Avenue
Youngstown 44504
(216) 747-3238

Southeast Running Club
Roger McKain
6549 Forest Glen Avenue
Cleveland 44139

PENNSYLVANIA

Allegheny Mountain RRC
Shirley McDaniels
721 Vallevista Avenue
Pittsburgh 15234
(412) 343-1327

Chambersburg RRC
Chuck Lesher
Route 10, Box 38
Chambersburg 17201
(717) 264-5390

Greater Pittsburgh RRC
Stuart Levy
818 MacArthur Drive
Pittsburgh 15228
(412) 341-4141

Harrisburg Area RRC
Park Barner
127 Wertsville Road
Enola 17025
(717) 732-1323

Mid-Atlantic RRC
Joe McIlhinney
908 Cottman Street
Philadelphia 19111
(215) 342-7600

Reading RRC
Bruce Zeidman
211 North Sixth Street
Reading 19601
(215) 375-4368

Delco Joggers
Byron J. Mundy
713 Beechwood Avenue
Collingdale 19023

Valley Forge RRC
Reverend Raymond K. Reighn
Pawling Road
Phoenixville 19460

SOUTH CAROLINA

Greenville TC
Bill Keesling
5 Rollingwood Drive
Taylors 29687
(803) 268-8967

TEXAS

Houston RRC
J. Geller
4132 Meyerwood
Houston 77025

UTAH

Beehive TC
Jan Cheney
289 South at 200 East
Kaysville 84037
(801) 376-5072

VIRGINIA

Tidewater Striders
Don Grey
6429 Gridle Way
Norfolk 23518

TENNESSEE

Chattanooga TC
Doug Hawley
Box 1167
Dalton 30720
(404) 226-3730

Eagle University RC
LTC Gerald L. Koch
101 Lacy Lane
Clarkesville 37040

VERMONT

North Country AC
Paul Mailman
12 Deerfield Drive
Montpelier 05602

Vermont Ridgerunners
Tom Heffernan
Box 116
Killington 05751

WASHINGTON

Club Northwest
Bill Roe
2557-25th Avenue East
Seattle 98112
(206) 325-3167

Walla Walla RRC
Russ Akers
959 Olympia
Walla Walla 99362

WASHINGTON, D.C.

DC Road Runners
Ray Morrison
120 Eastmoor Drive
Silver Spring, Md. 20910

WEST VIRGINIA

Country Roaders RRC
Paul D. Caseman
270 Buckey Hill Road
Wellsburg 26079
(304) 737-3340

WISCONSIN

University of Wisconsin at Milwaukee TC
Clark Bowerman
36545 Colonial Hills Drive
Dousman 53118

Indianhead TC
Doug Erbeck
707 Weshaven Road
Chippewa Falls 54709

WYOMING

Cheyenne TC
Greg and Mary Anne Niemiec
P.O. Box 10154
Cheyenne 82001
(307) 635-2003

Human Energy West
Bruce J. Noble
1063 Empanada
Laramie 82071

See page 33 for the address of RRCA, which publishes *Footnotes.*

In Support of Women

Women's Sports Foundation
1660 South Amphlett Boulevard, Suite 266
San Mateo, Calif. 94402
(415) 574-1600

A nonprofit corporation accepting tax-deductible gifts to encourage women in athletics of all kinds, through scholarships, sponsorship of competitions, free clinics, job opportunities. If you are a runner who needs help getting to a national woman's event, are not affiliated with a track club and need assistance in getting competitive training, or if you have ambitions in coaching in women's running, inquire about the current programs of the foundation.

HOW TO PROMOTE CLUB ACTIVITIES AND PARTICIPATION

The inevitable question: Members join in a flush of enthusiasm and skip the next potluck, the following fun-run—how do you maintain interest?

Running clubs have more opportunities than other single-interest clubs. They don't have to have formal meetings: the run is the meeting. They don't rely on fierce competition. But club organizers have to keep it interesting. Here's how some have:

—The Oregon Road Runners Club opens all its runs to members and nonmembers alike, but asks that non-AAU members join at the start of any event. Someone must be in charge of this program with friendly encouragement to join.

—Many clubs offer discounts on shoes and apparel through local merchants who advertise in the club bulletin. A club card is all it takes.

—"Jogathons" or fun-runs draw more participants when some sort of award is given for consecutive appearances.

—To encourage early or pre-entries in runs, door prizes or mystery drawings can be held from pre-entry forms.

—Certain club activities, such as annual picnics, can be free to members, with charges to nonmembers, to encourage memberships.

—There's no substitute for a well-prepared and clearly printed newsletter. Ink and paper and effort are cheap.

Joining

The National Jogging Association

Why do we need another national organization? Especially for a sport whose chief skill is putting one foot in front of the other? Well, ten thousand or more people seem to have found an answer, and have put up $15 each to belong to

Brian Maxwell takes a hand-off in the Lake Merced relays in San Francisco.

the NJA. It's a surprising phenomenon, and a surprising organization.

Here's what George F. Will had to say in his column in *Newsweek* in 1976:

Shortly after 6 p.m. Rory Donaldson lopes out of his row house in southeast Washingon, running west. . . .

Down Capitol Hill he goes, along the Mall, past the Washington Monument, around the Lincoln Memorial, and back up the Mall toward home, passing the gray mass of the Department of Health, Education, and Welfare. What Donaldson is doing is as important to the improvement of American health as HEW is.

Mr. Donaldson is the only full-time staff member of NJA, the editor of its tabloid newsletter, *The Jogger*, and its program director. He and his colleagues *believe* in jogging, and want to tell America about its benefits. For your $15 you'll get pep talks, information on books and equipment, encouragement in the form of an awards and achievement program. The newsletter comes out eight times a year; it's mainly reprints of articles from other publications, letters to the editor, humor, photographs. And you'll have the feeling you're a part of something good.

In 1977 the NJA offered a $15 discount on a top brand of running shoes as an inducement to join. Write for free information:

The National Jogging Association
1910 K Street, N.W., Suite 202
Washington, D.C. 20006
(202) 785-8050

There's always the suspicion that when a sport suddenly takes off in popularity the fast-buck artists won't be far behind. Have no fears about the NJA. With a publication as downhome as *The Jogger*, they have to be straight. And they've inspired George F. Will to this observation, anent the fact that Americans burn about 600 *billion* cigarettes a year: "So here's a jolly idea: the IRS can allow people to deduct, as a cost of preventive medicine, the price of their snappy doubleknit sweatsuits. The government subsidized tobacco, so why not jogging?"

seven

events
fun-runs, races, routes worth the trip

SELECTION:
1977 RIDE-AND-TIE

A week before the race, the Stewart Horse Camp was rimmed near the trees with only a few campers. Each campsite contained cues of what was coming: a horse trailer, a tent or two, running shoes, hanging bridles, dirty socks, nylon shorts, a stack of hay, ERG. As in other years, this Seventh Annual Levi-Strauss Ride-and-Tie brought together a curious mix of horsepeople and runners: runners with cowboy hats and cowgirls in Nikes. A handful were experienced in both horses and running. Like me, most were mainly either horsepeople or runners, each doing our best to look authentic to the other type. As the Sunday race approached, the camp swarmed with horses, trailers, flies, beer, and rumors. An incredible scene!

The race officially covered 38.95 miles in the Point Reyes National Seashore area—some swear it was closer to 42 miles. One hundred teams consisting of two alternating runners-riders and horse gathered for the mad dash for the narrow turn a quarter mile away at the end of the pasture. One partner rode the horse ahead up the trail, tied it to a tree and took off running, while the second partner caught up, mounted the horse and rode past his now-running partner, tied, took off, and so on in leapfrog fashion throughout the race.

That Ken Williams and former Olympian Tom Laris won in 4 hours, 19 minutes mattered less to most participants than the richness of their own unfolding story along the way. The modest eighth place finish by my partner, Jim Remillard, and our horse, Flying C Kenya, and me stands out less in my mind now than the adventure itself. Kenya was delighted to win the Best Conditioned award—a coveted honor among horses and horse people.

A number of terms accurately define the Ride-and-Tie, at least as I experienced it.

Unpredictable. Who could have known, for example, that the stitching on our right stirrup strap would rip out at eight miles—with me aboard while descending a winding trail down the 1,000 feet to the sea—and that I would survive with only a slightly stretched groin muscle. Nor could we anticipate Kenya's decision (fortunately a temporary one) three quarters of a mile from the finish line as we passed through the campground that *this* was really the finish.

Dangerous. Perhaps the greatest danger this year for those of us with tender, sensitive skin was the mile-long stretch of ten feet high poison oak bushes on each side of an 18 inch wide trail—with runners having no choice but to move aside (guess where) as faster moving horses galloped through. At least three runners hesitated a moment too long and took an *in*voluntary head-over-heels trip into the poison oak. Many of us are still itching, despite the best efforts of good friend Don Richey.

Ever try to bring a horse back into a trot for a downhill descent at the crest of a hill after it has been cantering hard up that hill? A rider just ahead of me didn't completely succeed. He did slow down the speed of the horse but not the cantering action. The result was more up and down than forward motion. He lasted about ten seconds. His horse went on alone and he ended up in the bushes. Luckily, someone caught the horse, and they ended up fourth.

Beautiful. Aches and pains were more than offset by fantastic scenery: a mile and a half on the beach itself, redwood forests, steep climbs up Bolinas Ridge with awesome views of the ocean behind, open pastures high above the sea, quiet streams, fernlined trails.

Social. A strong camaraderie developed in the campground, both among participants and among support crews who arrived the day before. About 25 friends from Chico [California] came to either watch or to help cool and rest the horse for the checks by veterinarians along the way. Our crew members also spread out to provide Body Punch to Jim and me every three to five miles. The bond among participants carries over from year to year, with new tales of triumph and woes shared from running or riding races of the past year.

Demanding. This was among the most difficult events I have ever undertaken. Riding and running required quite different skills—and muscle groups. Starting to run hard again after one to five miles of intense riding, for example, can be excruciating. Legs are tight, back is stiff. Swinging that leg back up over the saddle again for the umpteenth time—I can still relive the stiffness in my hips and thighs! And the 1,800-foot climb in a mile and a half at the 34 mile point! Even Kenya walked part of the way.

Complex. A marathon is relatively simple. You bring your shoes and you run—thinking of relatively few things along the way like pace, drinks, and perhaps how the competition is doing. The Ride-and-Tie is considerably more complex with respect to preparation and strategy. There are three bodies to train and to prepare for the start on race day. Carefully prepared tack for the horse. Crew members at the four vet checks with instructions and experience in horse care. Other crew members strategically scattered along the course to furnish us with replacement drinks (*horses hate the stuff*). Strategy about how long to ride before tying and vice versa early in the race, going uphill, going downhill, going into and out of the vet checks, as we approach the finish. (Exchanges occur between every half mile to five miles.) Pacing the horse as well as ourselves. Remembering to run with grace and ride with finesse as the press helicopters swoosh by. Framed for posterity.

Cooperative. Jim and I have developed a deep sense of intuitive understanding through participating in four Ride-and-Tie races the past 15 months. Smooth coordination of effort and communication is essential, not only between the two of us, but with the horse and the crew. For example, Thurlow McCloud saved our day. He was only about three quarters of a mile ahead, having ridden Jim's horse Saudii there to provide Body Punch as we passed, when our stirrup strap broke. By switching straps with him we were able to continue.

Competitive. While a spirit of common adventure and encouragement is evident among teams during the race, participants accept the challenge with care and intensity. This kind of competition approaches my ideal—it stimulates participants to elevate their efforts to higher levels of mental and physical performance than they had thought possible yet not all that much is at stake. Finishing high in the standings is great—the higher the better. But doing your best on that particular day—and simply taking in the rich adventure of it all—these are far more significant and lasting rewards.

—Walt Schafer,
Chico Running Club Newsletter,
July, 1977

Sooner or later, the least of the fun-runners, the shiest of the wallflowers, the busiest of the executives will come out for a competitive race. That doesn't mean at all that he or she wants to win anything. The idea, of course, is to be part of a happening; the challenge is to prove something to yourself.

Eventually you will win something. At first, a ribbon that says you finished. Then a shirt (your entry fee pays for this, but at least you have to register, show up, and finish). And on rare occasions it is given to the least of us mortals to carry off a prize. Our family got the trophy for the "fastest family" in the Bridge-to-Bridge Run in San Francisco in 1977 (the coveted Father-Mother-Daughter-Son-Son-Son Award, as we call it). More and more ways of encouraging people to come out and run are being tried every year.

The setting and the mood of the participants have the most to do with what makes an event memorable. Some of the country's most popular events are beginning to receive newspaper coverage (often because they are cosponsored by newspapers!), and so they have mushroomed. In Joe Henderson's list of favorites that follows, I have to disagree with at least one: the Bay to Breakers. The finish is a disaster area; registered runners don't receive the certificate that says they finished because nonregistered runners have grabbed theirs first. Joe says you shouldn't even bother to register. In fact, it's getting to be pretty common for race organizers to tell entrants, "Just say 'pending' where you have to fill in your AAU number." Yet I'll continue to run the Breakers every year—it's not the destination but the trip that's worth it.

THE BEST EVENT
The Trinidad Beach Run

I have no fear in nominating this event as the best one in the country: It's too far away from any population center to be overrun by entrants. Views of ocean and mountain swim into view at each turn of its 8½ miles. It combines shoe running with barefoot running. It's guaranteed cool and wet. It's not too long. And, with food and transportation thrown in, it's almost free!

Runners and pit crew assemble at the tiny town of Trinidad, some nine miles north of Eureka, California. Last minute entries may be filled out in the school gym, before the bus departs, taking entrants a few miles north to the starting line on California Highway 1. At approximately 1 p.m. on a late February afternoon, the chances are it's misting in this part of the country, and as the runners take off back down the coast a salt spray stings their faces. Some seven miles later they have navigated all the twists and turns and ups and downs of the road, with Clam Beach vaguely in view in the distance, and now they descend to the beach, remove their shoes, and deposit them on a large rock in front of Little River. Fording this stream, they strike out across a seemingly endless beach for the final mile and a half. The competitors are spurred on by the possibility of picking up a tee shirt (a recent addition to the prize list for the top 100 or so finishers). The bus then shuttles finishers back to the school, where sandwiches and oranges are consumed while the prizes are awarded. The entry fee is nominal for all this, and for $2 more one is treated to a beer bust in the evening. The strong running teams at Humboldt State nearby assure an interesting challenge for the competitive runner. Have I forgotten something?

JOE HENDERSON'S
TEN LONG-DISTANCE FAVORITES

The ten runs the editor of *Runner's World* would choose to participate in, given his druthers, are the following. Criteria: long, but not ultralong; open to all; with an established tradition; seasonally and geographically balanced:

San Francisco "Bay to Breakers"—7.6 miles, mid-May

Charleston Distance Classic—15 miles, early September

Cherry Blossom Classic—10 miles, early April (Washington, D.C.)

Falmouth—7.1 miles, mid-August (Cape Cod)

Honolulu Marathon—26.2 miles, early December

New York (City) Marathon—26.2 miles, late October

Paavo Nurmi Marathon—26.2 miles, mid-August (Upson, Wisconsin)

Atlanta Peach Tree—6.2 miles, July 4

Pike's Peak—14 miles up, mid-August (Colorado)

Trail's End Marathon—26.2 miles, late February (Seaside, Oregon)

Schedules of events are presented in *Runner's World*, but some of the smaller ones, such as the Trinidad, are announced only in club newsletters. For thorough coverage of events in the Midwest, South, and East, *Running Times* is the best over-all source:

Running Times
12808 Occoquan Rd
Woodbridge, Va. 22192
$10 per year (12 issues) Editor: Edward Ayres

The best coverage of events on the Pacific Coast is found in the Northern California Running Review, which is published monthly by the West Valley Track Club. You can write and ask for a free sample copy, or you can subscribe for $6 a year.

Northern California Running Review
P.O. Box 155
San Mateo, California

SELECTION:
SPECIAL OLYMPICS

In 1970, I was asked to serve as a District Coordinator for Special Olympics and being the person that I am, accepted the task and then found out what the task involved. A few other times in my life I had become involved in the unknown. I was asked to serve as a unit leader for 10-year-old boys in a camping education environment and had never been to camp as a child. After serving as one of the major leaders in our camping education program for three years, I was asked to serve as program director for a two-week camp sponsored by the Tennessee Society of Crippled Children. After that experience with 90 severely handicapped children and 40 very dedicated counselors and staff, I learned that the rewards received by those working with children who had few opportunities in life were far greater than the rewards received by the children who looked forward from year to year to this two-week camping experience.

When I accepted the coordinator position for Special Olympics, I knew that I could call upon Mel Rosen to help me. I knew that I would need a lot of help as I had never even attended a track meet, much less put one on, so Mel *did* help. He didn't even laugh at me when he tried to explain to me that I would need a "clerk of course" and that the duties of the "clerk of course" were not shuffling papers and keeping the records of wins and places as I had thought.

A human body moving with speed, agility and perfected coordination is a "thing of beauty" to me. The artist admires a painting, the engineer admires his bridge, while the physical educator finds pleasure in observing grace in human movement. With my professional interest in movement and my acquired interest in handicapped children, the two interests fused together and became "Track and Field."

As running and jumping are fundamental locomotive movements, the mentally retarded is quite capable of mastering track events. I worked with one young girl for six years in Special Olympics, as I saw that she had great potential at the age of eight when she ran the 50 yard dash in 5.9 and the best score of the meet was 5.8 run by a 17-year-old boy. At that time, I did not even know what a fast score should be. In attempting to get help for her, I learned that she could participate in the "All Comers Meet." Therefore, she and I attended every meet one summer. We went on to the International Special Olympics meet where she won three gold medals. Last summer I provided her with the opportunity to participate in the

---

A POTPOURRI OF CHALLENGING RUNS

The Most Rugged Race in the Northeast

The Escarpment Escapade, through Catskill State Park in New York, late July, 18½ miles of "rolling hills," spectacular views; 3½ hours can win.

Biathlons

Generally three miles on land followed by one-half mile by water, with a winning time around 25 minutes. *Running Times* reports two in August, at Middletown, Connecticut, and Wellesley, Massachusetts.

The Oregon Biathlon at Coffenbury Lake has been going strong since 1970, and attracts more than 200 competitors, also in August.

Triathlons involve cyclists as well, who obviously take on the longest leg, four to five miles. Coronado, Mission Bay, and Rancho Cordova are the sites of this event in California.

Ultramarathon

In addition to the John F. Kennedy 50-mile hike-run beginning in Boonsboro, Maryland, there are several unbelievable distance events in the East and scattered individual efforts elsewhere (see "The Ordeal," p. 158). Park Barner ran from

"All Comers Meet" and the AAU District and Regional meets. She no longer needs my motivation as she now runs with the Auburn High School team and has won second place in two events.

That young girl provided the thrill of winning, but working with the "All Comers Meet" one gets the feel of winning with every child's race or jump. Another little girl participated in the triple jump this summer and knowing it to be a difficult coordination for a young child, I asked her where she had learned. She replied, "You taught me last year." Then I remembered her to be the child that thought the triple jump was three jumps. She knew as little about track and field as I did seven years ago.

The smile on a child's face after an attempted event, a jump into the pit on the third trial when a young child's first two attempts resulted in a run into the pit, will help one develop new interest, even in "old age," if one loves movement and children.

—Mary P. Fitzpatrick,
Associate Professor
Health, Physical Education and Recreation
Auburn University
AORTA Newsletter
(Alabama), August, 1977

Washington, D.C., along the C&O Canal 186.4 miles to Cumberland, Maryland, in 1977, in 36 hours, 48 minutes, 34 seconds. He was forced to stop several times on the way, so he did not achieve a nonstop mileage record (for more unusual and unbelievable records, see Chapter 9, "Far Out").

Ride 'n Tie

An event growing in popularity in the West, through the sponsorship of the Levi Strauss Company: two-man teams proceed on foot and horseback, alternately riding and running (see "Selection," page 141).

The big daddy of all Marathons—the Boston—as rendered by Clive Davies

BONNE BELL RACES

Cosmetics manufacturer and fitness enthusiast Jess Bell, who looks like a top sergeant and is a cream puff when it comes to giving out prizes, has put women's running on the competitive map with his continuing series of 10,000 meter runs. He's lured joggers into races and made races exciting events for the media as well as for the dedicated runner. When you enter a Bonne Bell race, your fee will deliver a packet that includes T-shirt, sweat band, "Lipsmackers" (for chapped lips), and a badge to sew on your warmup jacket. Jess himself will probably be on hand to pass out bells to the winners. The Bonne Bell firm is one of a growing number of corporations who pay more than lip service to fitness — and they have been at it longer than most. For race information contact:

> Bonne Bell
> 18519 Detroit Avenue
> Lakewood, Ohio 44107
> Toll free: 800-321-9985 In Ohio: 221-9191

Chicago's jogging mayor, Michael A. Bliandic, leads his staff through the paces to help promote the first Mayor Daley Marathon, to be held annually on the last Sunday in September.

THE MAYOR'S MARATHON

In Chicago, this is how things are done: Runners Joe Flaherty and Wendell Miller met with Mayor Michael Bilandic in June. Bilandic called the Park District Superintendent and said, "Ed, these are good guys." On September 25, 1977, the first annual Mayor Daley Marathon went into the record books, with some 5,000 entrants paying $5 each to go to the Daley family charities. The 55-year-old, 184-pound Bilandic previewed the race by running it himself five days earlier—in 4 hours, 25 minutes, 23 seconds.

Sun-Times reporter Bill Granger wrote: "The

SELECTION:
THE BOSTON

Moving towards Wellesley, I passed a runner as a voice called out, "I'll say hello to Tom Ratcliffe for you back where I live in South Carolina." As the store manager at the Athletic Department in Berkeley in 1974, Tom had hired me to work there. I waved an acknowledgment of his statement and surged onward.

There were over a million spectators, many of whom were holding the entire entry list of runners that is published in the *Boston Globe* the day before the race. The people enjoy looking at your number, checking it on the entry list, and screaming your name. The runners enjoy the encouragement. This year my number was thirteen and people constantly yelled, "Hey, there goes lucky thirteen." One year I wore the word NIKE on the front of my shirt and people constantly yelled "Go, NIKE!"

Going up the hills I became hooked up in a personal duel with Vin Fleming, a local runner from the Greater Boston Track Club. The fans were screaming madly for him and together we began to pass runners on the series of four hills.

Halfway up the middle of the last hill, more popularly known as Heartbreak Hill, I heard a voice from a runner about twenty yards back. It was Tuttle screaming, "There's Rodgers—there's Rodgers." There he was: the Olympian American recordholder and pre-race favorite Bill Rodgers. Fleming and I passed him as we reached the top of the last hill just behind Boston College where I had run many track races during my college career.

As I reached Kenmoore Square next to Fenway Park where the baseball fans poured out from watching the Red Sox beat the Tigers, I caught another Fleming—Tom Fleming who had finished second twice and third once his last three tries at Boston. He gave me no fight as I headed towards the finish. A state police motorcycle accompanied me the last half-mile as the spectators were screaming the loudest I had ever heard in my life. I made a right turn and then a sharp left turn and there it was—the finish, the most welcome sight I had seen all day. The finish line official informed me I had finished fourth and was the first American.

—Ron Wayne,
NIKE News, Summer, 1977

start of the Mayor Daley Marathon was so thrilling that the envious crowd of reporters, supporters, and the curious burst into cheers and applause for the runners. In seconds, Washington St. was like a surging river that had just burst its dam. The runners even engulfed a poky car full of photographers, which escaped drowning in joggers only by drag-racing out of the way. The race start was almost a mystical moment full of fellowship and smiling at strangers: The Lane Technical High School band struck up "Semper Fidelis" and the theme from "Rocky," and one awed fireman spontaneously exclaimed, "I don't believe it!" . . . A cannon that was supposed to be fired at the crack of 8 o'clock didn't go off, despite a strong tug from Mrs. Eleanor Daley, the widow of Mayor Richard J. Daley. It went off unexpectedly after the runners were out of view and three persons were slightly injured by powder burns.

Although the winner's time was a respectable 2:17:52 (Dan Cloeter, 25, Fort Wayne, Indiana), this was clearly a day for amateurs—perhaps the first "fun-run" marathon. Joggers of all persuasions wanted to be part of the happening. Marlo ("That Girl") Thomas flew in from Hollywood to cheer on TV's Phil Donohue, who rose to the occasion with a PR of ten miles.

Sponsor: Flair Merchandising Agency Foundation. Probable date: last Sunday in September. Route: two roughly equal circuits out from the Loop and back along Lake Michigan. Mostly flat course on pavement.

FOR RACE ORGANIZERS

NUMBERS
Free samples and prices from:

Bock Industries Corporation
P.O. Box 2711
Colorado Springs, Colo. 80901
(303) 471-2299

Tearproof bib-type, also other race equipment:

Reliable Racing Supply
624 Glen Street
Glens Falls, N. Y. 12801
(518) 793-5677

DISPLAY CLOCKS
Pacedyne, 60 minute, battery-powered, 30 or 15 inches square ($149.95, $89.95):

SELECTION:
RECALLING A REAL-LIFE TARZAN

"Ellison M. (Tarzan) Brown, 61, who competed in the 1936 Olympics and twice won the Boston Marathon, was killed yesterday when he was run over by a car in the parking lot of a bar. Police said Brown was struck by a car driven by Phillip Edwards. . . . The incident occurred after Brown and Edwards had an argument."—*Boston Globe*, August 24, 1975.

. . . Ellison Myers Brown, whose grammar-school education lost frequent decisions to his ancestral preoccupation with trout fishing, obviously was surprised when asked what had motivated his Boston Marathon achievements almost 40 years ago.

"Why, I just love runnin'," Tarzan replied. "Runnin' marathons is livin' to run. Ain't no other reason for doin' it. I just loved gettin' out there and goin', and darin' those other guys to catch me. Sometimes they did, most times they didn't."

Hadn't he ever experienced the creed of The Cult, the joy that comes through pain?

"I know a little somethin' about pain," he said, "but I dunno as I got much joy out of it. Like the hernia I had. Not many people remember the hernia. I was runnin' and winnin' with that hernia for a long time. I run the Olympic in 1936 with that hernia, and I come back here and won two marathons in two days, Saturday and Sunday, with that hernia.

"Finally, I'm out runnin' near Westerly one day—I'm 'bout 20 mile out in the country—when all this pain hits me again like I've been havin' right along. Only this time it's tearin' at my guts, and I know somethin's real bad. I go sit down by the side of the road, all doubled up, and along comes this guy in a car. He picks me up and drives me home an' half hour later I'm on the operatin' table in the Westerly Hospital. I got a strangulated hernia. Man, I never even heard of one before, and I been runnin' 15, 16 races with one.

"So I guess you gotta say I know a little somethin' about pain."

The Indian's marathon motivations, then, were basic. Pain he knew well, and joy, too. But he does not relate them to companions romping hand in hand through a field of philosophical daisies.

Abundant joy was Tarzan's in winning the 1936 Boston Marathon, where he first emerged—unsung and fantastically untrained—from the Narragansett Reservation. It was his again in 1939, when he set a record with grace, speed, and stamina that are unforgettable.

In his original wild, undisciplined run to marathon immortality at Boston in 1936, Tarzan traveled so fast so early that halfway home he was 1,000 yards ahead of the field and shattering all the checkpoint records.

But to anybody with even a background in before-breakfast calisthenics, it was obvious that Brown was not in shape. His judgment of pace was also suspect. Although he quick-cooked his

Seagull Inc.
630 Cowper Street
Palo Alto, Calif. 94301
(415) 321-5230

Competitor Pacer Clock, 42 inches—supplier to 1976 Olympics:

Kiefer McNeil
999 Sweitzer Avenue
Akron, Ohio 44311

CLIPBOARD TIMERS, ETC.
Digital, liquid-crystal display, $69.95 to $159.95:

Sports Timing & Technology
3621 West MacArthur Boulevard #110
Santa Ana, Calif. 92704

STOPWATCHES
(For free catalog, see page 153)

---

rivals to a turn, he himself staggered and weaved down Beacon Street the final mile to victory like a shore-leave sailor who'd hit all the spots from dusk to dawn.

No philosophy guided or compelled Brown that day as might inspire a Ph.D. He was 20 and a marvelously fundamental human being. . . . "I wasn't thinkin' of just gettin' there. I was thinkin' that I wasn't gonna let anybody get there 'fore I did."

Two Aprils later, the Indian's star was descending with the rapidity of a cosmic fallout. His training methods were as primitive as the trap lines he set out each winter. He never disdained a beer hosted by the house or by his horde of local admirers. He trained half as much as his rivals. "I'm in great shape," he told a reporter before the 1938 event. "I can run 50 miles, I bet." Asked how he had achieved this physical peak, he replied casually: "Choppin' wood."

The cordage was stacked high by the Indian's woodshed, but the 1938 Boston race humiliated him. His ax-wielding brought him to the starting line with the torso of a finely-honed welterweight, but improper food and splurges of gourmandizing had left his intestinal tract acutely vulnerable to 26 miles of seemingly endless highway.

It was in this abject hour that Brown at last discovered "purpose," although the priority of that purpose might not withstand the scrutiny of a Ph.D.

"I was some mad when I got to the end—I was about 50th, and it was like I run a hundred mile—and I 'member lookin' over my shoulder at the crowd, all feelin' sorry for Tarzan Brown, and I says to myself: 'Take a good look. I'll be back next year and win this thing.'

"And I did, too!"

Tarzan Brown's revenge was a classic of technical competence and dramatic impact. The Indian came to the line in Hopkinton, mean and lean. He did not attack with an impetuous rush at the outset, as was his custom. Instead he waited for his prey with the cunning, patience and deadliness of the bushmaster. He withheld the intensity of his "purpose" until halfway down the pike from Hopkinton—at Wellesley Square, precisely. There he launched off in a furious blur of brown legs and churning arms. He began figuratively dismembering the opposition, including four past winners.

In that epic 1939 Boston Marathon, this proud descendant of a noble and warlike tribe made the run from Hopkinton to Boston in less than 2:29. . . .

"In my heart," said Tarzan, "I always felt I could beat any man livin' up to 50 mile, if I was in shape. 'Course I'd do different trainin' now, like the rest of 'em do. I didn't know nothin' 'bout trainin' or eatin' right. All I ever did was quit drinkin' beer when I was gettin' ready to race."

—Jerry Nason,
Runner's World,
December, 1975

Many races are now being "run" by people confined to wheelchairs. Left: a woman in a Bonne Bell Mini-Marathon. Right: a man in the New York City Marathon.

Many races are open to all ages. Here a young runner moves up on Mr. "Slow and Steady."

The start of the San Francisco Marathon at Golden Gate Park

MECHANICAL:

Olympia, Wrist
Fifths, quite good for joggers, 7 jewels, 30 seconds face or 60 seconds, $33.50.

Compass Sixty Special
For distance races, fifths, hand-held. $29.50

Hanhart Easy Reader
Tenths, 60 seconds. Special price: $38.50

Hanhart All-purpose
30 seconds face, special price: $38.95

Junghans 3-Circle
Seconds and tenths on separate dials from minutes. Special: $54.50

Hanhart Split 30
Two hands for better reading. Recommended by dealer. $68.00

Hanhart Swing
Same as above, with lanyard. $71.50

Hanhart Split Sprint
Ten-seconds face for sprint accuracy. $75.00

DIGITAL:
Arranged in order of price suggested by dealer listed below. Send for additional information re 10th or 100th second, cumulative or sequential split, time out, time of day, types of display.

Wrist:
Microsel Racer $69.95
Microma Chronograph $99.95 to $119.95

Hand-held:

Cronus Olympian	$29.95
Siliconix ET 105	39.00
Casio Time Comp	49.95
Siliconix ET 125	65.00
Cronus 3S	69.95
Cronus 3T	69.95
STT 300	79.95
Cronus 3ST	89.95
STT 200	124.95
Cronus 2D	125.00
STT I	159.95

In a race, even an injury won't stop a serious runner.

Watches may be ordered by mail from:

Track & Field News
Box 296
Los Altos, Calif. 94022

Ask also for free catalog of this and other equipment.

For viewing:
The Giant Stopwatch   from $995.00
Digital, 6 or 12 inch digits, accepts remote inputs, etc. From:

Zetachron, Inc.
1407 East Edinger Street
Santa Ana, Calif. 92705
(714) 558-2621

For automatic photo-finishes:
Accutrack Data available from:

Specialty Instruments Corporation
P.O. Box 623
Grand Prairie, Tex. 75051
(214) 252-7456

TIMERS
Free catalog showing complete line of stopwatches (such as the Heuer LCD Microsplit, $85) is offered by:

Feldmar Watch Co., Inc.
9000 West Pico Boulevard
Los Angeles, Calif. 90035
(213) 272-1196

Other digital-display watches are offered by Cronus, through dealers or direct from the manufacturer. Free color catalog available on electronic stopwatches from $29.95, from:

Cronus Precision Products, Inc.
2895 Northwestern Parkway
Santa Clara, Calif. 95051
(408) 988-2500

West Coast Dealer:
The Sharper Image
260 California Street
San Francisco, Calif. 94111

Ask about their new chronograph wristwatch, The Real Time, 100% stainless steel, waterproof, $69.00.

For wristwatches with four-function stopwatch capability, from $95, write for illustrated literature to:

Crystal Systems
P.O. Box 225B
Chardon, Ohio 44024

In *The Complete Book of Running*, James R. Fixx recommends the Wakmann Watch Company, 597 Fifth Avenue, New York, New York 10017; (212) 751-2926. He says that you'll receive a 25% discount if you identify yourself as a runner to the general manager, Hyman Kopf.

To measure a course:
Revolution counter for bicycle wheel, $12.00, from:

Clain Jones
3717 Wildwood Drive
Endwell, N.Y. 13760

To conform to AAU standards, get instructions (80¢) from:

Ted Corbitt
Chairman, AAU Standards Committee
Apartment 8H, Section 4
150 West 225th Street
New York, N.Y. 10463

Be a race promoter
Here's a way to promote local running activities and get in the limelight at the same time: Try to arrange a "mini-meet" to be held at halftime of pro-football games, especially in the exhibition season. The San Diego Track Club did just this during a 1977 San Diego Chargers—San Francisco '49ers exhibition. Mixed relays, masters events, and javelin throws were among the highlights.

Masters competitions in shorter races have also been held at halftimes of Golden State Warriors' games in Oakland, California.

Kirk Douglas got into the spirit of the Mayor Daley Marathon during the filming of *The Fury* with Lee Flaherty. The other major Chicago running events are the Lakefront 10-Miler in May for the benefit of heart patients, and the 20-Kilometer Fourth of July race.

SELECTION:
THE 24-HOUR RELAY

Are you a marathoner who would like to run all those miles one at a time for a change, or a miler looking for an excuse to train around the clock—one each hour? Then get some good buddies together for the annual 24-hour relay at Duniway Track [Portland, Oregon]. Anybody can do it. NOBODY is too slow. Here's all you do:

Get a bunch of runners together (up to ten—the more the better), pick a catchy team name if you're not all representing the same club or school, and be on the track at 10 a.m. Saturday, August 7. Each team should also bring a relay baton (cut a piece of plastic or aluminum tubing about an inch in diameter and a foot long), at least one helper to time and record miles, extra toilet paper for when the park's supply runs out, warm sleeping bags, lanterns and flashlights for those long night hours, and easy-to-digest, high-

energy snacks. We've ordered fair weather, but tents and rain gear are a sensible precaution.

The rules are simple. Pick the sequence your team members will run in. Every four laps, relay to the next runner and report your time to the recorders. After the last person on the team runs, relay to the first again and repeat the same sequence as often as you can. Drop-outs are permitted, but they cannot be replaced by substitutes. Dropping out is guaranteed to make you the least popular member of your team, as the others will have to run further, with less recovery time.

—*The Oregon Distance Runner*

Miki Gorman, a masters (over forty) marathoner from Los Angeles, was the first woman finisher in the New York City Marathon both in 1976 and 1977.

SELECTION:
THE LONG BLUE LINE

"The run for the Big Apple" [in 1976 in New York City, the first Five-Borough marathon] resulted in near world record performances by both Bill Rodgers and Miki Gorman. Utilizing a variety of resources including my personal viewpoint, newspaper accounts, personal interviews with the elite runners and an exciting movie of the race developed by Manufacturer's Hanover, I was able to relive the excitement of the front running.

At the very crack of Percy Sutton's pistol, Pekka Paivarinta, another of the "Flying Finns" nicknamed "The Cap," bolted off the line as if trying to beat the toll. He literally flew across the Verrazano-Narrows Bridge as his sponsors from Finnair applauded in his jet stream. Chris Stewart, like the Finn, a world class 10 km runner, and Japan's threat, Akio Usami, chased the leader across the Bridge and the remainder of the field was sucked across the New York Harbor. Ron Hill predicted that the Finn blasted out at a 4:30 mile up the long incline which was "bloody fast." Pekka hit 5 miles at a 4:45 pace and at 8 miles he was a full 42 seconds ahead of a pack of runners which included Shorter, Rodgers, Stewart, Fleming and Ian Thompson from England (the fastest active marathoner in history).

"The Cap" obviously had blazing speed and had a 2:12:10 marathon under his belt so he had to be respected. But his pace, described by Hill as "absolutely mad," brought about memories of a similar race. Shorter noted, "He did it before in Japan, he died again." At 10 miles he was still holding a 4:47 pace, but at 12 miles Rodgers and then Stewart pulled up even with him. "The Cap" was "Finnished" as far as front running was concerned but he certainly provided an element of suspense and gallantly hung on to place fifth.

Then it was Rodgers in the lead, but Shorter and Stewart were right behind him and the 6'6" Norwegian, Knut Kualheim, towered over all of them. He soon became the tallest drop-out. Rodgers and Stewart pulled away with Shorter in pursuit. For a two mile stretch they ran stride for stride, "beating each other's brains out." They were together as they approached the Queensborough Bridge, but then fleet Billy opened up a convincing lead. "Well, time to get going, Billy," he said to himself. Halfway across the Bridge he was already in command and then sailed along the East River, aggressively pulling away. Shorter confessed that "Rodgers just ran away from us."

As the Greater Boston Track Clubber navigated up river, he took the time to acknowledge Traum's efforts (he started the race at 7:00 a.m.) panting "atta boy, Dick" as he passed the last place runner who was also a big winner.*

Frank and Chris meanwhile matched strides along the East River and then the Olympic Gold Medalist boldly blasted away from him at precisely the moment they turned on to the Willis Avenue Bridge. As Billy doubled back from his brief visit to the Bronx he met Shorter, the man who always before had been America's number one marathoner. Frank acknowledged defeat with the comment "Nice going, Billy." The former champ was to fight on gamely for second place, finishing proud, although defeated. At that point for the charged up leader it was no longer a matter of who, but of how much. The conqueror of the Big Apple strided gracefully into the huge awe-stricken crowd outrunning the lead car which was slowed by the masses. He finished with knees churning, white gloves swinging, and tongue flapping in the wind like that of a dog returning from an exhausting, but mischievous adventure.

"Billy White Gloves" finished in 2:10:9.6, the 8th fastest time in world marathoning history. He was but 14 seconds off his own American record and the Olympic record set in Montreal by Waldemar Cierpinski. He was only 1:36 off the acknowledged world record set in 1969 by Au-

stralia's Derek Clayton, which Ron Hill suspects represents a "questionable authentic distance." Bill Rodgers now owns two of the eight fastest times in history. He won the 1975 Boston Marathon in 2:09:55, finished a close second to Shorter in the Olympic Trials in 2:11:58 in June, led the Olympic Marathon for 20 km in August before fading to place 40th, won the New York event in October and then on December 5th won the Baltimore Marathon in 2:14. Ron Hill, considered to be the world's premier marathoner in the early 70's, told me that Rodgers's effort on the hilly Baltimore course was worth a 2:11. "In my judgment," Hill acknowledged, "Bill Rodgers is now the top Marathoner of all time." When I recently approached Bill at a party concerning the comment he typically was embarrassed and disbelieving. But he did admit to having a strong desire to breaking the world's record.

A review of the "game film," in fact, shows three specific instances which cost Billy enough time that could have meant the difference in a world-record. The press car, apparently suffering from carbohydrate depletion, slowed down at the 59th Street Bridge and again near the finish forc-

Promoters of marathons and other special running events have wisely used the name-value of runners like Frank Shorter to bring the crowds out. The annual Pear Blossom Festival in Medford, Oregon, was honored by the fast winning time of Frank Shorter (right), here sharing his thoughts with a participant.

Runners take off across the Verazzano Narrows Bridge at the start of the New York Marathon.

ing the champ to slow down. Billy also took a wide swing approaching the Willis Avenue Bridge, adding another 10 yards to his journey. How fast could he have run if he and Shorter were fighting it out together rather than Billy being a decisive three minutes ahead of the pre-race favorite at the finish line? Billy modestly commented at the finish, "I did it, I feel great and the weather was ideal."

LETTERS OF THANKS

Hundreds of letters poured into the offices of the many race sponsors:

"I want to tell you how much my family and I enjoyed the Marathon. The fact that it ran right in our neighborhood, East Harlem, was extra special. East Harlem is a neighborhood that strangers are often fearful of, but the fact that a race was in our neighborhood gave the children a glimpse of the courage of life. I must say my neighbors were friendly and enthusiastic. As the runners passed everyone cheered and clapped. The neighborhood candy store gave out free candy bars. It was a moment I will always remember as we stood on 116th Street and First Avenue watching the determination of men and women, some quite advanced in age, and of course, the special courage of Richard Traum. [Dr. Traum has only one leg.] It gave the children hope that there is more in life and that if you try the impossible is possible. All of my sons want to start running and I might even take it up especially after seeing Miki Gorman who is older than me.... Everything worked out and some of the neighbors were stopping cars and helping the police. Another humorous note was when a woman was looking at the runner's numbers to get a good number to bet in the numbers game which is a long East Harlem tradition."

A 66-year-old amputee wrote to me: "I watched you and your runner on TV Tuesday night, and marvelled how this brave man could run with one good leg. It was the greatest thing I ever saw and it showed me real true courage and determination. After seeing this courageous man running it gave me new hope and vision."

Writer Leonard Harris wrote to Lew Rudin: "I'm not a member of any hierarchy, not in running or government. I am a part of the vast lowerarchy of New Yorkers who are still rooting for this town. Running through the five boroughs, hearing the cheers of neighborhood people, I felt proud and hopeful. And I know that the hundreds of out-of-towners who came to run got a new look at the city they'd heard so many nasty things about."

—Bob Glover, *Newsletter*,
New York Road Runners Club

In 1977, the shock waves from the first Five Borough marathon had not yet subsided as the cutoff day for entries passed. The race organizers had to discourage entrants by requiring them to answer a questionnaire satisfactorily before an entry form was sent! I asked two of the favorites, Ron Wayne and Brian Maxwell, for their impressions. Both suffered from the condition of the streets, but they pronounced it one of the best run events they had attended. "Billy White Gloves" repeated his 1976 effort, and so did the continuous wall of New Yorkers along the long blue line.

Dr. Traum running in the New York Marathon

SELECTION:
THE ORDEAL

It was only 8:30 a.m., but the distant mountains were already shimmering through the heat waves that rose from the floor of Death Valley. As I slapped Tate Miller's hand we exchanged places—he crawled out of the back of our support van and began running; I eased myself onto the mattress he just vacated. We had been going through this exchange ritual every half-hour since our 4:00 a.m. departure from Badwater, a pond of scumy, salt-saturated water that, at 279 feet below sea level, is the lowest point in the United States. Our destination was the summit of Mt. Whitney, 144 road and trail miles away.

We planned to continue these relays, leapfrogging across 133 miles that included Death Valley, Panamint Valley, the intervening Panamint Mountains, and finally the long, arduous climb through the eastern Sierra Foothills, until the end of the road at Whitney Portals. From there, we would hike up the 11 mile Mt. Whitney trail together. All of this was to be done against the clock, which would run continuously from the 4:00 a.m. start until we both touched the summit plaque.

This race course was first created and run in 1973 by that infamous pair of DSE runners, Ken Crutchlow and Pax Beale. Their time of 54 hours was the record until September, 1974, when Tate and I lowered it by three hours. It was our own record, which had stood for three years, that we were attempting to break.

But for now, our main concern was to get out of Death Valley before the sun rose high enough to saturate the still air with its August heat. During my half-hour shifts I was covering almost three and a third miles by running 9:05 miles. Tate was running the same pace during his shifts. We followed the road as it wound along the eastern side of the valley, following the contours of the mountain flanks that spilled onto the valley floor. I ran past highway signs identifying points of interest—Devil's Golf Course, Desolation Canyon, Furnace Creek. I hoped the ominousness of their names did not foreshadow our future. Looking westward across the valley, I saw miles of flat, dry, cracked mud. Intermittent sagebrush and occasional wooden crosses marking primitive gravesites offered the only respite from the glistening flatness until mountains, rising abruptly, defined the far side of the valley floor.

The temperature was rising as Tate and I continued our relayed running. At 10:23 when we completed the 42 miles to Stovepipe Wells, the ground temperature was 125° F. From there we would leave the valley by climbing over 4,956 foot Towne Pass. High, wispy cirrus clouds had helped filter the intensity of the sun. We later learned that those clouds kept the ground temperature down to 157° F., far below Death Valley's record of 201° F.

I was running as we began the 16 mile climb that would take us over the crest. My left ankle, broken twice within six months two years before, began to swell and throb. I made a mental note to begin taking an Excedrin along with the open-faced peanut butter and honey sandwich I was eating every other break. These gooey, calorie-rich sandwiches were to be the mainstay of my solid food diet during the run.

The road over the pass seemed to go on forever. Our pace slowed as we continued our relayed running. Neither Tate nor I wanted to be the first to walk. The bond that grows between two people as they share an ordeal does not preclude competition. My own ego kept me running as the gradient steepened.

The 4,000 foot marker was just ahead as I climbed out of the van to begin another turn. My hands were so cramped I couldn't even squeeze a water-soaked sponge over my head. Knowing I'd never be able to run for my entire half-hour, I suggested we begin 15 minute turns. Mercifully, Tate agreed. Tate was running as we finally reached the crest. Reverting to half-hour shifts, he began to stretch out his stride as the road curved downward into Panamint Valley. Almost all of our hard-earned elevation gain would be lost on the descent. During my shift my right knee, a chronic problem from an old skiing injury, could not take the punishment of descending on the steep asphalt and I was forced to walk. With Tate running and me walking/running, as my knee would allow, we limped into Panamint Springs at 3:15 p.m. We were past the half-way point and were almost four hours ahead of our previous pace. From here it would be all up hill, up to the 14,495 foot summit of Mt. Whitney.

An orange and violet sunset streaked the sky ahead of us as we followed the meandering road into the Sierra foothills. Tate finally gave up trying to run his entire turn—he began to allow himself the luxury of walking 10 of his 30 minutes.

Even though I was walking most of my turn, my condition was fast deteriorating—it was 90° F. outside but I was shaking from chills. The cramps had spread from my hands, up my arms, across my shoulders, down my back, and into my legs. I was probably suffering from an electrolyte imbalance, but I couldn't tell if I had taken too many potassium and sodium tablets or too few. I stopped drinking Gatorade and switched to plain water. Nothing seemed to help. I could only run for about 10 minutes before my entire body would cramp and I collapsed. The support crew would lift me into the back of the van, while Tate got out and began running. His strength, as we gained elevation and dusk enveloped us, was almost inhuman. He was running/walking his own shift and two thirds of mine.

Tate, hoping that all my body needed was time to regain its electrolyte balance, offered to try to go for two straight hours. Cramps prevented me from sleeping, but at 9:00 p.m. I felt much better and was able to take my two hour turn.

Thus we went through the night, trading off every two hours. A crew member walked ahead of us with a flashlight, clearing the road of snakes and scorpions. While walking, I tried to eat seed-less grapes, but threw up. When I tried to drink grapefruit juice and threw that up, I went back to drinking water.

We arrived in Lone Pine just before dawn— only 13 miles to go to Whitney Portals and then 11 miles up the mountain. Jogging past all of the darkened houses, I jealously imagined the inhabitants sleeping in warm, comfortable beds. The agony I was experiencing was incomprehensible to their resting bodies. But reflecting further, I realized the joy I would feel at the summit was equally incomprehensible. Jealousy became pity and I increased my pace.

When the sun rose, warming us and our spirits, we changed back to half-hour shifts. The sun's influence proved to be illusory as deep, deadening fatigue and the steepness of the road forced us to 15 minute intervals. After a half-hour rest at Whitney Portals, we began hiking up the mountain at 8:45 a.m. Two support crew members, having slept at 8,000 foot Whitney Portals to acclimatize to altitude, accompanied us up the trail. These "sherpas" carried our food, water, and cold weather survival gear in case we had to spend the night on the mountain. The initial, adrenalin-based rush of energy that propelled us up the lower part of the mountain soon dissipated. Fatigue, dizziness, nausea, and the increasing altitude slowed our pace.

One of the "sherpas" got sick at 12,000 feet and had to descend. The 97 switchbacks that led up to the trail crest just below 14,000 feet necessitated many rests. Above that it was a long traverse and then a scramble up loose rock. It was 3:50 p.m. when we staggered up to the summit plaque at 14,495 feet. We had beaten our record by 15 hours! We slapped hands and fell into an embrace.

—Bruce Maxwell, *DSE News*, San Francisco

SELECTION:
HEAR YE! HEAR YE!

Listen good townswomen of the lands around San Francisco Bay. On Saturday, October 22nd, at the stroke of 9:00 a.m., in Golden Gate Park, there will be a gathering of well-bodied women, the likes of which have never been seen in these parts. This congregation of fleet-footed milk-maids, untamed shrews, graceful gentlewomen and tempestuous trollops will all join in a running event of 10 kilometers, 6.2 miles in English measure.

FORE runners, the sponsors of this event, promise to provide timekeeping to the accuracy of the fall of the hourglass' sandgrains. Urchins and babes-in-arms will be tended for by responsible elders. So leave your hearth and potato fields! Milk the cow early and do the mending another day! Come to the Polo Fields in Golden Gate Park, San Francisco.

—*DSE News*, San Francisco

Jess Bell personally directs the 10,000 meter runs sponsored by his company, Bonne Bell. Here he is flanked by his assistants and (far right), Dr. Joan Ullyot, a top finisher at the 1977 San Francisco event.

eight

touring

how to make
running part of your travels

Planning a vacation? Why not look into the running possibilities of various locations first—and let everything else fall into place? Now it's not likely that you'll choose Wichita or North Platte on the strength of its jogging trails. But there are some outstanding places to run in this country and abroad—for scenic beauty, historical aura, or friendly natives.

Pointing to a marathon is an excellent way to justify a vacation trip: to Hawaii, for example, and of course to Chicago, Boston, or New York. And there's plenty to justify a pilgrimage to the jogger's mecca, Eugene, Oregon.

A surprising number of respondents to my questionnaire reported on jogging routes outside their immediate vicinity. A sampling follows of the best places to run in the world:

NOMINATIONS
The Best Places to Run
Outside the United States

The North Jersey Masters Track & Field Club reports that there isn't "anything like this in the world":

The Skatas, complete with clubhouse, similar to our golf clubhouses, with showers, pool, sauna, restaurant, in Goteborg, Sweden, site of the 1977 World Masters Championships. "The running paths are through the woods, covered with packed sawdust, which is ideal for running. The paths are marked for distances in different colors: 1 km, 5 km, 10km, etc. Overhead lights are installed for evenings and winter."

Lagoa, behind Ipanema and Leblon beaches, Rio de Janeiro, Brazil. Carol Gardner reports a steady stream of joggers around this lake all day, with the more serious ones taking off into the jungle mountains, Alta de Boa Vista. Clear air, sand and dirt paths, plenty of companionship.

Botanical Gardens, Sydney, Australia. Denis Burger says that although the gardens don't open until 7:30 a.m., "it's easy to climb the fence." From Sydney's finest hotel, the Wentworth, the route leads past the Opera House, around the harbor, and back.

Comrades Marathon course, between Durban and Pietermaritzburg, South Africa. Bob McGraw writes from Mowbray that this route is one of the finest anywhere and that jogging has come of age

SELECTION:
THE WILDWOOD TRAIL

It has to be one of the prettiest 17-mile runs in the Northwest. Which makes it one of the most scenic anywhere. And if you live in or around Portland, it's a shame if you don't avail yourself of it periodically.

. . . If you'd like some company and a tour guide, try calling Ken Weidcamp or Bill Gorman, both of whom count the Wildwood as one of their favorite runs. Each has gone the full distance four or five times this year, leading parties of from five to twelve runners.

. . . It's taken them approximately two and a half hours to complete the distance at a pace Ken estimates to average out at 8½ minute miles. "For the most part it's a very safe trail," is Ken's

evaluation, "with acceptable grades for both joggers and runners. There are sections approaching Pittock from the Forestry Center and further along where one wishes the upward pull would end. But, for the most part, it's an undulating course with a suitable trail width that allows runners to negotiate most of the distance shoulder to shoulder."

. . . Should you wish to explore the trail on your own, you can pick up a free map of Forest Park from Portland's Bureau of Parks and Recreation or the Chamber of Commerce.

. . . So run Wildwood! Where else can you traverse 17 miles of rain forest and restore your soul while you indulge your body? What a loss to have it in our midst and not enjoy it fully.

—Lionel Fisher, *Oregon Distance Runner*

in Durban and Johannesburg especially. A recent television-sponsored run in the latter city drew well over 10,000 entries. All amateur races and jogging are multiracial in South Africa. In Cape Town, the Spartan Harrier Club sponsors an annual 50-mile "Big Walk" from the tip of the cape to Cape Town.

The Imperial Palace, Tokyo. Photographer Burk Uzzle has circled this as well as dozens of other historical locations on assignments, and finds the ambiance of the palace and the quiet runners to be mutually supportive.

Bois de Boulogne, Paris. Here a series of races are held every December just before Christmas, called the Cross du Figaro. Some 20,000 participate in races from 3 to 12 kilometers, in a festive weekend. Edward R. Leydon also nominates:

The Marathon to Athens course, for interest beyond scenery and hot, dusty roads. As each runner finishes in the old Olympic Stadium, he is crowned with an olive wreath in the annual event.

The Danube, Vienna. Little running in evidence, virgin soil, reports Ed Burger: "Water is the next best thing to run with, and running with the Danube at your side evokes a primordial history."

The Avon, in Bristol, England, from the Downs to the Avon and along the river to the suspension bridge leading to Ashton Gate and Park, and back to Bristol, as nominated by George C. Martin.

English Gardens, Munich. The Greenville Track Club reports that this was a highlight in their experience in Europe.

Followers of Dr. Ken Cooper will find measured courses in both Holland and Brazil:

The Copacabana in Brazil sports a series of "Cooper" signs along the beach("jog" does not translate well into Portuguese, so Brazilians say that runners go out to "Cooper"). "Cooper" signs are also found in city parks and sports clubs in Sao Paulo, Porto Allegra, and other major Brazilian cities, as well as around the Maracana Stadium in downtown Rio de Janeiro.

Cooperbaans in Holland are located in the city parks. There are measured trails at these Cooperbaans, and also large signs that give de-

(above) In South America, jogging is frequently called "coopering"—a tribute to the impact of Dr. Cooper. In Rio de Janeiro, an English-speaking person will say "Let's cooper," even though there is no need to avoid confusion with the Spanish word "jogar," to play or to gamble. Here Ken and Millie Cooper flank a sign that gives (in Portuguese) aerobic point values for various distances.

(below) A Cooperbaan sign in Holland. Directions in Dutch tell the runner how to take the Cooper twelve-minute test.

tailed instructions on how to take Dr. Cooper's twelve-minute running test.

**For Information About
Other Locations Overseas**

In England, there are two publications to check about events and running locations:

    The Road Runners Club Fixture List
    J. Jewel
    296 Barkham Road
    Wokingham, Berks RG11—4DA, England

    Athletics Weekly
    World Athletics and Sporting Publications, Ltd.
    344 High Street
    Rochester, Kent, England

Edward R. Leydon, who supplied this information, says *Athletics Weekly* is the road runner's bible. "Athletics" in England means track and field, not sports in general.

Running in Russia

Jack Heycock reported in *Runner's Gazette* that his nine-day jogging tour from Leningrad to Moscow was a lonely affair, even though he circled the Kremlin at one point in the middle of a gigantic practice session for a May Day celebration. It's an excellent way to see the country, but he saw no other runners. One nice day: "It was a strange but glorious feeling to realize that here I

SELECTION:
ON THE TRAIL OF PHIDIPPIDES

The sun rises over the Euobean Gulf to the runner's rear as the mist clears ahead on the way to Athens. The sounds of battle drone in the east as the messenger heads to tell the rulers of the victorious tide in the fighting.

It's not 1977, it's 490 years before the birth of Christ, as the runner heads along the Plains of Marathon at full speed toward the city.

Phidippides, the legendary founder of the marathon race, sprints the 22 and a half miles to Athens and cries out, "Rejoice! We conquer!" After shouting his glorious news, he succumbs from the exhaustion of the run.

The mist clears, and it's not 490 B.C., it's 1977, and a 20th-century man runs the Plains of Marathon. The distant sound of battle and the voice of Phidippides echo in the runners' imagination.

Mel Slotnick, North Syracuse lawyer and member of the North Area YMCA, will soon get a chance to journey back to the time of Phidippides and the land of the gods. Slotnick, who has been involved in the YMCA for a dozen years, will leave in mid-October for a "Runners' Greek Odyssey."

To Slotnick, who has been running marathons for a number of years, this run over the Plains of Marathon is the ultimate experience for a distance runner. Slotnick has promoted marathons in the Syracuse area over the past few years.

In 1970, he said, the first "Salt City Marathon" was run in the Liverpool area. In 1972, the national marathon championships were held there, sponsored by First Trust and Deposit Co. Slotnick said he helped in the planning for the races in an effort to promote athletics and the YMCA work.

"One of the things that I thought might help our public image was to create a race that all athletes and members of the community could participate in," he said. He asked people in the community to go out and watch the runners or provide them with water or small amounts of food along the run.

When the North Area YMCA gets underway in the future in a brand new building, perhaps many more persons will become involved with running and marathons. Perhaps in the furure, some will even venture to the Plains of Marathon in Greece to repeat the run of the legendary Greek hero.

        Laurel Saiz in *Running On*,
        newsletter of Syracuse
        and Onondaga Company

was running a strange country completely alone, unmolested and delighting in the fact that for what little I was expending I was getting so much."

Inside the United States

The Reservoir, Central Park, New York City. The only circular track that doesn't become boring. 1.58 miles of well-trod earth, the skyline of the city standing guard like a forest on all sides, access at 360 degrees, and all kinds of variations to lengthen the route east, west, and south. Real cross-country running if you skip the trails on the way west and south.

The B. & O. Canal, along the Potomac, Washington, D.C. Site of many cross-country races and terminus for ultramarathons, this is one of those "start anywhere" courses favored by runners who don't like to drive to specific locations. Those who like to run mindlessly as far as they can—and then try to make their way back—will thrive on this meandering, pastoral course.

Georgetown—Capitol Hill, Washington, D.C. The Patriotic Jog par excellence. In one 6-8 mile

A jogger takes a turn around the reservoir in Central Park, New York.

run you can go by the Lincoln Memorial, the Washington Monument, around the Hill, back past the White House, stopping in at the Smithsonian if you have time. Stop also and play tennis at a much-neglected grass court in front of the White House. Honest.

A French fashion jog: collars over sweaters, scarves, open neck, Speedo warmups, cutoffs—in front of the Musee de Beaux Artes, Valenciennes, France.

The Charles River, from Boston to Cambridge and Brighton. The University Run, past Harvard, Massachusetts Institute of Technology, Boston College, perhaps out to Wellesley. The New England AAU conducted 318 races last year from two to 50 miles.

Ridgewood, New Jersey. The New Jersey Masters Track & Field Club nominates a route which runs through "the beautiful village of Ridgewood" and Saddle River County Park, with a terminus at Bergen Community College, where "we run all year, through the heat of summer and the snows of winter."

Stone Mountain Park, Georgia. Nominated by the Greenville, South Carolina, Track Club, among many wooded areas of the Southeast.

Percy and Edwin Warner Parks, Nashville, Tennessee. If 800 to 1,000 runners attend the two annual races here, it has to be good. There are 32 miles of paved road, 15 miles of gravel

There's good running at Malibu for anyone who can put one leg in front of the other, without fear of the elements or injuries. That's the essence of beach running.

within the parks, all sorts of activities going from archery to steeplechase for horses. "A fantastic place," says Larry Wallace; "all the activities enhance the run, but there's also solitude if you want it." The YMCA is the headquarters for the Nashville club, and there are two other parks (Centennial and Shelby) within running distance of downtown, as well as many tracks.

North Shore, Chicago. Lake Michigan, forest preserves, and, further north, the Green Bay Trail, provide excellent jogging even in the height of winter.

Brian's Head, Utah. Ten thousand feet and up, a majestic run with vistas in all directions. This and the following two were selected by Jack Welch, running publisher of *Running.*

Lake Mary Meadows, 11 miles south of Flagstaff, Arizona. State-owned Ponderosa forest has "a maze of dirt trails, roads, dry creeks, and cattle paths . . . turkey coyote, range cattle, horses, little prairie dogs, and elk. The runner and nature, running as it was meant to be."

Balboa State Park, San Diego, California. "I ran in the park just after dawn one spring morning. . . . The zoo was waking up, coming alive. . . . Roars and cries . . . something very primal about running along, like some antelope, listening to the jungle greet a new day."

Malibu, California. The combination of long white beaches, year-round warm water, and nearness to everything in the city make this and other southern California beaches excellent every-day jogging locations.

The San Vincente Strip. Apart from the beaches, the most popular jogging site in Southern California — grass track for several miles between Brentwood and Palisades Park above Santa Monica Beach. Not too far away, by Los Angeles standards — the UCLA campus, where TV and movie stars make their way around the track and into the surrounding neighborhoods. The rule that prevails here is *seek out the parks* — Griffith, Holmby, Malibu Creek, Will Rogers, Sepulveda Dam — or otherwise be content to run on your favorite city streets or along the beach. *Los Angeles* magazine suggests, I hope facetiously, that you get in touch with the Sierra Club for other routes. The AAU does sponsor races here, but in the past they have made a reputation

At eight o'clock in the morning, jogging over Westminster Bridge is unimpeded by any sort of traffic, and timing by Big Ben compares favorably to that of any stopwatch, coming and going.

for being particularly insensitive to the wants and need of the non-competitor.

Chico, California. Lower Bidwell Park bridle trails are where members of the Chico Running Club get their kicks—"where they filmed Robin Hood, with Errol Flynn." Under the massive oaks you can hear the faint clatter of armor of the Knights of the Roundtable on winter nights. This park, by the way, lays claim to being the largest municipal park in the country (larger than Golden Gate Park or Central Park).

Mount Tamalpais, Mill Valley, California. Show up at 9:00 a.m. on a Saturday at the halfway stop to Muir Woods, called Mountain Home, and you can join an informal group that takes off on trails all across the mountain, from seven to eleven miles. Beginners welcome: the front runners stop at various points to allow the group to re-form.

Among the regulars: Egil Krogh (remember his interviews with Watergate reporters as he circled a Washington, D.C., track?). "It's simply glorious to run this mountain early in the morning when the sun is just coming up over the East Bay. It's spectacular to ascend to an altitude of 2,200 feet, through the fire trails and roads and look out over the cloudbank settled over San Francisco in the summer." In the winter, or on rare fogless mornings in the summer, you can spy the Golden Gate Bridge. The most spectacular run, the Dipsea, skirts Tamalpais from Mill Valley to Stinson Beach.

The Cal Cross-Country Track, Berkeley, California. Something like first love. Leave Rim Road above Memorial Stadium, University of California, and head up Strawberry Canyon, past the softball fields, past the swimming pools, onto the narrow dirt path that finally dips away from the road and sends you into a fern laced forest— which modern signpost communications has labeled "Notice: Ecological Study Area." The path, now widened to a fire-trail, rises imperceptibly until after a mile you break upon a panoramic view of San Francisco Bay. Then walk through the eucalyptus, up 120 feet, to the beginning of the clay road that is the real course. A mile across the canyon and several hundred feet up you can clearly see your destination: a cluster of buildings of the astronomy department. By foot it's a good three miles to the top, so that the round trip back to the Stadium exceeds eight. On a Saturday you can time your return to glide through the open gates on the Cal side of the field and watch part of the last quarter of a Pac-10 football game.

The American River Path, at Sacramento, California. By far the most popular running route in the busy Sacramento area is the running/ bikepath along the American River. Twelve miles of scenic trails, asphalt and dirt (watch for horses). Finish at the Rio Americano High School, where a quarter-mile cinder track awaits you. At the eight-mile mark you can also stop at busy California State University—Sacramento, where there is an all-weather track. Interesting views of old Sacramento, good atmosphere, good vibes from runners of all kinds along the way.

Bush's Pasture Park, Salem, Oregon, four or

Woodminster Park in Oakland, California is known locally as the "woodmonster" because of its killing hills. But the final mile of the Woodminster Run, gently down a clearing in the woods, is the stuff of pastoral poetry.

lowing Laurel-and-Hardy episode in 1976, as described in the *Oregon Distance Runner*:

"This was one of the more interesting runs in recent memory. We were blessed with a lead patrol car, with lights a-blinking. Only problem was, he didn't know the course! The race turned into an impromptu handicap as the field of over one hundred realized they had been led astray, stopped, did an about face, and took off again. The first were suddenly last, and the last first, so the distance varied from 7 miles on up to about 8.5. Our crafty secretary, Ken Weidcamp, experienced his career high by tip-toeing around the correct turn, chuckling to himself 'It pays to know the course' and leading his faithful few followers with a sizeable lead for half the distance."

so blocks southeast (Mission Street, S.E.) of downtown. Ninety acres of grass fields and a few hills, Bush Park is used by 2:20 marathoners, YMCA "cardiac" joggers, and everyone in between. Runners looking for more miles and fewer people usually head out the bikepath, adjacent to River Road South, to Minto-Brown Island Park. Once inside the park, the runner discovers corn fields, a game preserve, and, oh yes, a land fill. (The latter seldom imposes.) There's also a figure-eight bikepath—almost entirely traffic free—which measures just 44 yards short of five miles.

Oak Hills Run, Portland, Oregon. A seven-mile loop in the countryside on the northwest side of Portland, this hilly course was the site of the fol-

Hagg Lake, Washington County, Oregon. Smooth asphalt road around Hagg (pronounced Haig) Lake, behind Scoggins Dam, about nine miles north of Portland. The 10.4 miles present a challenge, with plenty of hills. Oregonians advise to come prepared to sit in a boat afterwards and fish for your lunch—bring the family and make a day of it, as there's a variety of recreation for all.

Kapiolani Park, Honolulu, Hawaii. The Central Park of the Pacific, where there are more joggers per hour than any other place in the world. Convenient, smog-free, convivial atmosphere. Ken Cooper cites this park as evidence that Honolulu is "the jogging capital of the world."

Koolau Mountains, Oahu, Hawaii. Colonel Jim

Duncan of Auburn, Alabama, rates this high: "The beautiful paths along the crest of the mountain range are eerily quiet, serene, timeless." There are, of course, incredible places on the "big island" of Hawaii, but most travelers get no farther than the environs of Honolulu. Running anywhere in the South Pacific, after the early morning rain and before the day's heat, has a quality of naturalness difficult to imagine if all you've ever done is fit your jogging in before and after work.

This list is open-ended and highly subjective. I have included my favorites and those receiving strong recommendations or at least compelling descriptions by other runners across the country. The list is not arranged in any order of preference, but roughly geographically. The metropolitan locations are included for those who might find themselves by accident in those cities; the more exotic locations are intended for those who might wish to plan a vacation around one of them. Nominations for sites of your choice—especially with your personal evaluation and description—are welcome for future editions of this book.

Trails for Joggers?

Oregon has always been a state where the wishes of the populace seem to get translated into action faster than elsewhere. The Steve Prefontaine jogging trail in Eugene has become the model for ways of getting runners off the pavement and away from automobile fumes. A nine-mile jogging trail will soon be developed in Salem, Oregon, at a cost of $25,000, split fifty-fifty by the county and the city of Salem, with the Federal Bureau of Outdoor Recreation helping the city halfway. What? There's a bureau in Washington to support jogging?

Salem city councilman John McCulloch said, "I think Salem will have the best running facility of this type in the whole state . . . maybe in the whole country. I haven't heard of anything better." The surface is of bark dust, which is usable even in the continual winter rains of this area.

Can your city reach into the federal coffers for a jogging trail? McCulloch's best argument was, "There's no doubt in my mind that every noon hour, every day after work, and every weekend, it is going to be used. Everybody is going to be out there."

This trail in Marshall, California is not far from the course Michael Stubblefield describes in the selection "Have a Nice Saturday."

SELECTION:
HAVE A NICE SATURDAY. . . .

Friday night: Buy a map of (northern half, at least) California; a bottle of wine; sourdough loaf; cheese; fruit. Get a good night's sleep.

Saturday morning: as EARLY as you can get up. Skip breakfast. Put on your running clothes, some sweats, grab the map, food, and wine. Hop in your car (or on your motorcycle!) and head for Highway One, where it resumes its northward progress in Marin County (after temporarily merging with 101 north across the Golden Gate) and take the Mill Valley/Mt. Tamalpais exit (next exit past the second Sausalito exit). Turn left at the junction and then follow the road up to where it forks again—to the left and the Ocean, to the right and Mt. Tamalpais' summit. Take either route. They both eventually wind their ways to Stinson Beach, approximately 15 miles either way, give or take a mile. . . . The left fork will wind its way down the twisting, sinewy draw known as Green Gulch, past the farm of the same name, run by Zen Center, S.F. The road eventually opens out onto Muir Beach and then heads north, to Stinson Beach, flanked on its left by the Pacific Ocean far, far below the 100-foot vertical rock walls that often lie a few feet from the road; and on its right by the sensuous, upward-rolling slopes of Mt. Tamalpais, which lies some several miles and

Jogging in the city can be a tour if you are lucky enough to pick such locales as Vienna—here, the Karlskirche.

2,700 vertical feet above the fog and thundering waves and salty ocean air of the coast. . . . There are 11 miles of twisting, hairpin turns, decreasing radius turns, off-camber turns, turns of every description, before the road settles into Stinson Beach, a sleepy little resort town of artists, surfers, freaks, wealthy retired people, and, no doubt, runners. . . . Take that other fork in the road back down the road 11 miles and you will climb up, up, up those sensuous, rolling grass hills, following several ridges leading up to the summit of Mt. Tam. A few miles from the top, you again have a choice: the fork to your left will drop back down to the west, ending up at Stinson Beach; the fork to your right will take you to the summit, a breathtaking view of the entire north half of the Bay Area if the visibility is good, and well worth the hour-or-so detour before resuming your (vaguely) northward progress towards . . . not yet, it's a secret!

Once you reach Stinson Beach, by whatever route you have chosen to blow your mind, continue north on Highway One towards the town of Olema, some 17 miles up the road. . . . You will pass the Bolinas Lagoon on your left, a bird sanctuary long revered by bird lovers for the variety of its population. At the north end of Bolinas Lagoon there is a short detour of a mile or so if you want to visit the town of Bolinas (and you DO want to!). At this point you might want to get out and stretch a little. Have some tea or coffee at a Bolinas cafe. Then back to the Highway. Head north again. You will wind your way through large stands of coastal forest, punctuated by large expanses of rolling coastal hills, their long-dead spring grasses giving them a shimmering gold coat in the breezy, billowy, dry summer day (the fog, which you can expect in the early morning, should have begun to lift by now). You will pass many farms and solitary homes, each one of them driving home the fact that you wish you lived in such a lovely place to run and live. . . .

Once in Olema, proceed slowly through "town"—very, very slowly—and turn left at the Pt. Reyes National Seashore sign, a few hundred feet from the intersection of "downtown" Olema. Follow this route for about an eighth to a quarter of a mile and turn left into Park Headquarters, which will be on your left just after you turn in. Don't stop here! Keep going, up the short hill and around to the field which lies just a few more hundred feet. Drive all the way to the end of the road, until you come to a fork leading off to the right, and the stables. Park here in the big dirt parking lot on your left. Depending on the weather, either put on your sweats, or leave them in the car, OR take them in a knapsack, if a little coastal fog chills you; you can never tell by the weather in the parking lot, which is five miles inland, what it will be like once you reach the coast. . . . Divide up the food and wine amongst your merry band of two or more, lock up the car, hide the key and head for the beach! Take the Bear Valley Trail and follow the signs to the coast. The dirt road goes straight as an arrow through the last few hundred feet of inland grasses before diving into a dense, heavily forested paradise for runners. The road's surface, perfect for waffletype shoes under all but the soggiest of conditions, lets you stretch out a little in the cool, verdant green canopy of conifers and deciduous delights, before beginning a gentle climb up to Divide Meadow, whilst beside you a small, shallow creek burbles and gurgles its way down to the grassy plain from which you started. Divide Meadow is 1.9 miles into this 4.5 mile jaunt to the beach; from here it's all DOWNHILL (whew!—that little climb had you scared, didn't it?!). Relax: that was only a 400-foot ascent. . . . From Divide Meadow, you begin dropping down, down to the Ocean, though it isn't yet apparent, because you're still surrounded by towering trees, and acres and acres of ferns, mosses and yessss . . . *poison oak*. It lines the roads through most of Pt. Reyes' forests, so beware! Nettles, though less prevalent, still constitute a real threat along this particular stretch of road, so don't pet the plants! This 2.6 mile drop to the ocean is so quick, so effortless, so painless, so . . . beautiful, that you will be almost (but not quite) sorry when once the overhead umbrella of green opens up to a rich blue sky and those rolling nude hills that plummet down to the cliffs that line the narrow white strip of sand that disappears into the Pacific. . . .

Once in the clear again follow the road until it turns north and then pause here. You have a choice: there are only two ways to reach Kelham Beach, which now lies off ahead and below you, at the base of the cliffs that sharply delineate the edge of the field, and the continent, for that matter. One way is to take the trail that winds its way out to the observation point at Millers Point, overlooking Arch Rock. Underneath the lookout point, there is a small cave which has been carved out by thundering surf for thousands of years. You can usually climb down into the gulch and worm your way through this cave, out onto the southern tip of Kelham Beach. OR . . . you may choose to put off your sudden urge to reach the sand, and continue on towards Coast Camp, following the road north until you reach a huge, solitary eucalyptus tree on the left, about half a mile from the fork to the observation point. Here the trail leads down to the beach. OR, if you're STILL not tired, or aired out, then proceed on up the coast trail to Coast Camp, or beyond, to Limantour Spit (boy, *that'll* tire you out!). Otherwise, take the little trail at the tree down to the water and you'll find yourself roughly in the north middle of Kelham Beach. To your right, north, is Point Resistance. Go check it out and you'll soon see how it got its name! When the tide is low, you can wade into the big cliff-caves underneath the rock and work your way to the small, secret lagoon on the other side. To the south end of Kelham Beach is the aforementioned Millers Point, and the observation point which looks out to the Farallon Islands on a clear day. If you choose the *right* Saturday, or a Wednesday, which is sometimes better in the summer, you will own the beach. Go ahead! It's yours! Break out the wine and food and have a swim. Skinny-dipping (and skinny-RUNNING, for that matter) is okay out here. If you swim out far, remember the kelp and remember the undertow. The water is usually BRACING! After swimming and snacking, curl up on that soft, warm sand and have a siesta. . . . Give yourself plenty of time to digest things before starting back . . . and have a nice Saturday.

—Michael Stubblefield,
Editor, *Body Talk*

CAMPS

(Listings are for example only—they change from year to year. The vast majority run for 6-7 days, with a few larger camps having several sessions. Costs vary considerably, depending on accommodations, board, location—$125 is average. Numerous additional camps are designed for high school to college level and are not listed here. See *Runner's World*, May, 1977.)

Athletic Attic Adirondacks Family Running Camp, Lake George, N.Y.
Marty Liquori
c/o Athletic Attic
1135 East N.W. 23rd Avenue
Gainesville, Fla. 32601

Mid-Atlantic Running Camp, Medford Lakes, N.J.
Browning Ross
Sports East
240 South Broad Street
Woodbury, N.J. 08096

Stroudsburg Cross-Country Camp, Stroudsburg, Pa.
Jim Smith
229 Rocky Point Landing Road
Rocky Point, N.Y. 11778

Blue Ridge Trails, Tigerville, S.C.
Bill Keesling
Box 28544
Furman University
Greenville, S.C. 29613

Southeast running trails, famous guest runners:
Phidippides
Jeff Galloway
1544 Piedmont Road, N.E.
Atlanta, Ga. 30324

Florida Distance Camp, Brevard, N.C.
Roy Bensen
Athletic Department
University of Florida
Gainesville, Fla. 32604

Symposium on Running, Columbia, Va.
Fred Hardy
Box 6
University of Richmond
Richmond, Va. 23173

Wolfpack Cross-Country Pack, Raleigh, N.C.
James B. Wescott
Athletics Department
NCSU
Raleigh, N.C. 27607

Runner's Mecca, Brainhead, Utah
Rich Heywood
Box 2186
Mesa, Ariz. 85204

Montana wild country, guided runs:
Tom Kotynski
318 Stuart
Helena, Mont. 59601

YMCA High Altitude Training Camp, Catamount Ranch, Colo.
Don MacMahill
Cheyenne Family YMCA
1401 Dunn Avenue
Cheyenne, Wyo. 82001

Colorado Adventuring Distance Running Camp, Westcliffe, Colo.
Bill Crowell
Box 293
Westcliffe, Colo. 81252

Montecito-Sequoia Running Camp, Central Sierra Nevada, Calif.
1485 Redwood Drive
Los Altos, Calif. 94022

Jim Ryun Running Camps, Christian atmosphere, various locations:
P.O. Box 6266
Santa Barbara, Calif. 93111

National Running Week
December 26 to 31, Palo Alto, California, with events around the San Francisco Bay Area, clinics, workshops, tour of *Runner's World* offices, equipment displays, fun-runs, prominent guest speakers:

Box 366
Mountain View, California 94042

'Innerspaces of Running' Workshop
Led by Mike Spino, weekends November through April (Bahamas, 1977-78)

1345 Avenue of the Americas
Room 3305
New York, N.Y. 10019

nine

far out
the unusual,
the trivial, the sublime

When I asked for nominations for the best of this and the best of that, funny sayings on tee shirts, oddities, and unusual records, many respondents said there was too much trivia already! Well, I suppose the old gags are getting a little tired: "Joggers keep it up longer," "I may be slow but I'm ahead of you." You can now go into any major sporting goods store and order your personal message for 10 to 20 cents a letter, depending on the size of the letter. (If you have a design you want applied to your shirt, check first—some materials need more heat, more pressure.) And you can also buy preprinted shirts with all kinds of inspirational and nonsensical messages. Apparently most runners prefer to stick to shirts they have earned in races or to club shirts.

The nominations on the following pages are presented for your amusement and perhaps inspiration. You are invited to challenge this list by sending your nominations to the publisher for consideration in future editions.

THINGS TO SHOOT AT

Longest nonstop run:
Tony Rafferty, Australia, 140 miles
American record: Jared Beads, 121 miles
Most marathons:
Ted Corbitt, 55, New York: "more than 180" and "never entered a marathon he did not finish"
Back-to-back marathons:
Tarzan Brown, winner of two marathons in New England on successive days in 1936
Longest continuing run:
Siegfried Bauer, "world's healthiest man," 1,300 miles in 18 days (!), in New Zealand

NOMINATIONS

Best name for a road race: Macon Tracks (Macon, Georgia)

Best name for a running club: The Big Sky Wind Drinkers (Montana—the 99th club to join the RRCA)

Best name for a running shoe: The Street Fighter (Etonic)

Best name for a magazine column on jogging: Running Wild (George Sheehan, M.D., in *The Physician and Sportsmedicine*)

Best tee shirt, pairs: Blister Sisters—Blister Sisters Pit Crew (See photo)

Best tee shirt, front and back: Front: In Oregon, runners have the right of way. Back: (Imprint of waffle shoe)

Best cartoon on jogging: Snoopy (See illustration)

Best-produced newsletter: The Oregon Distance Runner

Most complete newsletter: The New York Road Runners Association Newsletter

Best name for a newsletter: Kukini (The King's Messenger—Hawaii Marathon Association)

Best name for shoe repair company: One More Company, a Briar Patch Enterprise (Shoe patch)

Best name for a family running club: Pamakids (San Francisco)

Best-organized club: Oregon Road Runners Club:

Corporate Address:
Ken Weidkamp, Secretary
14230 South West Derby Street
Beaverton, Ore. 97005
Founded February 17, 1970
Incorporated January 1, 1977

Some 1500 regular members and 700 family members, all listed with names and addresses, home and business numbers, with ages. A model bylaws—letterpress printed, typeset roster.

Best runner's recipe:

BRIAN'S BREAD

Starter Batter:

    1½ tsp. (one package) yeast
    2½ cups lukewarm water
    2   cups sifted flour
    1 tbsp. sugar
    1 tsp. salt

Bread:

    1½ tsp. (one package) yeast
    1½ cups lukewarm water
    1 cup starter batter
    2 tsp. salt
    2 tsp. sugar
    5–5½ cups flour
    ½ tsp. baking soda
    ¼ cup sesame seeds (to taste)

Starter batter directions: Dissolve one package of yeast in lukewarm water (about ½ cup will do). Once it is dissolved, add the rest (2 cups) of the water, the two cups of sifted flour, one tablespoon of sugar, and the salt. Then beat it all into a smooth batter. Let it stand at room temperature for three to five days. Stir two to three times a day. Be sure to cover it at night. If the batter starts to get too dry, add a little water. Store covered in the refrigerator when ready.

Bread Directions: Soften and dissolve the yeast in lukewarm water. Then add the starter, salt, sugar, sesame seeds, and about three cups of flour. Beat for three to four minutes until smooth. Cover, let rise in a warm place for one to 1½ hours. Mix the baking soda with 1½ cups of flour, add to the dough until stiff. Turn out on a floured board and knead for eight to ten minutes. Divide the dough in half, then let it rest for about ten minutes. Using buttered hands, shape the dough into long, thin loaves (if hands are well buttered, there is no need to grease the pan) and place on a cookie pan. Cut diagonal slashes on top, let rise for approximately 45 minutes to 1½ hours. When it's risen, bake at 400 degrees for 35-40 minutes. Makes two good-sized loaves.

Note: For a golden brown crust, brush with butter or margarine after about 20 minutes of baking. To replenish the starter, add one cup of water, one cup of flour to the starter batter that remains, then mix in one tablespoon of sugar and let sit for 12 hours, uncovered, at room temperature. Cover and refrigerate until needed. If the starter is not used within two weeks, add a teaspoon of sugar to stop the batter from going too sour.

    —Brian Maxwell, Assistant Track Coach,
    University of California, Berkeley

Brian Maxwell and Ron Wayne, two of the country's top marathoners, are members of the Bay Area Body Ammo Sports Club, in Berkeley. Homemade bread is a great aid to carbohydrate loading, if you don't like spaghetti or commercial bakery products. The problem is to be able to make it without too much fuss. The use of a starter and those little tricks like buttered hands make the whole thing feasible. Members of the club have pronounced it a great loader.

The only other nominations for runners' recipes were replacement drinks (see page 109). Any suggestions?

**SOURCES FOR
THE UNUSUAL IN BOOKS**

Major books on running and related matters are mentioned and reviewed throughout this catalog, but there are hundreds of other titles to appeal to individual tastes. An indispensable source for locating virtually any title in print in the sports world is the *Sports Book Directory*, published by World Publications, P.O. Box 366, Mountain View, California 94042. It is priced at 50¢, but the Directory offers a "Free Catalog" (value, $1.95) with "further description of any or all of the books in this directory." And you may have the Directory sent free to any name and address. Several quantity discounts are offered. The books listed include such things as *The Winner's Guide to*

(Facing Page) Does this man hold the record for jogging (unharmed!) the most dangerous trail of all? Watch out!

Dice and *The Complete Book of Cheerleading*, but also just about everything imaginable on exercise, yoga, diet, and running. There is no other source quite like this: Thank you, World Publications!

FILMS ON RUNNING AND AEROBIC EXERCISE

When you want to dress up a club meeting or have a focus for an instructional period preceding a fun-run, try a film. First check your nearest university film library, where you can also rent equipment. The list below is to whet your interest: some of these films may be difficult to get. Unless otherwise noted, they are available in 16mm, Super 8, or 8, and are usually in color.

Motivational/Instructional

Run Dick, Run Jane

20 minutes, rent $20 day. Focus on the medical benefits of avoiding heart attacks.

What Makes Millie Run?

14 minutes, rent $15 day. Reasons for college women to get in the run.

(The above two films are also available from the producer, Brigham Young University, Media Marketing, Provo, Utah 84602.)

Ryan Track and Field Series for Girls

Three films, 15 minutes each, rent $10 each per day. Purely instructional.

Available from Macmillan/Audio Brandon, 34 MacQuestern Parkway South, Mt. Vernon, New York 10550.

Ruth Anderson: Development of a Master Marathoner.

Ruth Anderson will rent her copy of the film to raise funds for the Long Distance Women's Masters Committee. For details contact her at 1901 Gaspar Drive, Oakland, California 94611; (415) 339-0563.

Special Emphasis

The Marathon

Marlin Darrah's exquisite portrayal of the Olympic trials at Eugene, Oregon, in 1976, featuring Shorter, Rodgers, Kardong. Mix of color and black-and-white, full sound, dramatic slow-motion sequences. Darrah also shot the 1977 Eugene marathon for a future film. 28 minutes, rent $30 day, $75 week; purchase $360, from:

Starting Line Sports
Box 8
Mountain View, Calif. 94042

New York City Marathon

Films of the 1976 and 1977 "Five Borough" marathon are available to clubs and organizations from:

Manufacturers Hanover
Attn: Patsy Warner
350 Park Avenue
New York, N. Y. 10022

The film of the 1976 marathon runs about 6½ minutes and is available either in 16mm or videotape. The film of the 1977 marathon runs about 12 minutes and is available in 16mm. The fee of $15 for each film's use goes to the New York Road Runners Club. Inquire also about films of succeeding marathons partially sponsored by the bank.

Run for the Record

12 minutes, rent $25, buy $195. Account of the 1977 Nike Marathon at Eugene, Oregon — Jeff Wells ahead of Don Kardong, Kim Merritt setting American women's record. Contact:

McKinley Productions
6003 Phinney North
Seattle, Wash. 98103
(206) 784-1099

Fifteen Degrees and Fast

Account of the 1977 NCAA Crosscountry Nationals. For details, inquire to McKinley Productions, above.

Inexpensive training films based on Olympic performances are available from Track & Field News, Box 296, Los Altos, California 94022. Write for catalog.

A twenty-minute film called *Coping with Life on the Run* about George Sheehan that Joan Ullyot calls "marvelous, very moving, the essence of running" is available from:

Sports Productions, Inc.
Locust Point Rd.
Locust, N.J. 07748
(201) 291-0300

Running for Life

28 minutes, rent $15 day. Results of Public Health research experiment with professors at University of Wisconsin—case history approach to study of heart disease. Produced by Indiana University. Available through most university film libraries.

Marathon Sequence from "Olympia"

13 minutes, rent $12 day. The famous sequence from Leni Riefenstahl's film on the 1936 Olympics. Available through most university film libraries.

Olympics—Twentieth Century

26 minutes, rent $14 day. Highlights from Olympics from 1936 to 1972, with emphasis on running events (Jesse Owens, Emil Zatopek, etc.). Available through most university film libraries.

Commercially available films on physical fitness:

How to Avoid Muscle Strain, 1949, 15 minutes, rent $10 day; physiology of muscles.

Cross-Country Runner, 1961, 14 minutes, rent $11 day; also on videotape; humorous overview.

Exercise & Physical Fitness, 1973, 17 minutes,

rent $18 day; imaginative production on cardiovascular system.

Movement: To Live Is to Move, 1976, 24 minutes, rent $25 day; motivational film for young people.

Girls' Sports: On the Right Track

Rent $25 day, purchase $250. Narrated by Katharine Switzer (first woman to run the Boston marathon, 1967, now an active promoter of women's running). A highly acclaimed film on women's self-awareness, excellent production values. Available from Phoenix Films, Inc., 470 Park Avenue South, New York, N.Y. 10016.

RUNNING STATISTICS

Ken Young
Institute of Atmospheric Physics
University of Arizona
Tucson, Ariz. 85721
(602) 884-3188

Ken Young has established the "National Running Data Center," whose object is to chart and set standards for performances in running at various age levels. The results of his work have been

SELECTION:
THE HASH HOUSE HARRIERS

Launched in 1972, the Washington club is the oldest U.S. chapter of the Hash House Harriers International, which had its origins among expatriates in Malaysia in 1938. Legend has it that an Australian in Kuala Lumpur named A. S. Gispert began jogging on Monday nights to sweat off the excesses of preceding weekends. He was joined by friends also seeking to "take the curse off Mondays," as Hashmen put it, and the group repaired to a local bar known as the Hash House following their runs.

The meetings evolved into "hare and hounds," and as the runners began exploring different routes around the Malaysian countryside, the Hash House's enterprising proprietor arranged to meet them at the finish line with a beer wagon. Overcome by his gesture, the Harriers named their club for his bar.

Although the Washington Hash is mainly composed of businessmen, bureaucrats, and professionals, like all Hashes it takes pride in being slightly disorderly and disreputable—a sort of genteel motorcycle gang. Serious runners belong, but they are periodically admonished not to treat the Hash runs as workouts. If there is tension in the club, it lies in the friendly wars between the "super jocks," so-called, and the "gentlemen," who look with scorn on anything that could be described as a training run.

The Washington Hash has also retained a steadfast prohibition against women runners despite pressures within and without the club to go co-ed as some outlaw chapters have done elsewhere in the world. Wives and girlfriends are invited to occasional picnics and parties, but the runs themselves are sacred. Club rules prohibit gambling, opium smoking, and "the introduction of females and bad characters on runs." The occasional member's wife who shows up dressed to run is greeted with stony stares.

All this is prologue to the historic night of August 15. There was no reason to expect anything out of the ordinary as 30-odd Hashmen gathered for the weekly run on a sultry Monday evening in rural Virginia. The appointed meeting place was a deserted gravel road off a country lane, but the runs are frequently held in secluded settings. At seven o'clock someone shouted, "On, on!" and the pack set off in pursuit of the hare.

The run, too, was run-of-the-mill. Long stretches on country roads followed by brief trampings through the woods. After crossing a stream, the trail led to the border of a lake and back to the gravel road where we had started.

Like the other Hashmen, I was tired and sweaty and looking forward to the beer. I stopped at my

published periodically in such magazines as *Runner's World*. For example, a person who could run 100 meters in 11.0 seconds at the optimal age of 22 would be performing comparably to one who could do it in 14.2 seconds at age 60. The optimal age for a miler is 25; if he could do a 4-minute mile then he could be expected to do a 5:07 at 60. The performance of a 5-minute miler at age 25 would be comparable to a 6:24 mile at age 60.

Ken has made some interesting statistical comparisons of the ability of women to lower their times in the short distances as against the long distances. So far it appears that women are not improving as rapidly in the endurance races, where their superior ability to metabolize glycogen is supposed to give them an edge over their male counterparts.

Marathon lists? Of course. If you're doing any kind of research into running, you've got to check with Mr. Young. Be sure to send a stamped, self-addressed envelope with your inquiry.

RELIGIOUS-ORIENTED ITEMS

Material related to the Bible: plaques, scrolls, poems, quotations, books:

car, put on a dry tee shirt, and walked slowly up the road to our starting point.

The first thing I noticed was a clearing lit by kerosene torches. "A touch of class," I thought to myself. On reaching the clearing, I received the shock of my running career. Flanking the entrance to a makeshift banquet table were two women, blond and generously endowed, wearing sarongs.

Could it be? It was. Dumbstruck, I advanced toward the pair. One of them embraced me, kissed me, and placed a plastic lei around my neck. "Aloha," she said huskily. "Good heavens!" I mumbled and stumbled toward the beer.

Recovering my composure, I watched this scene repeated as other runners trudged up the road, did a double take, then rushed toward the women. One escapee from the Hong Kong Hash, visiting Washington on business, practically had to be pried loose from his hostess.

Finally, the last runner had been welcomed, and the Hash settled in for the usual drinking and snacking. We were joined by the girls. I confess to wondering how much they had been paid for their services, but I was quickly disabused of this notion. These were no recruits from a go-go parlor, it turned out, but physical fitness instructors at a local health club and—will wonders never cease?—runners like ourselves.

Lighted by the flickering torches, the gathering took on the appearance of a routine Washington lawn party, except that each woman was surrounded by a larger-than-usual number of males. The girls discussed their careers and their running. One was planning to try a marathon and wanted advice on how to go about it.

I left before the party broke up and began the long drive home in a daze. Beside me on the carseat were two plastic leis. Should I say nothing and throw them away? I decided instead to give them to my daughters.

"What are these?" my wife asked suspiciously the next morning when she saw the leis on the kitchen table.

"Oh, the Hash last night had a Polynesian motif," I explained casually, "and I saved these for the girls." That seemed to satisfy her.

Other, braver men told their wives the full story—and immediately caught hell. Some wives wouldn't speak to their husbands for days. "I just don't see what that's got to do with running," one wife is said to have remarked.

Fair comment. But the Hash isn't really about running, it's about men, which is why the club has resisted female runners for so long. No, the Hash is about freedom, spontaneity, and small boys staying out after dark. . . .

—Steve Clapp, *Running Times,* October, 1977

The Physical Fitness Edition
11317 Earlywood Drive
Dallas, Tex. 75218

STATIONERY ITEMS

The "Eat and Run Calendar," designed and put together by Jan Ferris Koltun (Holt, Rinehart & Winston), keeps recipes and running tips before you as you turn the months over: a nice way to keep a log. Available through bookstores.

Interesting sets of notecards and posters with running motifs—black-and-white line-resolutions of striking photographs—are available through your Road Runners Club. Artist Herb Parsons obviously has a feel for how runners picture themselves and their preferred haunts. Of the six designs, two of a woman runner are the most dramatic, to my mind. For an order form (or to order sight unseen), write:

Bill Hoss, Jr., RRCA
747 Shepham Court
Virginia Beach, Va. 23452

Folded notecards, 4¼ x 5½ inches, with matching envelopes, are $2.25 for a dozen of one design. Posters, 11 x 17 inches, are $2.25 each.

More and more posters are coming on the market, as mementos of marathons or just plain decorations for bare walls. One with a zesty message comes (for $2.00) from Spiridon, the distributor for New Balance, the shoe manufacturer

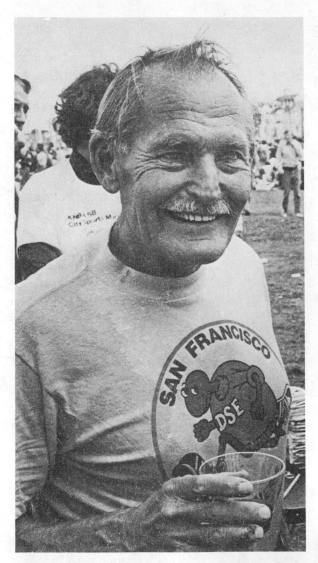

The Famous Dolphin South End Running Club Shirt, modeled by President Walt Stack

(see page 58). And it's big—20 x 29 inches. A kindly, white-haired grandmother, in grandmotherly clothes except for her New Balance shoes, stares straight at you. The caption reads: "When the going gets tough, the tough get going."

ASTROLOGY, BIOFEEDBACK, BIORHYTHM, SEX, SEXISM

In their search for the perfect run, competitive types will leave no stone (or pebble) unturned. Several firms are now offering devices to determine your best running days, to slow down your pulse rate, to pick your best races. But sex and perhaps sexism appear to be the most notable stimulants of the esoteric reasons for jogging.

People are now running to improve their sex lives, instead of worrying about how their sex lives might disturb their running. Dr. Laurence Morehouse, and a million tee shirts, proclaim that

One of the Herb Parsons stationery designs

Do a good deed today—teach a friend to jog.

runners are better lovers. Dr. Gabe Mirkin has been conducting a poll of the sexual experiences of runners for a serious study. As Dr. Rex Wiederanders points out, the production of testosterone is significantly lowered for eight or more hours after heavy exercise, but apparently this fact has posed no difficulties for males in prime health. A man in good aerobic condition, according to Dr. Richard A. Stein, has a lower pulse rate during coitus than a nonrunner, and hence may not be subject to psychological blocks from having had a previous heart attack.

And it seems that one of the healthiest reactions of the feminist movement has been from women defying the stereotypes and using their athletic prowess to shut up the MCP's, (male chauvinist pigs). (Secretly, even MCP's welcome the competition of women, simply because they really welcome women. The selection on pages 180-181 is a case in point.)

ten

epilogue

your personal log

At the back of the family Bible there used to be several blank pages where mother or father, grandpa, or grandma would record births, marriages, deaths, and a lot of other significant events in the life of what we now call "the extended family." If this happened in your family, you knew you had roots. It may seem trivial by comparison, but many runners have also taken to recording their life of jogging. Maybe it's that old impulse to keep a diary—resurfacing after years of being out of fashion. Especially if you go on to more serious running, however, it's psychologically helpful and instructive. Try it!

PERSONAL RUNNING HISTORY OF
_____

STARTED JOGGING ON _____ 19 _____ AT AGE _____

FIRST JOGGING ROUTE _____ MILES _____

ACHIEVED TEN-MINUTE MILE ON _____ 19 _____

RAN FOR THIRTY CONSECUTIVE MINUTES ON _____ 19 _____

MILEAGE PER WEEK: _____

FIRST SIX MONTHS _____

FIRST YEAR _____

REGULARLY _____

PERSONAL RECORDS:

ONE MILE _____ DATE _____ TIME _____

LONGEST DISTANCE _____ DATE _____ MILES _____

OTHER DISTANCES: _____ DATE _____ MILES _____ TIME _____

_____ DATE _____ MILES _____ TIME _____

FIRST ORGANIZED RUN/RACE _____ DATE _____

TIME _____ PLACE _____ RIBBON, ETC. _____

FIRST MARATHON _____ TIME _____

CHRONOLOGY OF RUNS/RACES:

EVENT	PLACE	DATE	DISTANCE	TIME MPM*

FAMILY RUNNING HISTORY

EVENTS	PLACE	DATE

FAMILY MEMBERS RUNNING TIMES

_____

_____

_____

_____

_____

_____

_____

*Minutes per mile, the usual way of speaking of a pace. For example, the marathon is usually won at a 5-minute pace or better (men), or 6-minute pace (women), and an 8-minute pace will just get you under 3 hours, 30 minutes. The difference between a jog and a run is sometimes defined as over or under a 7-minute pace. See "Basics," p. 13. It's encouraging to see how one's pace can be improved as soon as basic endurance is established.

FUTURE EVENTS

Even if you subscribe to a good running magazine and receive a local newsletter, it's easy to lose track of dates, entry fees, and especially closing dates for large races with a limited entry. (Many people have been disappointed in the New York Marathon, for example, by missing the "limit.") Use the following page to make a personal calendar of upcoming events you may want to enter. This will serve also as a reminder to update your log.

EVENT	DATE AND TIME	ENTRY FEE	ENTRIES TO:

MEDICAL HISTORY

Let's not get morbid or compulsive, but you may find it more encouraging to have your fitness figures at hand rather than buried in the files of your doctor's office. The first thing you should notice when you begin doing aerobic work regularly is a drop in your pulse rate and perhaps blood pressure. Runners who give blood often find the nurse doing a double-take when reading their pulse. You should be able to lower it to the 50's (normal: 72) after a year of running.

You're commonly advised to have a stress test if you start jogging after the age of 35 and after a relatively sedentary existence before that time. The major purpose of this procedure is to attempt to uncover any structural weakness in the heart, which might not show up until you try your first marathon. Many doctor-runners disagree: they feel that any possible damage you might do by running is more than compensated for by the general strengthening of your cardiovascular system. Experienced runners sometimes take stress tests as an ego trip. Whatever your feeling, there's more to a fitness evaluation than running on a treadmill. And a test may be just the thing to convince you something ought to be done!

Where can you get a complete test? "Multiphasic" examinations and annual "physicals" usually include a vital-capacity test and a pulse-recovery test, but that isn't enough. Thorough fitness tests are usually available only through the physical education department of a university such as Ball State in Muncie, Indiana. Several private firms now also offer "fitness tests" which include programs to match individual capabilities for exercise:

VITAL
One Embarcadero Center, Suite 1907
San Francisco, Calif. 94111
(415) 433-3286

Or:

CARDiO-METRICS
295 Madison Avenue
New York, N.Y. 10017
(212) 889-6123

(For suggestions on how to find a testing center near you, see page 114.)

And there are several firms which "plug in" to the instruments measuring a resting or recovering electrocardiogram (ECG), to give your doctor a computer analysis in a matter of minutes. This feature is especially important in suspected cardiac cases: readings can be taken at many more points around the body and diagnosed on the spot. Ask your doctor about this service. (For more on stress tests, see page 112.)

This is the type of information developed by the fitness testing program at the University of California at Davis, and it will serve as a chart of your medical history to be recorded in this book:

TESTING DATE	BODY COMPOSITION		VITAL CAPACITY
	% Body Fat	Fat Wt.	

	OXYGEN UPTAKE	BLOOD PRESSURE

TESTING DATE	CHOLESTEROL	TRIGLYCERIDES	GLUCOSE

There are many other medically important figures recorded in this particular program: other factors in pulmonary function, duration and speed of treadmill test, heart rate during and after the test, anaerobic threshold, and so forth. But these figures are the highlights and the clues to whether or not you're making progress or *need* progress. If you're stumped on where to go for a fitness test, write or call:

Adult Fitness Program
Physical Education Department
264 Hickey Gym
University of California
Davis, Calif. 95616
(916) 752-0729

In this case, test dates are scheduled every four weeks and take three to four hours. This program includes a prescription for diet and exercise to overcome any deficiency in your total health. A treadmill test alone will not give you this.

AEROBICS INTERNATIONAL RESEARCH SOCIETY

Ken Cooper's Institute for Aerobics Research in Dallas, Texas offers (for a small yearly fee, 50% of which is tax deductible) a monthy service that gives you a computer summary of the Aerobic point values of all your exercise — running, swimming, tennis, handball, basketball or whatever. Each month you receive an exercise log on which you chart your time, distance and other important statistics for each of your aerobic physical activities. Send the log in to AIRS and they'll send back a printout breaking down your month of exercise into daily and weekly aerobic points. Each printout also gives you a cumulative record of your aerobic points from the time you join AIRS. The data on each AIRS member will be kept in a computer at the Institute for Aerobics Research. Under Dr. Cooper's direction, the data will become part of the most extensive research on physical fitness ever undertaken. For further information, write to Mr. William Walker, Aerobics International Research Society, 11811 Preston Road, Dallas, Tex. 95230.

RUNNING AS A SOCIAL ACTION

At the end of your log—an epilogue. It could have been expected that this book would conclude with the usual charts and tables: metric conversions, pacing rates, training programs for a week, a month, a year. (All right, for the record: 5,000 meters is about 3.1 miles; so you know what 10,000 meters is. At an 8-minute pace your right foot will hit the ground about 800 times per mile, so you know how to measure an unfamiliar course. A pound is about 450 grams, so you know the difference between a training shoe and a racing shoe is only an ounce or two. What else do you really need to know?) It's hard to do arithmetical calculations in the middle of a long run, anyway. Try it! Your brain is being shorted oxygen. And that's what this epilogue is about.

You've now read all the reasons for running, conscious or unconscious. Consider the social reasons. In compiling this catalog, I've read hundreds of newsletters, magazines, books. I sent a questionnaire to a few hundred clubs, and was deluged with answers! I talked with and corresponded with some of the leading authors and organizers in the running movement, and was struck with their sense of camaraderie. I have jogged in just about every major city in the country (that's where I got started—I was on a promotion tour for a book and had to fill the empty hours). I will always remember the first five-borough marathon in New York in 1976. And what comes through all this to my eyes and ears is that running is bringing back that sense of *going out to the world* which civilization as we know it keeps trying to take away from us.

Snoopy said it best, in the pen of Charles Schulz: "Jogging is very beneficial/ It's good for your heart and your legs and your feet/ It's also very good for the ground/ It makes it feel needed."

When I go out running I discover how different the world looks when I'm not behind the wheel of a car or balancing myself on a bus. Distances I once thought measurable only on a speedometer I now think in terms of paces. I run through parts of the city I once had mentally shielded from view. I am aware of people noticing me going along the street. I am in touch with the world as never I imagined. It needs me.

index